The Top 5 Most Influential Explorers: Marco Polo, Christopher Columbus, Hernán Cortés, Ferdinand Magellan, and Sir Francis Drake

By Charles River Editors

About Charles River Editors

Charles River Editors was founded by Harvard and MIT alumni to provide superior editing and original writing services, with the expertise to create digital content for publishers across a vast range of subject matter. In addition to providing original digital content for third party publishers, Charles River Editors republishes civilization's greatest literary works, bringing them to a new generation via ebooks.

Signup here to receive updates about free books as we publish them, and visit charlesrivereditors.com for more information.

Introduction

16th century portrait depicting Marco Polo

Marco Polo (1254-1324)

"I have not told half of what I saw." – Marco Polo

A lot of ink has been spilled covering the lives of history's most influential figures, but how much of the forest is lost for the trees? In Charles River Editors' Legends of the Middle Ages series, readers can get caught up to speed on the lives of important medieval men and women in the time it takes to finish a commute, while learning interesting facts long forgotten or never known.

Marco Polo (1254-1324) is an instantly recognizable name, and he is known for his travels, but it's safe to say that his influence and importance has been greatly overlooked in the nearly 700 years since he died. Born in Venice, Marco Polo was in a fortuitous position to participate in the Mediterranean trade, but he was still a young man when he went on the journey that would make him famous and greatly inspire the Age of Exploration.

Though he was destined to become famous, Marco Polo was simply following in the footsteps of his own family, and it's believed that he was already a teenager before he met his father and uncle, who had been traveling to the Far East and, according to Marco Polo, had met Kublai Khan, the famous grandson of Genghis Khan. A few years later, they set off for Asia again, this time with Marco Polo, and they would not return to Venice for 24 years. When they came back, they had allegedly traveled about 15,000 miles and brought back plenty of riches and treasure.

Marco Polo was hardly the only European merchant or trader who traveled to the Far East, but it was his written account of his travels that would generate extreme interest in Asia. Having described such a rich land full of desired resources, Marco Polo's travels became a source for European cartographers of the era, and they became the impetus for men like Christopher Columbus, who added his own annotations to Marco Polo's account and used it as a reference for his own legendary expedition in search of the Far East. Centuries later, historians have scoured over the account and what was written in an effort to validate its authenticity, leading to sharp debates today.

This book chronicles the life and travels of the Venetian merchant, while analyzing how his account influenced subsequent explorers. Along with pictures of important people, places, and events, you will learn about Marco Polo like you never have before.

Posthumous portrait of Columbus

Christopher Columbus (1451-1506)

"At two o'clock in the morning the land was discovered…As I saw that they were very friendly to us, and perceived that they could be much more easily converted to our holy faith by gentle means than by force, I presented them with some red caps, and strings of beads to wear upon the neck, and many other trifles of small value, wherewith they were much delighted, and became wonderfully attached to us." – Christopher Columbus's diary, October 11-12, 1492

The most seminal event of the last millennium might also be its most controversial. As schoolchildren have been taught for over 500 years, "In 1492 Columbus sailed the ocean blue." In October of that year, the Italian Christopher Columbus immortalized himself by landing in the New World and beginning the process of European settlement in the Americas for Spain, bringing the Age of Exploration to a new hemisphere with him. Ironically, the Italian had led a Spanish expedition, in part because the Portugese rejected his offers in the belief that sailing west to Asia would take too long.

Columbus had better luck with the Spanish royalty, successfully persuading Queen Isabella to commission his expedition. In August 1492, Columbus set west for India at the helm of the Nina, Pinta and Santa Maria. Befitting a legendary trip, the journey was star-crossed from the beginning. The Pinta's rudder broke early on, and just days into the journey Columbus' compass stopped pointing due north and started pointing to the Earth's magnetic north pole, something the Europeans knew nothing about. Columbus knew that the uncertainty of the expedition's destination made his crew nervous, so he hid his compass' "malfunction" from his crew. Additionally, after 30 days of sailing, the expedition still had not sighted land, so Columbus started lying to his crew about the distance they sailed each day, telling them they had sailed fewer miles than they actually had so as not to scare them even more.

On October 7, 1492, the three ships spotted flocks of birds, suggesting land was nearby, so Columbus followed the direction in which the birds flew. On the night of October 11, the expedition sighted land, and when Columbus came ashore the following day in the Bahamas, he thought he was in Japan, but the natives he came into contact with belied the descriptions of the people and lands of Asia as wealthy and resourceful. Instead, the bewildered Columbus would note in his journal that the natives painted their bodies, wore no clothes and had primitive weapons, leading him to the conclusion they would be easily converted to Catholicism. When he set sail for home in January 1493, he brought several imprisoned natives back to Spain with him.

Everyone agrees that Columbus's discovery of the New World was one of the turning points in history, but agreements over his legacy end there. Although his other three voyages to the New World were far less successful and largely overlooked in the narrative of his life, Columbus became such a towering figure in Western history that the United States' capital was named after George Washington and him. Conversely, among the Native Americans and indigenous tribes who suffered epidemics and enslavement at the hands of the European settlers, Columbus is widely portrayed as an archvillain.

This book chronicles Columbus's life and his historic voyages, but it also examines the aftermath of his expeditions and analyzes the controversy surrounding his legacy. Along with pictures of important people, places, and events in his life, you will learn about Columbus like you never have before.

Hernán Cortés de Monroy y Pizarro (1485-1547)

"Among these temples there is one which far surpasses all the rest, whose grandeur of architectural details no human tongue is able to describe; for within its precincts, surrounded by a lofty wall, there is room enough for a town of five hundred families." – Hernán Cortés

During the Age of Exploration, some of the most famous and infamous individuals were Spain's best known conquistadors. Naturally, as the best known conquistador, Hernán Cortés (1485-1547) is also the most controversial. Like Christopher Columbus before him, Cortés was lionized for his successes for centuries without questioning his tactics or motives, while indigenous views of the man have been overwhelmingly negative for the consequences his conquests had on the Aztecs and other natives in the region. Just about the only thing everyone agrees upon is that Cortés had a profound impact on the history of North America.

Of course, the lionization and demonization of Cortés often take place without fully analyzing the man himself, especially because there are almost no contemporaneous sources that explain what his thinking and motivation was. If anything, Cortés seemed to have been less concerned with posterity or the effects of the Spanish conquest on the natives than he was on relations with the Mother Country itself. Of the few things that are known about Cortés, it appears that he was both extremely ambitious and fully cognizant of politics and political intrigue, even in a New World thousands of miles west of Spain itself. Cortés spent much of his time in Mexico and the New World defending himself against other Spanish officials in the region, as well as trying to portray and position himself in a favorable light back home.

While those ambitions and politics understandably colored his writings about his activities and conquests, scholars nevertheless use what he wrote to gain a better understanding of the indigenous natives he came into contact with. Even then, however, what he wrote was scarce; Cortés's account of his conquest of Mexico is comprised of five letters he addressed to the Holy

Roman Emperor, Charles V. As Adolph Francis Bandelier noted in the Catholic Encyclopedia in 1908, "Cortés was a good writer. His letters to the emperor, on the conquest, deserve to be classed among the best Spanish documents of the period. They are, of course, coloured so as to place his own achievements in relief, but, withal, he keeps within bounds and does not exaggerate, except in matters of Indian civilization and the numbers of population as implied by the size of the settlements. Even there he uses comparatives only, judging from outward appearances and from impressions."

This book chronicles Cortés's life, but it also examines the aftermath of his conquest and analyzes the controversy surrounding his legacy. Along with pictures of important people, places, and events in his life, you will learn about Cortés like you never have before.

FERDINAN·MAGELLANVS·SVPER·ATIS
ANTARCTICI·FRETI·ANGVSTIIS·CLARISS

Ferdinand Magellan (1480-1521)

"Most versed in nautical charts, he knew better than any other the true art of navigation, of which it is certain proof that he by his genius, and his intrepidity, without anyone having given him the example, how to attempt the circuit of the globe which he had almost completed... The glory of Magellan will survive him." – Antonio Pigafetta

Ferdinand Magellan, known in his native Portugal as Fernão de Magalhães and in Spain, where he moved later in life, as Fernando de Magallanes, was unquestionably one of the more remarkable figures of the so-called Age of Discovery, a period in which Europeans spread their political and commercial influence around the globe. Accordingly, his name is often invoked alongside that of Columbus, but the nature of his achievements has sometimes been misunderstood. Magellan has sometimes been credited with "proving the world was round," since he and his crew were the first Europeans to reach Asia via a westward route. But such a claim is based on a popular misconception, referred to by historian Jeffrey Burton Russell as the "myth of the flat earth": the belief that medieval Europe had erroneously believed the earth was flat. In reality, essentially no educated Europeans of the late 15th and early 16th centuries doubted the spherical shape of the earth, which had been persuasively established by the scientists of ancient Greece – even down to Eratosthenes's relatively accurate measurement of its circumference in the third century B.C. It is also not quite true that Magellan himself circumnavigated the globe – in fact, he died in combat in the Philippines, leaving his surviving crew to complete the voyage. It is, on the other hand, certainly the case that Magellan was one of the most accomplished navigators of his time, and that he crucially charted territories previously unexplored by Europeans.

Perhaps the most important fact about Magellan, though, is that he succeeded precisely where Christopher Columbus before him had failed. While Columbus has gone down in history as the discoverer of America (for Europeans), finding a new continent was never his true goal: in fact, America came into Columbus's life as an unanticipated and troublesome obstacle on his planned journey to Asia. He had staked his career and his nautical reputation on the theory that the breadth of the body of water separating Europe from Asia was far less than most geographers had predicted. While most thought that a ship heading west toward Asia would run out of supplies long before arriving. As it turned out, Columbus was wrong and his detractors were right: the figure for the circumference of the earth first arrived at by Eratosthenes was more or less correct, and were there nothing in between Europe and Asia, sailors attempting to reach the East by the West would starve in mid-ocean. Yet as Columbus unwittingly demonstrated, there was something in between: namely, the adjoining continents of North and South America. When Columbus arrived in the Caribbean islands scattered between these two continents, he believed he was on the edge of Asia, and initially interpreted the northern coast of Cuba as a part of China. Only toward the end of his career, as he sailed along the coast of what is now Venezuela, did Columbus begin to acknowledge that he was in fact on the edge of a new continent, but in his bewildered state he associated it with the earthly paradise of Christian legend.

The dramatic story of the exploration and conquest of the Americas, carried out initially by the Spanish and later continued by the Portuguese, Dutch, French, and English, has captured the historical imagination like few others. But for the Europeans of the time, the establishment of trade routes to Asia remained the most important commercial ambition of all, and a consideration of Magellan's career helps remind us of this. He sailed forth around the same time that Cortés was beginning his initial expedition into Mexico, and he reached the Pacific around the same time that Cortés was penetrating the core of the great Aztec empire. Both fulfilled some of Columbus's ambitions: Cortés by conquering rich new empires for the Spanish crown, Magellan by establishing a westward route to the Spice Islands of the Indian Ocean. For sixteenth century Europe, the latter accomplishment was probably more important, and there is a simple reason for that. East Asia was at the time the economic center of the world; it was wealthier and more commercially advanced than Europe, and possessed luxury goods that were in high demand among wealthy Europeans. In economic terms, the opening up of new trade routes with Asia is a more significant development than the conquest of the Americas, and indeed the development of the new American colonial economies is unimaginable without the expansion of commerce with the East. For example, a large proportion of the gold and silver mined in the minerally rich territories of the Andes and Mexico did not remain in Europe – they were traded to China and India for silk, tea, spices, and other exotic commodities. The colonial Mexican economy, after the establishment of Spanish settlements in the Philippines, became a conduit for the trade of such goods between East Asia and Europe.

So Magellan, who bypassed South America on the way to the Indian Ocean, reminds us what the fundamental goal of European expansion in the 16th century actually was: access to the widely coveted riches of Asia. The settlement of the Americas may be seen to some extent as a byproduct of this larger geopolitical and economic development, which would culminate centuries later in a period of European dominance over Asia, which had for over a thousand years been the wealthier and more commercially influential continent. Magellan's story lacks the dramatic martial flair of the stories of the conquistadors like his exact contemporary Cortés, but he remains an exemplary figure for having connected the two opposite ends of the earth in a period we might think of as the first era of globalization. Moreover, although he sailed under the Spanish flag, his Portuguese origins bring home the centrality of Portuguese navigation in the processes that forged the modern world and the modern globalized economy. Often neglected because of the later dominance of Spain and England, Portugal contributed decisively to the commercial and political reorientations of the early modern world.

This book chronicles Magellan's life and his historic expedition, analyzing the aftermath of his expeditions and his legacy. Along with pictures of important people, places, and events in his life, you will learn about Magellan like you never have before.

Sir Francis Drake (1540-1596)

"There must be a beginning of any great matter, but the continuing unto the end until it be thoroughly finished yields the true glory." – Sir Francis Drake

A lot of ink has been spilled covering the lives of history's most influential figures, but how much of the forest is lost for the trees? In Charles River Editors' British Legends series, readers can get caught up to speed on the lives of Great Britain's most important men and women in the time it takes to finish a commute, while learning interesting facts long forgotten or never known.

The life of Sir Francis Drake, or, more precisely, the tale of it, is one of those prime examples that history is written by the winners. Drake was the most famous sailor of the Elizabethan Era, and he has long been considered a hero by the English. His successes against the Spanish as a captain and a privateer were legendary, and Drake was celebrated for fighting the Queen's enemies, sinking their ships, and capturing the treasure that would otherwise be used to finance attacks on England. Drake vigorously pursued every mission given to him by Elizabeth I, and brought all his skill, experience and training to bear against her enemies. He was recognized at court for his valor, praised in story and song, and remembered for the kind of personality and esprit de corps that the English have long desired and celebrated in their military heroes.

While that might have summarized Sir Francis Drake's life from an English perspective, that's not at all how the Spanish remember "El Draque" ("The Dragon"), the 16th century's most notorious pirate. Referred to as "the main cause of wars" in one 1592 letter to the Spanish King Phillip II, Drake harassed Spanish ships in several oceans and was so despised by the Spanish that Phillip II placed the equivalent of a 7 million dollar bounty on his head. This should come as no surprise, given that Spanish accounts tell of a captain who attacked and boarded Spanish merchant ships to steal their treasure and made off with it in the kind of haughty and dramatic ways that have become standard fare in pirate lore. El Draque also had no qualms about killing those who refused his requests. At the same time, Spain was hardly above using privateers and piracy themselves, as one English writer would later put it, "The Spaniards had carried barbarism to such a pitch in seizing our ships and condemning their crews to the galleys, that Queen Elizabeth was never averse to meeting murder and plunder by more than the equivalent in retaliation."

Which version of Drake's life is more accurate? As usual, the reality falls somewhere inbetween. For most of his career, Drake was unquestionably a privateer and not a member of any organized Navy, thus answering to nobody except the Queen, and had he failed, he might have been shackled in irons and imprisoned. It was due to the fact he was successful that he was instead given a seat of honor at Elizabeth's own table in her own court. While privateers were used by all European powers during times of war, Drake also happened to target enemy ships when no state of war existed, thus clearly veering into the realm of piracy. Naturally, Elizabeth's enemies claimed that he was engaging in piracy with her blessing, which was probably true at times and untrue at others.

While contemporary accounts reveal two very different sides of the same man, Drake's legacy has since been shrouded in legend, with tales concerning buried treasure, encounters with Native Americans, and his famous circumnavigation of the globe. This book looks at the life, career, legends, and controversies of the Elizabethan Era's most famous captain. Along with pictures of important people, places, and events in his life, you will learn about Sir Francis Drake like you never have before, in no time at all.

Marco Polo
Chapter 1: The World in Marco Polo's Age

Today Venice is best known for its unique layout and canals, but Venice was the most prominent trading center in the medieval world, a status it had earned as early as the 9th century. Over the course of the 11th and 12th centuries, the merchant classes gained power, spurred by bankers and an economic system that facilitated long-distance trade in the city. In 1032, the seat of the doge, or hereditary leader of the city, was a position assigned by merit rather than birth, and the Great Council of Venice was established in 1172, making Venice a true republic.

Venice and Venetian Territory circa 1000 A.D. in red

During the 13th century, Venice remained a republic and offices in the Great Council were open to men in the merchant classes, but by the end of that century the power structure in Venice was significantly less open and the city operated as an oligarchy controlled by a small number of wealthy, powerful merchant families. These families would establish a secret service to help them consolidate power and maintain control over the city.

In addition to Venice itself, the Republic of Venice established Venetian territory elsewhere along the coast of the Adriatic Sea, as Venetian traders maintained bases in the Balkans, Tunis and Constantinople, as well as ports further east. Using this territory, Venetian merchants brought goods from the east to Europe, relying upon efficient seafaring vessels to transport their merchandise, which ranged from spices and pomegranates to minerals, fabrics, and even slaves. Marble and other materials scavenged from ancient buildings also made its way across the Mediterranean. Venetian traders also shipped their goods by water west to Marseilles, London and other ports, using galleys so efficient in sailing from one place to the next that the journey from Venice to Constantinople took only a few weeks.

Relatively early in the city's history, Venetian traders and other European traders began to maintain trade relationships with traders on the Silk Road, an overland trade route that linked China and the Mediterranean. The Silk Road encompassed both the Far East and Near East, including Beijing and Baghdad, and traders moved goods from east to west and west to east. Prior to the Mongol conquests, the route was relatively dangerous and frequently plagued by thieves, high tolls and other challenges. While the Venetians did not travel the Silk Road, they did have contacts in North Africa and elsewhere with caravan traders.

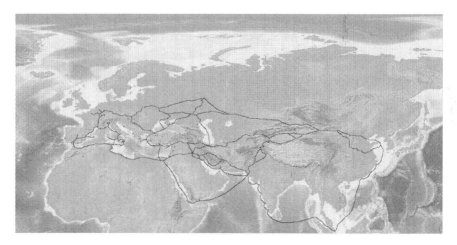

A map of overland trade routes used in the 9ᵗʰ century by the Radhanites

During the course of the 13th century, the Mongols conquered much of the eastern world under Genghis Khan, who united a huge portion of the eastern world by forcefully subduing and taking large regions. In areas that simply surrendered, violence was limited and local governors were allowed to retain their roles. At its height, the Mongolian Empire controlled more than 9 million square miles and 100 million people, and upon Genghis Khan's death, his empire was split between his grandsons. While the Mongolians did not maintain the unity of their empire, they continued to provide a sort of Pax Mongolica, even while separated into four distinct khanates. During his reign, Kublai Khan fought others in his family dynasty to retain his power, having been elected Great Khan alongside his brother. Over time, Kublai Khan consolidated and expanded his empire.

Kublai Khan

As Great Khan, Kublai Khan ruled the Mongolian Empire from his capital in modern-day Beijing, with a court that included Mongolians, Arabs, and Persians from throughout his empire. While Genghis Khan may have been a warrior, Kublai Khan was a man of culture, intellect and curiosity, and his court was a luxurious one rich in art, music, and goods.

Under the rule of the Mongolian Empire, trade along the Silk Road was both easier and more efficient than ever before. Toll gates were removed and traders could move freely from place to place. It was said that even women could travel safely with goods without fear of harm. Most importantly, the Mongolian emperors welcomed foreigners and traders in their empire and their courts.

Chapter 2: The Polo family

The Polo family first appears in Venetian records in the late 10th century, and they were apparently already wealthy mine owners during this time, as well as regular travelers between Venice and Dalmatia on the eastern coast of the Adriatic (in modern day Croatia). Members of the Polo family were among the nobility and commanding ships for the Republic by the 12th century. Thus, by the time the two Polo brothers (Marco's father and uncle) set off on their journey, they had the financial and social standing required to make such a trip.

Niccolò and Maffeo Polo were Venetian merchants and noblemen who eventually established successful trading facilities in the Crimean port of Soldaia (modern-day Suldak), Constantinople and a western trading post in the Mongol empire. During the 1250s, the pair left Venice for Constantinople, leaving behind their families. When they left, Niccolò's wife was either pregnant or had just given birth to an infant son.

Though the Byzantine Empire still existed in the 13th century, it was a shell of its former self, and Constantinople had been taken by the Venetians in 1204, maintaining a substantial Venetian presence thereafter. Niccolò and Maffeo likely felt at home in the city when they arrived, and the two remained in Constantinople until 1259 or 1260. At that time, political tensions in the region made a move essential because the Ottoman Turks were attempting to take Constantinople. As it turned out, the Venetian quarter in Constantinople was destroyed soon after the Polos departed. While they planned to return to Venice, pirates in the Black Sea blocked their path, so they moved on, establishing the family business in Soldaia. Soldaia, located in Crimea, was under the control of the Mongol state at the time and thus part of the Mongol Golden Horde.

15th century manuscript depicting the Polo brothers leaving Constantinople and heading

East.

While this was the Polo family's first contact with the Mongol Empire, it was far from their last. They moved on to Sarai and may have become familiar with the Mongol court camped there. When they met the Western khan, Barka, they gave him gifts of the jewels acquired in Constantinople and were rewarded with gifts twice as valuable. Here the brothers worked as traders in the court, encountering few Europeans but many traders from the East, including Muslims and Jews. Concerned about a potential civil war in the Mongolian ruling family, they moved further east, they next traveled to what is now Uzbekistan, conducting a difficult journey that Marco would later recount for the memorable fact that the brothers had to learn to tolerate the Mongol abhorrence of bathing and the taste of fermented mare's milk (koumiss). Despite these customs, the brothers remained there for three years, working as traders and dealing in various fabrics and jewels.

In 1264, the two brothers, now quite wealthy, joined a diplomatic group to visit the court of the Mongol ruler Kublai Khan, the grandson of Genghis Khan. Both could speak Mongolian by now, and they had developed a close relationship with many in the city of Bukhara, Uzbekistan. The ambassadors convinced the Polos that the Mongol Khan would be quite interested in meeting Europeans. The journey took two years and the pair, along with the others in the delegation, likely traveled in a caravan of carts and horses. The court of Kublai Khan was in Dadu, modern-day Beijing, where he ruled as the leader of the Great Khanate, comprised of Mongolia and China. He ruled as khan from 1260 onward and as the Yuan emperor of China from 1271 onward. Kublai Khan founded the Yuan dynasty in China, which ruled over China, Mongolia and Korea.

Depiction of Niccolò and Maffeo in Bukhara being invited to travel east.

While the Pope had denounced the violent actions of his grandfather, Kublai Khan's empire was remarkably peaceful and, even by Western standards, quite civilized. Kublai Khan received the Polo brothers with great curiosity, provided them with lavish quarters, and asked many questions about life in the west, particularly about Christianity and the Catholic Church. While the Polo brothers likely believed they were the first Europeans in the khan's court, there had been other traders, merchants and knights in the past. Kublai Khan's court welcomed foreigners, but retained a strong Mongol identity even in China.

After meeting the brothers, Kublai Khan assigned a Mongol ambassador to return to Europe with them. The ambassador was to take a letter to the Pope requesting that 100 Christian missionaries come east to debate the worth of Christianity and educate the Mongol court about life in the West. While he did not promise to renounce other faiths, he did tell the Pope that he and his men would accept the Church if convinced of its worth. He also requested the oil of the Holy Sepulchre, which was believed to cure all ills. Of course, this might not have been as earth-shattering as it seems at first glance. At the time, the Mongolian pantheon of deities was quite large, and it's likely that Kublai Khan was merely holding out the possibility of recognizing Jesus as one of the deities in the pantheon.

The letter also included a golden tablet, or paiza, allowing the brothers and the ambassador to travel and obtain lodging and goods throughout the empire. By holding the paiza, local rulers were required to provide rooms, horses and escorts to the travelers. But even with the paiza, the journey back to Venice took three years traveling by sea and overland, along with a stop in the Western-controlled kingdom of Jerusalem along the way. And as luck would have it, the Mongolian ambassador did not complete the journey to Venice, having become quite ill only 20 days into their voyage.

While oil from the Holy Sepulchre was a manageable and accessible commodity (if not always authentic), there is no evidence that either Niccolò or Maffeo expected to return with a large contingent of Christian mercenaries. Such a journey with a group of that size would have been nearly impossible during the 13th century.

Niccolò and Maffeo returned to Venice in 1269 or 1270; and upon coming home they learned the papal elections were quite delayed. Thus, they were not able to deliver the message from Kublai Khan until after the next papal election in 1271, and they eventually opted to continue on their mission regardless of the situation with the papacy.

Depiction of the brothers delivering Kublai Khan's message to the Pope

This also happened to provide an opportunity for a family reunion, as the brothers' return to Venice reunited Niccolò with his son Marco. Marco's mother had died when he was quite young, and he was living with an aunt and uncle in Venice. The family had apparently had no contact in many years, and Niccolò was apparently startled to learn of his wife's death and his 15 year old son. Marco Polo was likely unaware that his father was even alive throughout his life. During his short stay in Venice, Niccolò remarried, and his new wife quickly became pregnant.

Chapter 3: Marco Polo's Journey

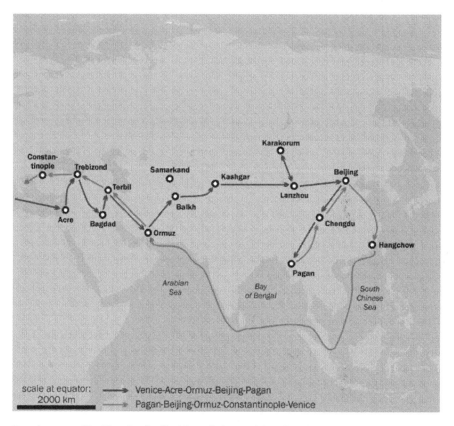

scale at equator: 2000 km
——► Venice-Acre-Ormuz-Beijing-Pagan
——► Pagan-Beijing-Ormuz-Constantinople-Venice

Born into a wealthy Venetian family, Marco Polo certainly enjoyed a privileged childhood. Venice was a religious city, with the day divided by traditional prayers, but it was also rife with crime and intrigue. Notably, the Polo family was relatively free of scandal throughout the thirteenth century.

Venice was then, as it is now, surrounded by water, and the Venetians were a close-knit community. Amongst the merchants, strong and trusting relationships enabled easy investment and trade relationships. Merchant travelers, like Marco Polo's father and uncle, were not uncommon, and though they were often away for many years, they retained their identity as Venetians and their standing in the city. Venetians spoke a distinct Latin-based dialect, but many were multi-lingual.

While travel was uncommon in much of Europe, Venetians embraced a more international life. Technological advances, including the compass, ships and water mills, improved life in Venice and for the Venetians. The city's Arsenal, or shipyard, turned out large numbers of fast-moving galley ships which served the dual purpose of being both merchant vessels and battleships. Venice was constantly at war along the Mediterranean, often over its trade interests. The Republic of Venice operated the ships and provided protection while the travelers were expected to carry their own food, bedding and necessities. Even still, short sea journeys were often difficult and dangerous, and battles were common.

The city celebrated a number of formal rituals, including a ceremonial Marriage to the Sea and the installation of a new Doge. At 14, Marco Polo certainly witnessed the ceremonies and festivities when the new Doge was chosen. Members of the merchant guilds of the city, elaborately dressed, proceeded through town. These rituals, unique to the city of Venice, helped to strengthen ties within the community.

Marco Polo is believed to have been about 15 years old when his father returned, and he was apparently considered old enough to join his father and uncle on their second journey east to the court of the Khan two years after their return. While Niccolò and Maffeo had made a rather haphazard and slow trip east the first time, this time they hadt he advantage of traveling with the paiza. Having made the acquaintance of the new pope, Pope Gregory X, the three traveled first to part of modern-day Lebanon to speak to the papal legate in the Kingdom of Acre. They had made the acquaintance of Teobaldo Visconti on their earlier journey. From there, they were allowed to travel to Jerusalem in search of the oil of the Holy Sepulchre requested by Kublai Khan.

Depiction of Pope Gregory X

In Jerusalem, the Polos acquired the oil, and they received a letter that the Pope wished to have them present to Kublai Khan. They also returned to Acre to pick up two friars, Nicolau de Vicense and Guilielme de Tripule, who joined their party to bring news of Christianity to the east as requested by the khan. The friars, appointed by the Pope, were granted the rights to establish churches, ordain priests and make bishops. Clearly Gregory X was pleased by the opportunity to establish the Church in the Mongol Empire.

From Acre, the group of merchants and explorers traveled through Persia and then northward into Tartary. While the Polos pressed on, the papal delegation, including the two friars, was so frightened that they turned back before the group reached Armenia. The Polos, however, were still quite certain that they could successfully make the journey east, and that it would provide them with both wealth and power.

Marco would later note that he was unimpressed by what he found in Armenia and Turkey. He remarked on Muslim customs with great distaste, only briefly mentioning the nomadic nature of many of the people of the region, but as a trader he was impressed by their fine carpets. As the withdrawal of the papal delegation suggested, this part of the trip was the most dangerous part of their journey, as they moved overland through potentially unfriendly and (at least in their minds) uncivilized regions. They did not have the comforts of organized caravans and caravan services while they were in Turkey, and the culture was hostile to western Christians.

However, once they entered Mongol territory, their journey would proceed with greater ease thanks to the golden tablet. By this point, they had also found it easier to travel without the conspicuous papal delegation. Marco noted the surprising environment of religious tolerance throughout the Mongol Empire; while obedience to Kublai Khan was required, there was no state religion and no religion was favored over any other. Islam, Buddhism, Nestorian Christianity and the Mongol faiths all co-existed in relative peace throughout the Mongolian Empire.

The Polos may have become the most famous Europeans to travel to Asia, but they were far from the first. Earlier travelers had made it just as far east, and some even produced accounts of their visit. Benjamin of Tudela, a Spanish Jew, had written an account of his visit to Asia in the 12th century, but it was not widely circulated. Franciscan monk Giovanni de Pian del Carpini and a companion made it significantly east of Baghdad in the 1240s and were received at the Mongol court. He was the first Christian missionary to go that far east, and he produced the *Historica Mongolica* upon his return to Europe. Another Franciscan, William of Rubruck, also traveled east and recorded his observations about the Mongolians, noting the devotion and piety of Buddhist monks in his account.

When the travelers reached the city of Mosul (present day Iraq) on the Tigris River, Marco Polo witnessed his first true desert trading post. Traders of all faiths and nationalities sold and bartered in Mosul, and Marco was introduced to new trade goods, including unbleached cotton muslin from India. He also encountered a new religion, Nestorian Christianity, which distinguished between the human and divine Christ in a way the Catholic Church did not. Marco, raised a Catholic, identified the Nestorians as heretics. In this early stage of his journey, he remained a Venetian Christian, demonstrating he was, as yet, unchanged by his perceptions and experiences. At the same time, it must be kept in mind that Polo was writing for a Christian audience back in Europe, making it sensible that he would portray Christianity in a favorable light and look down upon foreign religions.

While Baghdad was just 200 miles from Mosul, the stories in Marco Polo's account suggest he never visited the city. The Polos did visit Tabriz, known for its pearl market, but again they were far from the only Europeans in the city. Genoese traders frequently visited Tabriz for pearls and other goods, which actually offered Marco some respite from foreign culture. Marco was quite concerned by the beliefs and actions of Muslims, so he was relieved by the existence of a Carmelite monastery in Tabriz.

The travelers next moved into Persia, visiting Kerman. While some of Marco's account of his travels is clearly inaccurate, other sections reveal a precise awareness of his own surroundings. He describes the journey from Kerman in some detail, and over time, his account suggests that he began to feel at home in Persia, remarking upon the fine, large sheep and oxen and the falcons used for hunting. The Polos also had a near brush with disaster when they encountered the Karaunas, raiding bands of marauders and assassins, during their stay in Persia. The travelers narrowly escaped the Karaunas and went on to Hormuz, a trade and port city on the Persian Gulf.

The Polo family planned to go from Hormuz to India by sea, but they found the ships unsafe and heard news of recent deaths on both land and sea. Thus, they returned to Kerman and planned to make their journey overland along the Silk Road. Instead of horses and carts, they would rely on the best means of travel in this desert climate, the two-humped bactrian camel. They carried goods on donkeys, but they were particularly concerned about access to water on their journey. Larger groups joined together to form trade caravans for safety. Marco recounts visits to desert oases on their way with some delight, noting in particular how beautiful the women were. While oases were often home to larger communities, caravan stops provided food, lodging, water and stables for animals and were, in many areas, spaced approximately every 20 miles. As they moved east into Afghanistan, the environment changed, becoming more lush and fertile. In Afghanistan, Marco noted the ruins of the great city of Balkh, which had been destroyed by Genghis Khan in 1220.

Marco became ill during his time in Afghanistan, and this illness marked the first change in his observations and perspective. The most likely explanation appears to be tuberculosis, which was rampant in Venice during his childhood. The family spent a year in the mountains of Afghanistan staying in the wealthy city of Badakhshan, and the fresh mountain air and sunlight improved Marco's health, though it's also possible he may have controlled the coughing and symptoms of tuberculosis by ingesting or smoking opium. Even today, that region of Afghanistan remains a notoriously prime poppy-growing area.

When the Polos moved on, they next passed through a very isolated region, Pemir, largely inhabited by sheep. The facilities and caravan inns they had enjoyed earlier in their journey were no longer available, and they had to travel over large areas with little access to food or water. The family reached Khotan and restocked, enjoying the fertility of the Buddhist region as well as access to food and other supplies. Marco did not, at this point in his journey, show any interest in learning about the religion, simply identifying them as idolators. Not long after leaving Khotan, the family reached the desert of Lop, the hardest and driest stage of the journey, as well as one of the most dangerous. After passing through the desert of Lop, they reached the border of China.

For the first time at the border of China, Marco noted the similarities between Christianity and Buddhism, and he instantly recognized the use of similar rituals and festivities. He examined cultural practices like cremation and gradually, during his stay in Tangut, began to shed his own European identity and engage in significant self-exploration.

In Kamul (modern-day Hami, China), Marco enjoyed the hospitality of the people, which extended to offering wives and daughters to guests. This custom helped to reduce the risks of a closed marriage system within the village without challenging the economics of the community. Marco's observations of women and sexual behavior would continue throughout his travel chronicle. The travelers spent a full year in another trading post, clearly working as merchants, but Marco provided no details of this time. However, they had now been on the road for three years and were still approximately 2,000 miles from the court of Kublai Khan.

Eventually the Polos moved on until they entered Mongol territory. Marco described the nomadic existence, the carts and the homes of the Mongol people in some detail. The homes or ger could be broken down and transported from place to place along with the herds. He found the women to be loyal, diligent and hard-working, while polygamy was practiced and men fathered large numbers of children. They were well-fed, enjoying a varied and rich diet. Marco also described their religious rituals and beliefs in some detail, and, all told, his writing makes clear that he admired the Mongolians and viewed them as civilized. Moreover, he idolized the fierce Mongol warrior of the time of Genghis Khan.

"Now am I come to that part of our Book in which I shall tell you of the great and wonderful magnificence of the Great Kaan now reigning, by name CUBLAY KAAN; Kaan being a title which signifyeth "The Great Lord of Lords," or Emperor. And of a surety he hath good right to such a title, for all men know for a certain truth that he is the most potent man, as regards forces and lands and treasure, that existeth in the world, or ever hath existed from the time of our First Father Adam until this day. All this I will make clear to you for truth, in this book of ours, so that every one shall be fain to acknowledge that he is the greatest Lord that is now in the world, or ever hath been." – *The Travels of Marco Polo*, Volume 1

Marco, his father and his uncle continued their journey, visiting the summer palace of Kublai Khan in Xanadu, which Marco described in detail. The elaborately detailed and decorated summer palace was made of marble and surrounded by large gardens and a royal zoo for the khan's enjoyment. The rooms were painted with pictures of animals, birds and flowers. Walls enclosed some 16 miles of gardens, including fountains and rivers, and within the gardens was a second smaller palace placed in a grove of trees, made of cane and fixed tightly together to make it watertight. Silk robes secured the palace to the ground like a tent. Like the Mongolian homes or ger used by the lower classes, the palace could be broken down and moved from place to place with little difficulty, and at the end of summer, the cane building was broken down as the khan moved to his winter accommodations in the city of Beijing.

The palace gardens were also home to great herds of albino horses and cattle, reserved solely for the use of the khan and his family. Festivals celebrated the albino mares in the khan's herd and marked the end of the summer season and the return to the winter palace.

Marco was simply amazed by the palace and its surroundings, noting:

"The Hall of the Palace is so large that it could easily dine 6000 people; and it is quite a marvel to see how many rooms there are besides. The building is altogether so vast, so rich, and so beautiful, that no man on earth could design anything superior to it. The outside of the roof also is all coloured with vermilion and yellow and green and blue and other hues, which are fixed with a varnish so fine and exquisite that they shine like crystal, and lend a resplendent lustre to the Palace as seen for a great way round. This roof is made too with such strength and solidity that it is fit to last for ever.

Between the two walls of the enclosure which I have described, there are fine parks and beautiful trees bearing a variety of fruits. There are beasts also of sundry kinds, such as white stags and fallow deer, gazelles and roebucks, and fine squirrels of various sorts, with numbers also of the animal that gives the musk, and all manner of other beautiful creatures, insomuch that the whole place is full of them, and no spot remains void except where there is traffic of people going and coming. The parks are covered with abundant grass; and the roads through them being all paved and raised two cubits above the surface, they never become muddy, nor does the rain lodge on them, but flows off into the meadows, quickening the soil and producing that abundance of herbage."

While the summer palace brought Marco into contact with the khan's court, he did not meet the khan until they reached modern-day Beijing, home to the court of Kublai Khan. The palace complex, designed by a Muslim builder, was immense; it contained storage space for arms, stables, workshops and more than four hundred rooms. There were also wide roads and excellent drainage systems, which kept the palace clean and comfortable. It was, by the standards of Venice, a remarkably clean and spacious complex.

The palace was so finely decorated that the nobility carried fine white slippers to wear indoors and carried small vases as spitoons to protect the carpets. Paintings decorated every wall, and even the roofs were brightly colored, creating a vivid impression from quite a distance. Outside of the palace, wide streets were laid out in a grid. Gates allowed sections to be closed and reduced the risk of crime. A large city clock announced the time, and a curfew was in place to further control behavior. In comparison with the tight alleys and canals he knew, the city was exceptionally safe.

The palace could accommodate large banquets, to such an extent that Marco suggested (probably incorrectly) that these lavish banquets were attended by as many as 40,000 people. Huge enameled vessels held beverages and food at the banquets. Enamel was unknown in the west, and Marco provided a description to help his viewers understand the wealth of the palace.

The three travelers, wearing their finest garb, approached the emperor at once after reaching Beijing. While they certainly dressed in elegant Venetian clothing, the attire of the khan and court exceeded anything seen among the European nobility. Marco described garments of silk and cloth of gold, liberally embellished with pearls. Contemporary accounts from Yuan dynasty China support his descriptions of the lavish court dress. They prostrated themselves before Kublai Khan, who welcomed the Polo brothers back with a great feast and was quite pleased to see them. In turn, the brothers presented Kublai Khan with the letters they had carried from Acre, bearing the papal seal. They also gave him the oil of the Holy Sepulchre, collected in Jerusalem. Finally, Niccolò presented his son, giving Marco into the service of the Mongol emperor. The relationship between Marco and Kublai Khan would continue, with remarkable trust and closeness, for the next 17 years. Kublai Khan was already in his early sixties by the time the Polo brothers reached the court on their second visit. While Marco describes him in flattering terms, of fair size and well-formed with a fair face and black eyes, contemporary portraits reveal that Kublai Khan was somewhat overweight and beginning to show his age. He appears kindly but imposing in portraits of the period and not as "well-formed" as Marco Polo described.

The Polo brothers delivering the Pope's letter and presents to Kublai Khan

Kublai Khan was a remarkably cosmopolitan ruler and immediately impressed the young Marco. Raised by his mother, a Nestorian Christian, he had a wide tolerance of diversity, even by Mongolian standards, and he embraced the wide and varied customs of those he ruled. Under the influence of his second and favorite wife, Chabi, Kublai Khan embraced Tibetan Buddhism. Chabi's influence continued throughout Kublai Khan's life. While earlier Mongol rulers had limited the participation of Chinese and other non-Mongols in the court, Kublai Khan gave them positions in the court, and his advisors included Mongols, Chinese and Persians. He assigned scholars to teach Mongolian students in China the Chinese language and culture and even went so far as to support the creation of a new written language in an attempt to unify the linguistically diverse empire. While Mongol leaders were traditionally brutal, Kublai Khan maintained order and loyalty with generous rewards.

Chabi was the most influential of Kublai Khan's wives, but each of his four primary wives maintained their own palace and household, consisting of many young women and eunuchs. As he did elsewhere, Marco paid special attention to the women in the court. The khan also had access to a large number of concubines, chosen from the most beautiful women in the empire. Naturally, only the loveliest young women were selected to serve the emperor, and a group of six girls served the emperor for three days before being replaced by another group of six. The less beautiful of those brought to the capital were taught skills and served in the courts of the emperor's wives. The young women were often married to barons in the court, after having served the emperor.

Given this arrangement, it should come as no surprise that the khan fathered many children.

Marco mentions 22 sons by his four wives and an additional 25 by his concubines, among which his eldest son, Chinkim, was intended to be his successor. The Great Khan's reproductive success was not unique, and Marco went on to attribute the glory of the Mongol empire to the practice of polygamy.

Kublai Khan also proved an adept administrator, even introducing paper money and thus replacing gold, silver and copper coins with printed money. The court welcomed merchants and traders, recognizing them as a vital source of tax revenue and income in the court, and merchants were required to trade valuable goods, including gems, cloth and gold, for paper currency in the court. Worn or damaged paper currency could be exchanged for new paper at the mint. Marco Polo described the system in detail:

"Now that I have told you in detail of the splendour of this City of the Emperor's, I shall proceed to tell you of the Mint which he hath in the same city, in the which he hath his money coined and struck, as I shall relate to you. And in doing so I shall make manifest to you how it is that the Great Lord may well be able to accomplish even much more than I have told you, or am going to tell you, in this Book. For, tell it how I might, you never would be satisfied that I was keeping within truth and reason!

The Emperor's Mint then is in this same City of Cambaluc, and the way it is wrought is such that you might say he hath the Secret of Alchemy in perfection, and you would be right! For he makes his money after this fashion.

He makes them take of the bark of a certain tree, in fact of the Mulberry Tree, the leaves of which are the food of the silkworms,—these trees being so numerous that whole districts are full of them. What they take is a certain fine white bast or skin which lies between the wood of the tree and the thick outer bark, and this they make into something resembling sheets of paper, but black. When these sheets have been prepared they are cut up into pieces of different sizes. The smallest of these sizes is worth a half tornesel; the next, a little larger, one tornesel; one, a little larger still, is worth half a silver groat of Venice; another a whole groat; others yet two groats, five groats, and ten groats. There is also a kind worth one Bezant of gold, and others of three Bezants, and so up to ten. All these pieces of paper are [issued with as much solemnity and authority as if they were of pure gold or silver; and on every piece a variety of officials, whose duty it is, have to write their names, and to put their seals. And when all is prepared duly, the chief officer deputed by the Kaan smears the Seal entrusted to him with vermilion, and impresses it on the paper, so that the form of the Seal remains printed upon it in red; the Money is then authentic. Any one forging it would be punished with death.] And the Kaan causes every year to be made such a vast quantity of this money, which costs him nothing, that it must equal in amount all the treasure in the world.

With these pieces of paper, made as I have described, he causes all payments on his own account to be made; and he makes them to pass current universally over all his kingdoms and provinces and territories, and whithersoever his power and sovereignty extends. And nobody, however important he may think himself, dares to refuse them on pain of death. And indeed everybody takes them readily, for wheresoever a person may go throughout the Great Kaan's dominions he shall find these pieces of paper current, and shall be able to transact all sales and purchases of goods by means of them just as well as if they were coins of pure gold. And all the while they are so light that ten bezants' worth does not weigh one golden bezant."

The presses that produced currency also produced books, including a variety of books on astrology. Ironically, while Marco Polo was aware of the production of books and their circulation, he did not deem the khan's printing press worthy of particular mention. It would take over 150 years after Polo's journey for Johannes Gutenberg to invent the printing press in the West, and that would be considered one of the most important inventions of the millennium.

Marco took note of another technological innovation in the Mongolian Empire:

"It is a fact that all over the country of Cathay there is a kind of black stones existing in beds in the mountains, which they dig out and burn like firewood. If you supply the fire with them at night, and see that they are well kindled, you will find them still alight in the morning; and they make such capital fuel that no other is used throughout the country. It is true that they have plenty of wood also, but they do not burn it, because those stones burn better and cost less."

These "black stones" are still widely used for fuel today. They were, of course, coal. Marco Polo is credited with providing or returning the knowledge of coal to the west.

Large parts of the Mongolian Empire were not particularly fertile, but the government managed the food supply, releasing grain as needed. If weather conditions led to famine, the khan released grain from his own stores, collected as taxes the previous year. If the livestock had suffered, he provided families from his own stores. In the event of a difficult year, taxes on the region could be waived to ease the hardship. Even merchants benefited from charity, being freed from fees and taxes if a ship sank due to a lightning strike. Bread was distributed at the palace daily to the needy. The welfare programs established under the khan provided adequate food for some families for a full year, and clothing was also provided to the poor from the royal stores. While the khan certainly ruled as a dictator, he was a benevolent one who cared for his people. Marco Polo wrote, "And this applies, let me tell you, to all kinds of corn, whether wheat, barley, millet, rice, panic, or what not, and when there is any scarcity of a particular kind of corn, he causes that to be issued. And if the price of the corn is at one bezant the measure, he lets them have it at a bezant for four measures, or at whatever price will produce general cheapness; and every one can have food in this way. And by this providence of the Emperor's, his people can never suffer from dearth. He does the same over his whole Empire; causing these supplies to be stored everywhere, according to calculation of the wants and necessities of the people."

Kublai Khan also established a network of couriers as an ancient form of a postal service, enabling messages to travel as much as 200-250 miles each day. Stables provided fresh riders and horses every 25 miles, and in the event of urgent news riders would travel at night. Meanwhile, runners covered shorter distances, carrying the message a few miles at a quick sprint. This effective network allowed news to travel quickly throughout the empire.

Life at the court consisted of grand banquets and even grander hunts, and Marco was especially impressed by falconry. He had first witnessed the use of birds of prey during his journey, but never on the scale present at the court of Kublai Khan. Kublai Khan also had a variety of large cats, including a tame lion who lay at his feet. Perhaps unsurprisingly, Polo was less impressed by the court astrologers, which consisted of two types that Marco both linked to the devil. He added a story to explain the evil of the court astrologers, stating that they ate the flesh of those condemned for crimes. But even as he deemed them evil, he seemed entranced by their power, and Marco fancifully described them as capable of lifting large numbers of cups without touching them at the khan's banquet.

Like his father and uncle on their first trip, Marco quickly mastered the languages of the Mongolian empire, both written and spoken, which made him a valuable tool in Kublai Khan's court despite the fact he never learned or spoke Chinese. During his first months in the court, he also mastered writing and archery. The Polo family had not intended to remain at the Mongolian court for long, but they soon found themselves wrapped up in the court and unable to leave the control of their friendly but determined overlord. This obligation to Kublai Khan would continue for many years.

Not long after settling into his role in Kublai Khan's court, Marco was sent on a six-month journey as a royal messenger. He traveled without his uncle and father for the first time, but he did have a Golden Tablet and the blessing of Kublai Khan. While they have not survived, Marco maintained careful notes of all that he heard and saw during his travels, in the hopes of distinguishing himself as an ideal messenger for the khan. When he returned to the court, he recounted his trip to Kublai Khan in great detail, impressing the leader and increasing his own status within the court.

After this first successful outing, Marco was assigned other administrative tasks across the Mongol Empire, and it is most likely that he served as a tax collector for the khan. He went from Beijing to Hangzhou, traveling along the Grand Canal, and the trip took him through much of Asia. On his journey, he crossed the Guangli Bridge, today called the Marco Polo Bridge, and he eventually reached Tibet. It was here that his admiration for the Mongols failed upon witnessing the devastation throughout the countryside, and it did not escape his notice that the primary form of currency in Tibet was salt.

As he had at other times, Marco took a special interest in the women and the customs attached to female sexuality. Throughout Tibet and further east, he found once again that hospitality extended to the female family members. Marco first encountered tea during this visit, but his description is vague.

He traveled onto Karagian, in the Yunnan Province of China. Karagian was quite distant from the centralized part of the Mongolian Empire, and while the Pax Mongolica was officially in place, this was a rough and uncivilized region. This part of the trip is most memorable for Marco's account of a fearsome "serpent":

"In this province are found snakes and great serpents of such vast size as to strike fear into those who see them, and so hideous that the very account of them must excite the wonder of those to hear it. I will tell you how long and big they are.

You may be assured that some of them are ten paces in length; some are more and some less. And in bulk they are equal to a great cask, for the bigger ones are about ten palms in girth. They have two forelegs near the head, but for foot nothing but a claw like the claw of a hawk or that of a lion. The head is very big, and the eyes are bigger than a great loaf of bread. The mouth is large enough to swallow a man whole, and is garnished with great teeth. And in short they are so fierce-looking and so hideously ugly, that every man and beast must stand in fear and trembling of them. There are also smaller ones, such as of eight paces long, and of five, and of one pace only.

The way in which they are caught is this. You must know that by day they live underground because of the great heat, and in the night they go out to feed, and devour every animal they can catch. They go also to drink at the rivers and lakes and springs. And their weight is so great that when they travel in search of food or drink, as they do by night, the tail makes a great furrow in the soil as if a full ton of liquor had been dragged along. Now the huntsmen who go after them take them by certain gyn which they set in the track over which the serpent has past, knowing that the beast will come back the same way. They plant a stake deep in the ground and fix on the head of this a sharp blade of steel made like a razor or a lance-point, and then they cover the whole with sand so that the serpent cannot see it. Indeed the huntsman plants several such stakes and blades on the track. On coming to the spot the beast strikes against the iron blade with such force that it enters his breast and rives him up to the navel, so that he dies on the spot."

Scholars agree that Marco had just encountered a crocodile for the first time, and he went on to note that the animal was valued both for its meat and medical purposes. He also noted the presence of elephants and "unicorns", which were not the mythical horned horse but rather rhinoceros.

Continuing his travels, Marco Polo came in contact with tattooed peoples of China, describing the process in some detail. "The people of this country all have their teeth gilt; or rather every man covers his teeth with a sort of golden case made to fit them, both the upper teeth and the under. The men do this, but not the women. The men also are wont to gird their arms and legs with bands or fillets pricked in black, and it is done thus; they take five needles joined together, and with these they prick the flesh till the blood comes, and then they rub in a certain black colouring stuff, and this is perfectly indelible. It is considered a piece of elegance and the sign of gentility to have this black band. The men are all gentlemen in their fashion, and do nothing but go to the wars, or go hunting and hawking. The ladies do all the business, aided by the slaves who have been taken in war."

As he noted, the practice was quite dangerous, and many people died during the process of being tattooed. Marco's travels extended into Vietnam, where lions posed so serious a risk to travelers and merchants that they slept on the river and relied upon wolves for protection. After his long journey, Marco began a slow route back to the capital, traveling primarily by river and canal on his return.

In Huangzhou, called Quinsai at the time, Marco found a Chinese city built on canals, much like Venice, and he claimed to have served there as governor, but there is no evidence in the Yuan dynasty records. There was a large lake to one side of the city and a river to the other, and bridges connected roads throughout the region. While he was not welcomed to the city and could not speak Chinese, he was personally entranced by Huangzhou. The city had been conquered by the Mongols, but it had not lost its Chinese identity and resented the Mongol occupation. Other contemporary accounts support Marco's stories about the grandeur and wealth of Huangzhou. The population of the city may have reached as many as 1.5 million.

Marco commented on the pleasure barges on the lake, well-dressed courtesans in the city and the eunuchs working in administrative positions. He was seemingly unaware of the custom of foot binding, which would lead some scholars to question the authenticity of his account and whether he had actually made it to China. However, Chinese noblewomen were typically secluded indoors and did not and could not travel about the town, so the women Marco encountered in Huangzhou were courtesans, merchants and workers rather than the noblewomen who experienced foot binding. While Marco had noted the curfew in Beijing, life in Huangzhou began in the wee hours of the morning and continued nearly 24 hours a day. The work week was ten days long, with a single day of rest following each week. Marco left Huangzhou suddenly, without explanation; he may have simply been called back to the court of Kublai Khan.

Conditions in the Mongol Empire worsened while Marco was in Huangzhou. Kublai Khan's favorite wife Chabi had died, along with his eldest son and heir. Moreover, the elderly khan's own health worsened, and he became an alcoholic, gaining substantial amounts of weight. His judgement also began to fade, and he embarked on a series of poorly planned attempts at the conquest of Japan which were recounted by Marco. While the Chinese and others conquered by the Mongolians were largely peaceful peoples, the Japanese were particularly known for their skill in battle and the ferocity of their warriors. The conquest of Japan and an attempted conquest of Java both failed.

Kublai Khan's weakness put the Polo family at risk, and Marco reunited with his uncle and father after leaving Huangzhou. The three traveled widely, joining with merchant caravans for protection, and faced with growing strife in the Mongol Empire and the weakening status of Kublai Khan, they set out for a voyage by sea to India. They had begged Kublai Khan's permission to return to Venice but were granted permission only to travel throughout the Khan's lands; their travels, therefore, were technically on behalf of Kublai Khan. The Arab and Chinese ships that sailed between India and China were comfortably outfitted with cabins for merchants and, unlike Venetian vessels, were well-provided. Separate watertight holds reduced the risk of shipwreck and made the journey less dangerous.

The Polos traveled first to Indonesia, where Marco recounted the animals, including rhinoceros and elephants, but he was particularly fascinated by pygmies, writing, "I may tell you moreover that when people bring home pygmies which they allege to come from India, 'tis all a lie and a cheat. For those little men, as they call them, are manufactured on this Island, and I will tell you how. You see there is on the Island a kind of monkey which is very small, and has a face just like a man's. They take these, and pluck out all the hair except the hair of the beard and on the breast, and then they dry them and stuff them and daub them with saffron and other things until they look like men. But you see it is all a cheat; for nowhere in India nor anywhere else in the world were there ever men seen so small as these pretended pygmies." Though he described the pygmies as a type of monkey that were hunted and later displayed as a curiosity, the pygmies were, of course, actually unusually small humans who were common both in Africa and Indonesia during the period. His accounts of Indonesia also included detailed descriptions of cannibalism, and he remained in at least occasional contact with Kublai Khan.

From Indonesia, Marco moved on to India, where he was quite taken with the pearl trade and described pearl fishermen who signed short-term contracts and dove for pearls. The local inhabitants embellished their garments with pearls and even made pearl garments by stringing pearls together. Pearl fishing was a risky trade with "great fishes" attacking the pearl fishermen. Marco described magicians, or brahmins, who controlled the "great fishes" to prevent these attacks. The king also wore a collar covered in pearls and gemstones.

As he had elsewhere, Marco noted the sexual behavior of the people of Bettala, including the 500 wives of the king. The women of Bettala were, according to Marco, especially beautiful, but that wasn't the most interesting characteristic of women there. It was in Bettala that Marco first described the practice of suttee or widow-burning, in which widows threw themselves on the funeral pyre with their husbands. This action was praised, and women who did not commit suttee were scorned by the society.

Marco also described devout yogis who fasted for years and slept naked on the ground, and once again, he was especially interested in the sexual practices of the yogis. Members were tested with sexual temptation, and if they responded physically, they were cast out from the group. Marco retained a surprising objectivity in his description of the people, suggesting that he was moving away from his own upbringing's cultural biases.

While Marco's understanding of faith and culture increased, he continued to express the faith of his childhood. In India, he, along with a group of pilgrims, visited the tomb of St. Thomas in Madras. St. Thomas was believed to have brought Christianity to India, and both Christians and Muslims made pilgrimages to the burial site, where the earth was credited with the ability to cure malaria. While St. Thomas predated Islam, the Muslims of the region viewed him as a great holy man. Marco also saw coconuts for the first time on this visit and described them as a nut that provided both food and water.

In India, Marco began to explore Buddhism in earnest. He had first encountered Buddhism in the Mongol court, but they practiced Tibetan Buddhism. Indian Buddhism was a more ancient form than Tibetan, and Marco was drawn to the practice. When he wrote his account of the travels, Marco included a short retelling of the Buddha's life that was short but mostly accurate and fair. He treated the subject with great care and respect, naming it the equal of Christianity and not defining their practices as "idolatry" or blasphemy.

Environmental conditions troubled Marco during his time in India. He described the excessive heat in the country. The animals were equally remarkable, including birds of all sorts and "black lions". He encountered new plants, fruits and vegetables during his stay. "There are in this country many and diverse beasts quite different from those of other parts of the world. Thus there are lions black all over, with no mixture of any other colour; and there are parrots of many sorts, for some are white as snow with red beak and feet, and some are red, and some are blue, forming the most charming sight in the world; there are green ones too. There are also some parrots of exceeding small size, beautiful creatures. They have also very beautiful peacocks, larger than ours, and different; and they have cocks and hens quite different from ours; and what more shall I say? In short, everything they have is different from ours, and finer and better. Neither is their fruit like ours, nor their beasts, nor their birds; and this difference all comes of the excessive heat."

As Marco moved west through India, he encountered Arab pirates who preyed on merchants of all nationalities He clearly felt a connection to the victims, describing how they swallowed gems to protect them from pirates. When pirates boarded, they killed relatively few, but the merchants were humiliated and suffered great financial losses. Trade on the western seas was made very difficult by these pirates, and those who later annotated Marco's account noted that piracy was still an issue in the region during their day as well. Marco described several other locations in India, but he may have relied upon second-hand information for some of these. Still, his accounts remain as one of the few Western portrayals of this portion of the world during the 13th century.

Marco may have kept incredibly detailed notes of his travels, but he was primarily concerned with returning to Venice and continued his journey with that aim in mind. Thus, regardless of his concerns about pirates, Marco sailed across the Indian Ocean to the island of Socatra. In Socatra, he was most taken by the amazing variety of plants and animals in the region, describing it as "the most enchanted place on earth". The rich and wealthy fishing industry in Socatra included both tuna and whaling. Arab whalers used fatty tuna as bait, harpooning the whales to kill them. Europeans were familiar with whaling, commonplace in Scandinavia.

After visiting the Ganges River, Marco moved on to Africa or at least claimed to have done so. He visited Zanzibar and described giraffes: "They have also many giraffes. This is a beautiful creature, and I must give you a description of it. Its body is short and somewhat sloped to the rear, for its hind legs are short whilst the fore-legs and the neck are both very long, and thus its head stands about three paces from the ground. The head is small, and the animal is not at all mischievous. Its colour is all red and white in round spots, and it is really a beautiful object."

While he had likely encountered African traders and African slaves in Venice, this was his first exposure to African culture. He describes the people as both large and strong, but gratefully notes that they do cover their "natural parts". The women are not, in his opinion, attractive. While his physical descriptions are harsh, he goes on to call them great merchants and traders, as well as strong and able fighters who take on elephants. "They have among them excellent and valiant warriors, and have little fear of death. They have no horses, but fight mounted on camels and elephants. On the latter they set wooden castles which carry from ten to sixteen persons, armed with lances, swords, and stones, so that they fight to great purpose from these castles. They wear no armour, but carry only a shield of hide, besides their swords and lances, and so a marvellous number of them fall in battle. When they are going to take an elephant into battle they ply him well with their wine, so that he is made half drunk. They do this because the drink makes him more fierce and bold, and of more service in battle." His physical description may have been marked by racism, but he treats the people as equals in a mercantile economy.

Marco eventually returned from India and his travels, taking his place once again in the court of Kublai Khan. Along with his father and uncle, the three set out on another mission for Kublai Khan. A young Mongol princess needed to journey by sea to her new husband. They would take the princess to Argon and were, at last, granted permission to return to Venice after completing their mission. Kublai Khan required that they promise to return to him after some time in their home. They agreed, but it was clear that Kublai Khan was near death and they had no intention of keeping any such promise. Marco, now 38, was excited by the potential of a return home.

Kublai Khan outfitted their ships and provided them with generous gifts before they left on their journey to Argon, including enough gems and gold to cover their expenses for ten years. Thus, the Polos would return to Venice wealthy men. This mission to Argon and the delivery of the Mongol princess Kokachin is also confirmed by Yuan dynasty sources, and the details in both Marco's account and Yuan sources are the same (though the Yuan sources omit the names of the three emissaries).

The group sailed for 18 months and the journey was exceptionally difficult. Marco does not describe their voyage in detail, other than to tell that the majority of those traveling died on their trip. By the time they arrived, the King of Argon had died, so the Polos opted to marry the princess to his young son, unsure of the right course of action. The princess delayed their journey for some time, and they remained in the court for nine months before finally leaving with gifts from the ruler of the region, Quiaticu, including paizas or golden tablets to provide them with protection and assistance. They left Quiaticu in 1294.

Kublai Khan died at the age of 80 in his palace in February 1294 and was succeeded by his grandson Temur. While Marco Polo had been anxious to return to Venice, the death of Kublai Khan ended any chance of a return to the Mongol court and Beijing. Thus, the three Polos continued their long journey home, still protected by the paiza. In the small kingdom of Trebizond, they were robbed of a significant portion of their fortune, some 4,000 gold coins. From Trebizond, they went to Constantinople and on to Negrepont. In 1295, they reached the city of Venice.

Chapter 4: Life Back Home

Marco, Niccolò and Maffeo returned to Venice permanently changed by their journey. Having been gone for over two decades, they could barely speak their native language after years without practice. They wore Mongol-style clothing, including brightly colored caftans, layered over loose-fitting trousers. They may even have worn their hair in the Mongol style, with parts of the head shaved and long braids. They were not recognized when they arrived home, and their family in Venice had no way of knowing if they were alive or dead and likely assumed them dead after so many years.

Niccolò and Maffeo's brother had made provisions for them in his will before his death, and when they returned they were immediately made the executors of his estate. This measure provided the returning members of the family with the legal standing that they needed in the city. Maffeo's wife was alive, as was Niccolò's second son, Maffeo Polo. Still facing doubt, the three threw a grand banquet. During the course of the banquet, according to legend, they tore apart multiple sets of rich clothing before finally appearing in their Mongol caftans. They cut into the caftans, revealing rich stores of gems and gold sewn into the fabric. Only after this display were they welcomed back into Venetian society.

Marco brought knowledge of a number of significant technological advances back to Italy with him, including paper money, coal and eyeglasses. The eyeglass lenses also provided the innovation necessary for the telescope, and the introduction of gunpowder revolutionized warfare. He kept the paiza, given by Kublai Khan, for the rest of his life and was served by a Mongol servant named Peter in his home in Venice.

While Venice had been a thriving republic when Marco left 24 years earlier, he returned to a less successful city. Under interdict by the Pope for some time, the city could not even celebrate religious festivals, and wars and famine also threatened the city. The people of Venice blamed members of the ruling families, particularly the Dandolo family, for their difficulties. Making matters worse, the Christian kingdom of Acre, where the Polos had began their journey, had fallen to the sultan of Egypt, so a lack of Christian trading outposts in the Middle East reduced Venetian access to trade in the region. In response, the Venetians increased trade throughout western Europe.

Sometime after Marco's return to the city, tensions between Venice and longtime trading rival, Genoa escalated. Genoa controlled both the spice and grain trade, bringing in goods from distant regions, including India. Venice allied with Pisa against Genoa and initiated a draft. All men between 17-60 could be drafted, and Marco volunteered to serve. Clearly not a prime age for fighting by now, Marco may simply have found Venice boring after a life of travel and adventure.

During the naval battle with the city of Genoa, Marco Polo was captured and taken prisoner, but like other wealthy prisoners, he was quite well-treated and his prison was a luxurious one. His family in Venice worried about his well-being, and Niccolò and Maffeo attempted to ransom him to secure his freedom. With concern about Marco's well-being and the family's future, Niccolò remarried. While Marco was in prison, the family bought a new palazzo in a comfortable Venetian neighborhood. The gems and goods brought from the east likely financed this purchase.

In prison, Marco met a writer of adventure stories and romances named Rustichello of Pisa who had likely been captured by the Genoese in 1284 and had been imprisoned for a number of years. While Marco spoke a number of languages, none, including his native Venetian, were appropriate for a literary venture, but Rustichello was fluent in French, a popular literary language of the time.

While in prison, Marco, with Rustichello's assistance, began work on the book about his travels. This autobiography included many stories of Marco's travels throughout the Mongol kingdom, as well as those of his father and uncle. He also included second-hand accounts of a number of regions and some stories which were, without a doubt, purely fictional. Marco dictated his autobiography to Rustichello, and the two should be considered co-writers, but as the book progresses it moves further from conventions of travel and adventure stories. This suggests that Marco may have taken a greater hand in its writing, and Marco may have relied upon some of his own travel notes, as well as his memory, when dictating his adventures to Rustichello.

While Rustichello could write French, he did so poorly. Verb tenses varied, and he moved from first to third person narration frequently. The poor grammar and language of the text subsequently caused substantial difficulties for translators. The original manuscript produced by Rustichello in prison does not survive, and early surviving copies vary widely, with alterations to the text in many instances. Modern scholars divide these manuscripts into two groups, A and B. Manuscripts in the B group are believed to be truer to the original and less altered by translators. Marco may have added to the manuscript later in life, continuing to alter the text until the time of his death.

Marco was released from prison in 1299 when the two warring cities signed a peace treaty and returned to Venice, rejoining his father and uncle and serving on the Great Council. Now in his 40s, Marco married after his return in a marriage arranged by the family. There is no record of what the 45 year old, who had taken such keen interest in the foreign women he had seen, thought of his own marriage, but Donata's dowry was generous and the match was a good one for the Polo family. Marco and Donata had three daughters in the coming years.

Niccolò Polo died around 1300, leaving his son and brother to continue the family business in Venice, but neither traveled to Asia again. They did, however, travel around Europe, and Marco carried copies of his story with him when he traveled in Europe for business, giving them to nobles he encountered. Contemporary accounts suggest he frequently spoke of his adventures.

While the war with Genoa was over, conflict with the papacy continued. In 1309, a papal bull excommunicated the entire city of Venice, sparking a rebellion in the city that caused turmoil. However, Marco and his family were largely uninvolved.

Maffeo Polo died in 1310 leaving no children, and thus his estate passed to his nephews. Marco's brother Maffeo died soon after, leaving Marco the heir to the Polo family fortune. Later in life, he became obsessed with wealth, and he continued to work as a merchant, amassing a significant fortune. While he made loans to family, court records show that he sued when he was not paid. Two of his three daughters had married by 1318, and he integrated their husbands into the business, even favoring them over others in the Polo family.

In his later years, Marco was no longer an adventurer, but he maintained relationships with other world travelers. Pietro d'Abano visited Marco, and the two conversed about their travels and astronomy. D'Abano's writings shared stories from "Marco the Venetian" and helped to spread Marco's reputation. While Marco was relatively well-known by the end of his life, his work was typically considered to be fiction. A Dominican recounted a story in which friends suggested he recant parts of the book which were lies. Marco responded that he had only written half of what he saw and experienced.

15ᵗʰ century depiction of Pietro d'Abano

Marco Polo died in Venice in 1324, leaving significant wealth to his heirs and naming his wife and daughters co-executors of his estate. He also released a number of people from their debts to him and freed a Mongol slave that had been with him since his return, leaving him a generous bequest. He provided for his wife and a dowry for his unmarried daughter. The remainder of his estate was to be divided between his two married daughters.

Many of the items listed were typical possessions of a Venetian merchant, but there were several that were unique to Marco Polo. The golden tablet of Kublai Khan was still in his possession, as was a "Buddhist rosary". Finally, he still owned a Mongol headdress or bochta. It is likely that this was a gift from the Mongol princess he had accompanied on her journey. His will does not mention a significant quantity of gemstones, but these may have remained with the estate. Marco was buried in the tomb he had built for his father Niccolò.

None of his family took up his travels after his death. His daughter, Fantina, battled in court throughout her life to preserve her own wealth, but the family took little interest in the account of his travels. Marco's tomb disappeared during the course of the 18th century, along with the remainder of the Church of San Lorenzo in Venice. While the monument is lost, it is likely that the bones of Marco Polo and his family were integrated into the foundations during the rebuilding of the Church of San Lorenzo.

Less than fifty years after Marco Polo's death, the Mongol dynasty ended. Kublai Khan's grandson and successor died in 1307, and during the coming years the Chinese population pushed the Mongols back into the steppes. The great Mongol tribes who had developed the court of Kublai Khan were now once again simply a nomadic tribal people. Ironically, even as Marco Polo's travels would motivate explorers to try to head to China for lucrative trade, the Ming dynasty that followed was not interested in trade and contact with the west. China began to isolate itself, and merchants no longer traveled freely along the Silk Road. While a few travelers visited China, no one could repeat or replicate Marco's experience.

Chapter 5: Fact or Fiction?

119 early manuscripts of the Travels of Marco Polo survive, but only a few circulated in Venice. Nobles, scholars, and monks were the first readers of the text, but many who could not read may have also learned of Marco's travels orally. The Travels may have been translated into Tuscan within just years of its writing. A Dominican monk, Francesco Pipino, translated the text into Latin between 1310 and 1314. His translation edited the text for a religious audience, removing sexual references and providing the Travels of Marco Polo with a distinctly Christian perspective. It later appeared in German, English, Catalan, Aragonese, Venetian, Latin and even Gaelic. Circulation increased after the invention of the movable printing press. The first printed text appeared in 1477 in Germany, followed by another German edition four years later. Pipino's Latin translation provided the basis for a French translation in the 16th century.

Even as Marco Polo's account began the process of making its way across Europe, the Venetians widely considered him a fiction writer at best by the end of his life, and that perception continued into the 14th century. Even translators believed the stories to be fictional, because other adventure and travel stories, like that of John Mandeville, were pure fiction. Mandeville simply combined stories, often relying upon ancient sources, and he had not traveled on his own. Mandeville's account of his imagined travels was more popular than Marco Polo's for many years, and the two were frequently grouped together.

The Travels of Marco Polo includes Marco's factual observations, noting plants, animals and people that he saw with his own eyes. In the text, he insists that he was present at certain times and places. While descriptions of his own experiences can mostly be considered truthful, he also includes other information that he certainly believed to be true, including second-hand information, local mythology and his own opinions. The role he played in the Mongol court enabled him to provide observations about the character and personality of the ruler, Kublai Khan. To understand why so many thought Marco Polo had written fiction, it's necessary to keep in mind that he was not only trying to create a factual account but an imaginative and exciting text describing his travels and journeys.

While aspects of the Travels of Marco Polo were factual or at least reflected Marco's own perceptions and experiences, Rustichello added a number of stories to the Travels of Marco Polo that frequently drew upon Christian miracles and were unrelated to Mongol, Chinese or Indian culture. Marco Polo also continued the belief that a hidden Christian kingdom, led by a ruler named Prester John, existed somewhere in the east, perhaps in India.

Marco Polo did include a number of second-hand accounts in the Travels, some of which are clearly noted as such and others that are not. He records details of the battle in Japan and the Japanese people though he did not visit Japan personally; his knowledge of the battle was purely second-hand. He described Madagascar but did not claim to have visited the island, and after recounting his own stay in Zanzibar, he shared what he knew of Ethiopia but did not visit the region himself.

Marco also tells of the islands of Male and Female on his visit to India. According to him, the men and women of these two islands only spend a few months together each year. The remainder of the year, men remain on the island of Male and women on the island of Female. He describes the women as devoted mothers focused on raising their children, and girls remain with their mothers while boys are raised as children on the island of Female. The island of Maliku remains largely matriarchal and may have provided the basis for Marco's description of Female.

Marco Polo also likely exaggerated the role he, his father and uncle played in the government of Kublai Khan, and he almost certainly did so at some points in his account. He describes them playing a vital role in the Battle of Xiangyang, but the Polos were not present in China at the time of the siege and could not have assisted during the siege. Marco also claims to have been governor of Yuanzhong, but contemporary sources do not support this assertion. He does claim to have worked for Kublai Khan as a young man, but contemporary accounts suggest that the khan routinely employed young men of all nationalities. The three certainly served in diplomatic and administrative roles during their stay.

Regardless of how his contemporaries treated his account, Marco Polo's travels played a crucial role for subsequent explorers. Since Marco frequently discussed distances between places he traveled, navigators and cartographers used his account to help them broaden the scope of their maps and learn more about the geography of the world. His account directly inspired Fra Mauro's map of the known world in the 15th century.

In 1492, Columbus carried a copy of the Travels of Marco Polo on his journeys to the New World. He hoped to find Marco Polo's China and its rich trade goods, including spices that Marco mentioned in his accounts of India. This edition exists today and is heavily annotated in his own hand. A later Venetian explorer, Antonio Pigafetta, circumnavigated the globe and wrote his own account of his voyage, inspired by Polo's writing.

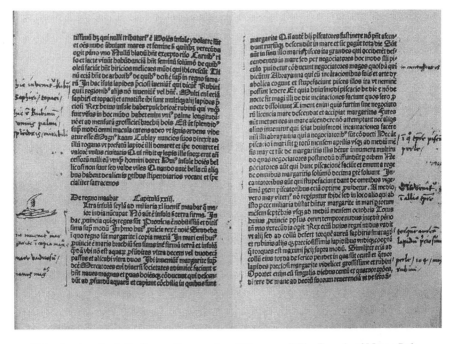

Columbus's notes in Latin, on the margins of his copy of *The Travels of Marco Polo*

Portions of Marco's book were integrated into other travel and adventure stories, including Purchas His Pilgrimage. These excerpts inspired well-known works, including Samuel Coleridge's Kubla Khan.

By the 17th century, Marco Polo was much more well-regarded and often referred to as the one "who discovered new countries". He appeared in an ecclesiastical history of Venice late in the 17th century, and during the early 19th century, Marco Polo's accounts were recognized as fundamentally factual. Scholars compared the Travels of Marco Polo to annals of the Mongol and Chinese courts and found clear similarities in the depiction of court rituals, merchant practices and religion. Large annotated editions of the Travels appeared and became popular in the 19th century.

Interest in Marco Polo's Travels as a relatively accurate reflection of his experiences continued throughout much of the 20th century. A longer version of the text was discovered in the 1920s and translated in 1938. This new translation more accurately captured Marco's enthusiasm and his voice than earlier translations.

Only a few scholars questioned his account. In the 1990s, Frances Wood produced an article analyzing the validity of Polo's account. Her arguments included Marco Polo's failure to mention the Great Wall of China, but the Great Wall was not mentioned in Chinese chronicles until 1579 and was built during the Ming dynasty, sometime between 1368 and 1644. Marco Polo did not mention the Great Wall because it did not exist as we know it during his time in China. Any evidence of the earliest efforts at a Great Wall would have been relatively minimal during his years in China. His lack of knowledge regarding tea and chopsticks are also noted as possible discrepancies, but Marco functioned primarily within Mongol society. His understanding of Chinese society was limited by his lack of exposure to it.

While Marco Polo's account is not purely factual, it provides a rare window into the culture of the Mongol Empire, and its intrigue led Marco to accustom some of that culture himself over the course of his life. Just as importantly, The Travels of Marco Polo opened up an unknown world to readers.

Bibliography

Bergreen, Laurence. *Marco Polo: From Venice to Xanadu*. New York: Vintage Books, 2008.

Polo, Marco. *The Travels of Marco Polo*. MacMay, 2008.

Christopher Columbus
Chapter 1: Origins and Early Years

Christopher Columbus is one of the most famous and controversial figures in history, so it is fittingly paradoxical that very little can actually be established about his life with certainty. As an initial indication of how little history truly knows of the man, even his name is a subject of disagreement, partly as a result of his itinerant life and partly as a result of the array of reputations that have come to surround him in different parts of the world. Christopher Columbus is an adaptation of the Latinized version of his name, "Christophorus Columbus," which has become prevalent in the English-speaking world, but the name Christopher Columbus would go unrecognized in Spain and Spanish America, where he is known by the Hispanized version of his name: "Cristóbal Colón." While these two versions are the most widely used today, both are adaptations of his actual given name, which was probably Christoffa Corombo, as it would be pronounced in the local Genoese dialect presumably spoken in his family; a closer version to the original is the standard Italian Cristoforo Colombo.

Tthere is little agreement on a common name for the famous sailor and explorer, but the question of his family's origins has also inspired a great deal of debate over the years. While his birth and early upbringing in Genoa is well-documented in contemporary materials, scholars have repeatedly claimed that his ancestors came from elsewhere. In part, this would seem to be a consequence of his status as a national hero and an object of patriotic pride in subsequent centuries. Thus, scholars have variously claimed that his family bloodline traced back to Catalonia, Portugal, and Spain, the latter two both being places where he spent formative periods of his career and which had a vested interest in claiming him more fully as a true son. None of these theories have gained ascendancy among mainstream scholars, nor has an intriguing claim that Columbus's origins were among the Sephardic Jews of the Iberian peninsula. A large part of the evidence for this claim is that Columbus was reticent in later life about his family backgrounds – and why, some scholars have contended, would he have been so reticent unless he were hiding something? And what would he be hiding if not Jewish origins, a major liability in the vigorously Catholic Spain of the late 15th century, which was in the process of expelling all of its Jewish inhabitants? Regardless, the absence of evidence surely does not itself constitute evidence, and the desire to tie Columbus more fully to one or another national or ethnic background mainly provides an index of the way his figure and voyages have been used to serve many purposes.

Those questions aside, there is little doubt that his birthplace was Genoa, and most scholarship has put his year of birth around the latter half of 1451. Genoa was an independent republic at the time, a sea port whose economy revolved around trade routes stretching in various directions across the Mediterranean Sea. In this milieu, it is not surprising that Columbus chose the life that he did. While in other parts of Europe (including Spain), a young man seeking adventure might have opted for a military career, seafaring and trade were an obvious choice in Genoa, which even had its own small colonies in the Greek islands. Columbus later claimed to have first gone to sea at the age of 10, but his first known voyages were on merchant ships to the island of Chios, a Genoese colony in the Aegean Sea which was a port of entry to the Eastern Mediterranean, which in turn was the nearest point of arrival of exotic products from Asia.

Columbus was also born around the time of the fall of Constantinople to the Ottoman Turks, whose newly powerful empire threatened trade routes to Asia. In the environment in which he grew up, there were immediate reasons, both economic and religious, to be concerned about the new balance of power. On the economic front, for several centuries, Italian merchants had been able to travel safely to the East and bring back valuable trade goods (the most famous of these was Marco Polo, whose accounts of various Asian kingdoms Columbus read). Now, having conquered Constantinople, the Muslim Turks were dangerously positioned to dominate the highly lucrative trade with the East. Meanwhile, on the religious front, the Ottomans were now not only in control of the holy city of Jerusalem but threatening the Southeastern quadrant of Christendom via their new foothold on the European continent. Both commercial and religious leaders were beginning to call for a new crusade to reestablish Christian control in the East. For some, the rising Muslim power was a sign of the coming apocalypse, anticipating the final struggle between Christ and the Antichrist.

In any case, the economic goal of extending trade routes and the religious goal of expanding Christendom would remain intertwined in Columbus's later activities. A further effect of the fall of Constantinople was the arrival to Italy of thousands of Christian refugees from the former Byzantium, including Greek-speaking scholars carrying with them classical Greek manuscripts. By most accounts, their arrival was one of the major catalysts for the Italian Renaissance, and the new availability of scholarship would exercise an influence on Columbus, a man of extensive scholarly curiosities.

In his early expeditions, Columbus sailed as far north as the ports of Bristol, England and Galway, Ireland, and possibly even all the way to Iceland. These trips would crucially shift his orientation from the Mediterranean to the Atlantic, a sphere of travel and trade that had been unfamiliar to him when growing up. His realignment toward the Atlantic, and thus toward the West, was completed when he settled in Portugal around 1476, ironic given that Columbus started looking west as the Portugese were fixated on looking east. His arrival in Portugal was initially accidental, according to most reports. Although Genoa was at peace with Portugal, his ship, bound to England, was attacked and destroyed just beyond the straits of Gibraltar, and Columbus was reportedly forced to come to shore clinging to an oar. The castaway was treated well by the Portuguese villagers he met on shore, and he proceeded to Lisbon, Portugal's capital, where he fell in with the city's small community of Genoese merchants and sailors. He remained based in Lisbon for the next decade, marrying a Portuguese woman and having a son, Diego.

Painting depicting Columbus and his son Diego

Chapter 2: Columbus in Lisbon

Columbus's enterprise of sailing to the Indies emerged directly out of the cultural and economic environment he discovered in Lisbon. As John Noble Wilford has observed, "Ideas do not emerge in a vacuum. Even a man of his intuition, zeal, and self-assurance could not have conceived of such a scheme in a time much earlier or a place much different from Portugal in the late fifteenth century". Columbus's previous world had been that of the richly diverse but limited and fully charted Mediterranean; his world now was that of a country deeply engaged in exploration and expansion.

Since the fall of Constantinople, Portugal had begun to exploit its position at the edge of the Atlantic to set out to largely unmapped territories in search of new routes, new resources, and ultimately, a new path to the East that would circumvent the Ottoman blockade. But even prior to conceiving that goal, the Portuguese had been at the vanguard of oceanic exploration, and by the 1420s had already arrived at and established settlements on the Atlantic islands of Madeira and the Azores. The intellectual architect of Portuguese exploration was Prince Henry the Navigator, who was motivated by religious zeal to send expeditions down the Atlantic coast of Africa, initially hoping to check Muslim power on the continent and make contact with Prester John, a legendary Christian king in Africa (the legend was probably a garbled version of the Christian kingdom of Ethiopia). In the decades prior to Columbus's arrival in Lisbon, Portuguese expeditions had pushed farther and farther southward down the West African coast, opening up new trade in gold, ivory, and African slaves along the way. By the 1450s, the goal of circumnavigating Africa to reach Asia had been conceived.

Henry the Navigator

Furthermore, the Portugese were being strongly encouraged by the Catholic Church. In the 1450s, the Pope issued papal bulls promising Portugal that at least among Catholic nations,

Portugal would be given a trade monopoly in lands they discovered in Africa south of the Sahara. That was all the motivation the Portugese needed: by then, the Portugese had already sailed to Sierra Leone, on the western coast of Africa about half of the way down the continent. And in 1488, the Portugese explorer Bartolomeu Dias became the first European to sail around the Cape of Good Hope, discovering much to his amazement that the Indian Ocean was connected to the Atlantic Ocean. One of the missions of Dias' expedition was to sail to India, which was a stated objective despite the fact the Portugese did not realize they could sail around Africa to Asia. Dias did not reach India, but in 1497, Portugal's most famous explorer, Vasco da Gama sailed around Cape Good Hope, sailed north up the eastern coast of Africa and then sailed to Calicut, India, arriving in 1498.

Columbus would make his name by promoting a different route than that sought by the Portuguese, but the Portuguese explorers and traders had prepared the way for his ideas in several ways. First, the increasing confidence about long-distance sea travel, based in part on improved nautical technology and cartographical accuracy, made the notion of connecting distant regions by sea far more plausible than it had been even a hundred years earlier. For much of the Middle Ages, it was assumed that any routes connecting Europe and Asia would be land routes. Medieval cartography had always shown the possibility of sea routes, since they showed the three known continents of Europe, Asia, and Africa to be surrounded by a continuous body of water, but sea travel was regarded as far too dangerous and untested. The Portuguese explorations of the 15th century began to make this conviction look like an unfounded prejudice.

A second obstacle had been the belief, held since ancient times, that the Southern Hemisphere was an uninhabitable torrid zone where life could not thrive. Now the Portuguese had traveled much farther to the south than any Europeans before them and had found the climate pleasant, the vegetation abundant, and the ground rich in mineral deposits. These discoveries found confirmation in the rediscovered work of the ancient Greek geographer Ptolemy, who had painted a relatively pleasant picture of the tropical zones of Africa. In fact, the Portugese would find so many inhabitants of Africa that when the Pope issued his papal bulls granting the Portugese a trade monopoly in lands they discovered in south Africa, he gave the Portugese the "right" to make "Saracens, pagans and any other unbelievers" slaves. Over the next 300 years, an estimated 10 million African slaves would be transported to the New World.

Columbus did not only imbibe the environment of Portugal's era of exploration – he also took part in it. Some time around 1481, he participated in a voyage to the Guinea coast of West Africa, where he was impressed by the great abundance of gold that had been mined. During the same period, he supposedly heard multiple stories from Portuguese mariners suggesting that mysterious objects and even the bodies of unusual-looking men had been found washed ashore in several of Portugal's Atlantic settlements. Columbus also took advantage of his Atlantic expeditions to study winds and currents, the patterns of which apparently suggested to him the feasibility of westward travel out into the ocean.

Just as importantly, he became aware of the work of an Italian geographer based in Florence, Paolo Toscanelli, who on the basis both of recent Portuguese reports and of his prolonged studies of ancient cartography calculated that the shortest route to Asia lay across the Atlantic. Columbus apparently became aware of Toscanelli through the Florentine scientist's correspondence with a Portuguese acquaintance, Fernão Martins. Columbus himself wrote to Toscanelli in the early 1480s expressing enthusiasm for a westward route to the Indies and soliciting more details. Toscanelli was encouraging in his reply but died soon after writing it, leaving Columbus to continue his calculations on his own.

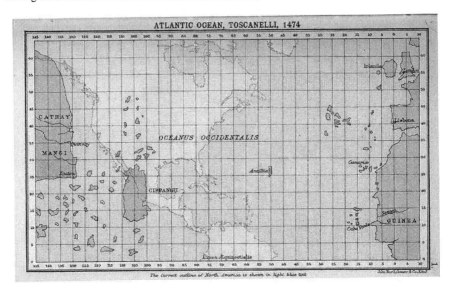

Toscanelli's map, calculating Asia's position across the Atlantic. Cathay was the word for China.

As Columbus's discussions with Toscanelli and Toscanelli's map make clear, the notion that Columbus "discovered that the earth was round" and had trouble finding backers for his enterprise because most of his contemporaries believed he would fall of the edge of the flat earth is one of the most blatant falsehoods of the many myths that have come to surround his biography over the centuries. The spherical shape of the earth had been assumed by educated Europeans for nearly two thousand years by the time Columbus arrived on the scene, and the groundwork for his enterprise had been laid by generations of geographers who worked with a relatively accurate picture not only of the earth's shape but of its dimensions.

The claim that the ignorant Spaniards and Portuguese of the 15th century believed in a flat earth seems to have been first introduced by the American writer Washington Irving, whose deliberately mythmaking 1828 biography made Columbus into a visionary advocate of empirical science in the face of medieval obscurantism. This characterization was at best highly exaggerated and at worst an outright falsification: Columbus certainly drew some of the evidence for the feasibility of his plans from the empirical discoveries of Portuguese explorers, but he also drew heavily on the traditional authorities, including the Bible, Aristotle, Ptolemy, Pliny and the more recent cosmography of Cardinal Pierre d'Ailly.

Columbus's true disagreement with many of his contemporaries had to do with a different question: the true circumference of the spherical earth, and the relative amount of its surface covered by land and by water. Different geographers and cosmographers had come to different conclusions, even though the Greek astronomer Eratosthenes had in fact calculated the earth's circumference quite accurately in the 3rd century B.C. In addition to the lack of empirical verification through circumnavigation, Eratosthenes's estimate had failed to become the consensus position because of confusion over the different systems and units of measurement used successively by Greeks, Romans, Arabs, and medieval Christians. Such confusion contributed to Columbus's calculation of a much shorter distance between the western tip of Europe and the eastern tip of Asia: when reading the estimates of medieval Arab cartographers, he took them to support the much smaller figure, when in fact they were simply working with a longer unit of measurement.

In any case Columbus developed his estimates from various sources, including Ptolemy, d'Ailly, Toscanelli, and certain obscure passages in the Bible, ultimately concluding that Asia lay at a distance of just under 4,000 kilometers. Here the Irving myth of Columbus the scientific pioneer becomes truly ironic: his estimate was as far off as could be, since the real distance was about 20,000 kilometers. As historian Edmund Morgan put it, "Columbus was not a scholarly man. Yet he studied these books, made hundreds of marginal notations in them and came out with ideas about the world that were characteristically simple and strong and sometimes wrong, the kind of ideas that the self-educated person gains from independent reading and clings to in defiance of what anyone else tries to tell him."

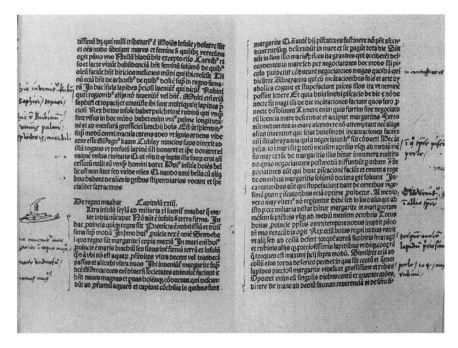

Columbus's notes in Latin, on the margins of his copy of *The Travels of Marco Polo*

The experts who ridiculed Columbus, far from being ignorant flat-earthers, were actually working from highly accurate measurements and had good reason to believe that Columbus's expedition would run out of water and supplies before reaching Asia. They only lacked one important piece of information: there was another land mass between Europe and Asia. This fact would both foil Columbus's initial goal of reaching Asia and ultimately place a different set of tasks before him.

Chapter 3: The Search for a Royal Sponsor

It was only natural that Columbus would first present his proposal to the Portuguese monarchy, which had sponsored so much exploration over the previous decades and had been reaping increasing rewards from their African trade routes. He did so for the first time in 1485, and after an initial rejection, returned with a second proposal in 1488, which met with an even more definitive rejection. In addition to the skepticism of King John II's official advisers, who correctly argued that Columbus's estimate of the distance to Asia was far too short, his plan was in competition with an alternative proposed route that would pass around the southern tip of

Africa. This was clearly the safer option, and once the Portuguese navigator Bartholomew Diaz rounded the Cape of Good Hope and reached the Indian Ocean in 1488, Columbus's hopes for Portuguese support were dashed.

Since Portugal could already reach India, Columbus was forced to turn to rival powers for potential sponsorship. He made unsuccessful proposals to his home republic of Genoa and to Venice, both major seafaring powers whose Atlantic ambitions proved too modest, and to England, which also passed.

As it turned out, Columbus chose an auspicious moment to make his proposal to the so-called Catholic Monarchs of Spain, Ferdinand and Isabella. The two had married in 1769, uniting several previously separate kingdoms on the Iberian peninsula, most importantly the large kingdoms of Castile and Aragon. In the meantime, they had set out to reunite the peninsula under a fervently Catholic monarchy, which involved ridding their territories of non-Christian subjects. These efforts would come to a head in 1492 with the conquest of the southern kingdom of Granada from its Muslim rulers and the expulsion of all Jews who refused to accept baptism.

It was in this environment of territorial expansion, burgeoning military and political confidence, and evangelizing fervor that Columbus first brought his proposal to Spain. Partly due to his interest in the Bible and partly due to the religious nature of his audience, the proposal to sail west to the Indies that Columbus made to Ferdinand and Isabella was based on his interpretation of the Second Book of Esdras (2 Esdras 6:42), which Columbus interpreted as meaning the Earth was comprised of six parts of land to one of water. Although the monarchs, on advice from their official cosmographers, rejected the Genoese mariner's plan once again, they also provided him with a certain amount of encouragement, offering him a stipend if he chose to stay in Spain. Clearly, although they were uncertain about the plan, they did not wish Columbus to sell his ideas to a rival power such as Portugal, whose maritime advantage the Spanish crown was desperate to weaken.

Depiction of Ferdinand and Isabella

Two years later, in the wake of the successful Granada campaign, Columbus returned once more to Ferdinand and Isabella with his proposal and finally met with success. They accepted the terms he had proposed to all of the governments he had courted: three ships to undertake the voyage, the title of Admiral of the Ocean Sea, the title of Viceroy of any new lands he might claim for the Spanish crown, and the right to 10% of any revenue generated as a result of the trip. He and the Spanish monarchs signed their contract in the city of Córdoba, not far from the recently conquered Moorish capital of Granada. From there, he set out towards the small port of Palos de la Frontera, where he began to gather supplies and recruit crewmen.

Historians have long wondered why Columbus chose this small port, with limited resources, rather than the larger ports of Seville or Cádiz. One theory is that the resources in those two places were occupied with the thousands of Jewish refugees leaving Spain in the wake of the monarchs' edict of expulsion. In any case, Columbus hired the best ships he could find in Palos, contracting two caravels called the Niña and the Pinta from the Pinzón family and the third, which he called the Santa María, from cartographer Juan de la Cosa. Columbus referred to the Santa María as La Capitana ("The Flagship"), the Pinta was Spanish for "The Painted", and the Niña (Spanish for " Girl") was named after her owner, Juan Niño of Moguer. The real name of the Pinta is lost to history, while the Niña was actually named the Santa Clara.

The three ships set out on August 3, 1492.

Chapter 4: The First Voyage and its Impact

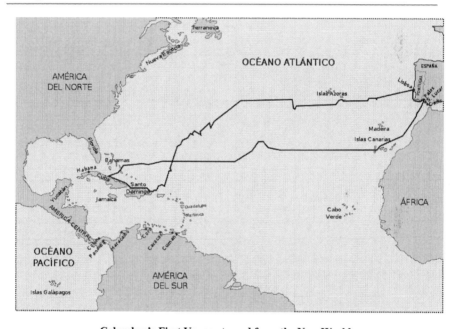

Columbus's First Voyage to and from the New World

Columbus would make history in October 1492, but the journey that landed him in the New World consisted of both crucial setbacks and a good deal of luck. The three ships would end up spending a total of just over two months on the Atlantic between continents, longer than what Columbus, with his optimistic measurement of the distance to Asia, had hoped for, but not so long as to cause mutiny or starvation.

The Castilian-sponsored expedition worked with several advantages. First, they were able to stop for supplies in early September in the conveniently placed Canary Islands, the one archipelago off the coast of West Africa that belonged to Castile rather than Portugal. Because the Portuguese crown had obtained papal guarantees of control over a large swath of the Atlantic seaboard, Columbus and his men had to be careful to avoid territories controlled by the rival power – not least because he did not wish to reveal his intentions to potential competitors. The Canaries provided a critical stopover for the expedition.

A second advantage, possibly but not certainly understood in advance by Columbus, were the "trade winds" blowing out of the East that prevailed as the ships sailed westward from the Canaries. The constant favorable wind allowed them to proceed at a brisk pace.

Finally, once they had proceeded some 300 leagues to the West of the Canary Islands, Columbus and his crew found themselves, to their surprise, in the midst of a highly pleasant, temperate climate, which seemed to improve as they proceeded.

Despite those advantages, the voyage is better known for its more harrowing circumstances. Just days into the journey from Spain, the rudder on the Pinta broke, disabling the ship and largely leading Columbus and his men to believe it had been sabotaged as a result of the fact the Pinta's owners and crew had not wanted the ship to be used in the journey. Columbus wrote of the incident in his journal (in which he refers to himself in the third person as Admiral), "It was believed that this happened by the contrivance of Gomez Rascon and Christopher Quintero, who were on board the caravel, because they disliked the voyage. The Admiral says he had found them in an unfavorable disposition before setting out. He was in much anxiety at not being able to afford any assistance in this case, but says that it somewhat quieted his apprehensions to know that Martin Alonzo Pinzon, Captain of the Pinta, was a man of courage and capacity."

After fixing the Pinta in the Canaries, the voyage ran into more trouble shortly after leaving from that point. On September 8, 1492, Columbus noticed his compass needle was no longer pointing due north, instead varying a half point to the Northwest and varying gradually further as the expedition continued. Columbus tried to keep this secret from the crew, which sparked even more anxiety when his pilots took notice. Columbus insisted that the needle was simply pointing to some invisible point on the Earth, and his reputation for knowing the stars allayed his crew's concerns. Unbeknownst to Columbus, his needle had started pointing to the Earth's magnetic north pole, something the Europeans knew nothing about.

The expedition was already getting antsy to spot land by mid-September, as evidenced by the journal entry Columbus made on September 14, 1492. "Friday, 14 September. Steered this day and night west twenty leagues; reckoned somewhat less. The crew of the Nina stated that they had seen a grajao, and a tropic bird, or water-wagtail, which birds never go farther than twenty-five leagues from the land."

Two days later, Columbus already noted in his journal that he had taken up the practice of recording that the ships had sailed less distance than they actually had. He also continued to find evidence of land even as land sightings evaded his crew. "Sunday, 16 September. Sailed day and night, west thirty-nine leagues, and reckoned only thirty-six. Some clouds arose and it drizzled. The Admiral here says that from this time they experienced very pleasant weather, and that the mornings were most delightful, wanting nothing but the melody of the nightingales. He compares the weather to that of Andalusia in April. Here they began to meet with large patches of weeds very green, and which appeared to have been recently washed away from the land; on which account they all judged themselves to be near some island, though not a continent, according to the opinion of the Admiral, who says, 'the continent we shall find further ahead.'"

Columbus noted the uneasiness of his crew on September 23. "Sunday, 23 September. Sailed northwest and northwest by north and at times west nearly twenty-two leagues. Saw a turtle dove, a pelican, a river bird, and other white fowl;--weeds in abundance with crabs among them. The sea being smooth and tranquil, the sailors murmured, saying that they had got into smooth water, where it would never blow to carry them back to Spain; but afterwards the sea rose without wind, which astonished them. The Admiral says on this occasion 'the rising of the sea was very favorable to me, as it happened formerly to Moses when he led the Jews from Egypt.'"

One of the first major false sightings of land took place on September 25, as recounted by Columbus. "At sunset Martin Alonzo called out with great joy from his vessel that he saw land, and demanded of the Admiral a reward for his intelligence. The Admiral says, when he heard him declare this, he fell on his knees and returned thanks to God, and Martin Alonzo with his crew repeated Gloria in excelsis Deo, as did the crew of the Admiral. Those on board the Nina ascended the rigging, and all declared they saw land. The Admiral also thought it was land, and about twenty-five leagues distant. They remained all night repeating these affirmations, and the Admiral ordered their course to be shifted from west to southwest where the land appeared to lie. They sailed that day four leagues and a half west and in the night seventeen leagues southwest, in all twenty-one and a half: told the crew thirteen leagues, making it a point to keep them from knowing how far they had sailed; in this manner two reckonings were kept, the shorter one falsified, and the other being the true account. The sea was very smooth and many of the sailors went in it to bathe, saw many dories and other fish."

By October 10, Columbus's crew was on the verge of losing all hope. "Wednesday, 10 October. Steered west-southwest and sailed at times ten miles an hour, at others twelve, and at others, seven; day and night made fifty-nine leagues' progress; reckoned to the crew but forty-four. Here the men lost all patience, and complained of the length of the voyage, but the Admiral encouraged them in the best manner he could, representing the profits they were about to acquire, and adding that it was to no purpose to complain, having come so far, they had nothing to do but continue on to the Indies, till with the help of our Lord, they should arrive there."

Thankfully for Columbus, the expedition actually sighted land the following night, on October 11, 1492. Ironically, after all the false reports about sighting land, Columbus was initially skeptical when the crew actually did see land, writing on October 11, "The crew of the Pinta saw a cane and a log; they also picked up a stick which appeared to have been carved with an iron tool, a piece of cane, a plant which grows on land, and a board. The crew of the Nina saw other signs of land, and a stalk loaded with rose berries. These signs encouraged them, and they all grew cheerful. Sailed this day till sunset, twenty-seven leagues. After sunset steered their original course west and sailed twelve miles an hour till two hours after midnight, going ninety miles, which are twenty-two leagues and a half; and as the Pinta was the swiftest sailer, and kept ahead of the Admiral, she discovered land and made the signals which had been ordered. The land was first seen by a sailor called Rodrigo de Triana, although the Admiral at ten o'clock that evening standing on the quarter-deck saw a light, but so small a body that he could not affirm it to be land."

Scholars have long attempted to determine which of the many tiny islands that now make up the Bahamas and Turks and Caicos Islands it might have been, but the mystery remains. It is known from Columbus's and other accounts that the inhabitants of the island called it Guanahaní; Columbus, upon setting foot there and claiming it for the Castilian crown, called it San Salvador (Holy Savior). While the excitement of landfall was obviously enormous, it should be recalled that Columbus was likely very puzzled by what he encountered: naked or semi-naked people with no apparent material wealth beyond the odd trinket or piece of jewelry, and with no permanent abodes of a recognizable European type. He had set out, after all, in search of what was then the wealthiest and most economically advanced region of the world: Asia, which he believed to be ruled by the fabulously opulent Great Khan described by Marco Polo. Columbus's earlier communiqués, then, are somewhat unreliable in that they comprise an attempt to make the best of unexpected circumstances. Since he has found none of the great sources of wealth he sought, he instead celebrates the gentleness, simplicity, and innocence of the people he has discovered, as well as the tropical abundance of the land.

According to Columbus's journal, these were his exact words upon coming into contact with the indigenous natives:

"As I saw that they were very friendly to us, and perceived that they could be much more easily converted to our holy faith by gentle means than by force, I presented them with some red caps, and strings of beads to wear upon the neck, and many other trifles of small value, wherewith they were much delighted, and became wonderfully attached to us. Afterwards they came swimming to the boats, bringing parrots, balls of cotton thread, javelins, and many other things which they exchanged for articles we gave them, such as glass beads, and hawk's bells; which trade was carried on with the utmost good will. But they seemed on the whole to me, to be a very poor people. They all go completely naked, even the women, though I saw but one girl. All whom I saw were young, not above thirty years of age, well made, with fine shapes and faces; their hair short, and coarse like that of a horse's tail, combed toward the forehead, except a small portion which they suffer to hang down behind, and never cut. Some paint themselves with black, which makes them appear like those of the Canaries, neither black nor white; others with white, others with red, and others with such colors as they can find. Some paint the face, and some the whole body; others only the eyes, and others the nose. Weapons they have none, nor are acquainted with them, for I showed them swords which they grasped by the blades, and cut themselves through ignorance. They have no iron, their javelins being without it, and nothing more than sticks, though some have fish-bones or other things at the ends. They are all of a good size and stature, and handsomely formed. I saw some with scars of wounds upon their bodies, and demanded by signs the of them; they answered me in the same way, that there came people from the other islands in the neighborhood who endeavored to make prisoners of them, and they defended themselves. I thought then, and still believe, that these were from the continent."

Columbus's log and his early letter to his financier Luis de Santángel, which are the earliest accounts of the "discovery," project a politically expedient confidence and optimism since he did not wish to lose his contract with Ferdinand and Isabella, but Columbus was likely very confused by what he found. The people and their way of life clashed with what he expected, and the disposition of the many small islands he found was difficult to reconcile with the maps of the East Asian coast he had so avidly studied. His most important goal was to reach *terra firma*, since it was there that he would find the great trading empires whose wealth he wished to tap into. Thus, the early accounts contain a number of strategies of interpretation that attempt to fit what he has found into his preconceived framework. First of all, he attempted to map the territories he found in the Caribbean, however improbably, onto Asian geography as he understood it. The northern islands of the Bahamas, he imagines, may be part of the island empire of Cipango (Japan); the long coast of Cuba, where he arrived next by heading to the Southwest, must be part of China. Second, in his repeated emphasis on the gentleness and peacefulness of the natives, he is also insisting on their status as "natural slaves," an intellectual category used in the ancient world to justify slavery. More specifically, he concluded, they must be among the peoples from whom the Great Khan drew his many slaves; at the same time, he set the stage for the slavery-based colonization that would soon overtake the Caribbean islands and, within a few decades, wipe out their entire indigenous population. In fact, Columbus began this trend by essentially kidnapping six Guanahaní natives, in his words, "so that they will learn to speak," i.e. become interpreters for the expedition.

On San Salvador and several subsequent small islands, Columbus proceeded in the same way: he claimed the territory for Spain, announcing to the uncomprehending inhabitants that they were now subjects of the King and Queen, engaged in small-scale barter with the natives, giving them what were for them unusual glass beads and bells in exchange for parrots, javelins, and other local objects, and looking around for anything that seemed to be of real value, according to his standards. Here he was soon successful, or so he thought, because some of the "Indians," as he called them (in an error whose effects on nomenclature remain to this day) were wearing small pieces of gold as nose rings and earrings. This was, to Columbus's mind, his first indication of the famed wealth of the East: gold was so abundant that even these poor and marginal peoples possessed some.

No sooner did he catch sight of gold than he began asking after its origin. His inquiries propelled him toward the large island of Cuba, which he was desperate to interpret as part of the mainland coast. He called it La Juana, and after a brief stop, proceeded to the island he would call La Española (anglicized to Hispaniola). It was here that the Santa María ran aground on a shallow coral reef and was damaged, leading to the establishment of the first permanent Spanish settlement on Christmas Day, 1492, which was duly named La Navidad. The marooned men were treated generously by the local Taino Indians, and it seemed as safe a place as any to lay a settlement; furthermore, there were reports that they were close to the enormous gold deposits they were looking for. It was perhaps because of this that the men were eager to stay behind in La Navidad rather than proceed onward.

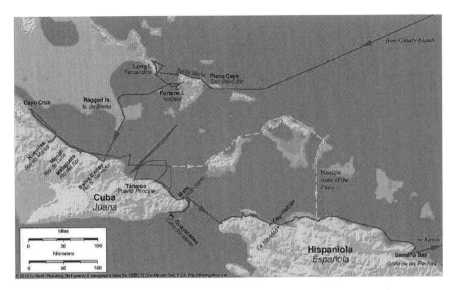

Columbus's exploration during the First Voyage

For reasons that are not entirely clear, Columbus decided at this point to proceed with great haste back to Spain, as he announced in his log on January 8, 1493. Since he believed that he had ultimately come close to a source of great wealth, he may have wished to return with reinforcements in the instance of any hostilities. After all, Columbus believed the great armies of the Khan could have been nearby. Furthermore, Columbus may have sought to reassure the Spanish Crown of his success and guarantee his share of the wealth that he now felt confident about extracting from the lands he had encountered.

Whatever the explanation of his choice to end his first voyage, it marked a turning point in his career. He had so far spent over five months at sea and three months exploring with no major setbacks, no mutinies and no hostile encounters with the natives. All of this was about to change, and the early idyll of friendly encounters with generous "Indians" would come to an end abruptly on January 13, on the eastern end of La Española, in what is now the Dominican Republic. The Spaniards, as was their habit, had come ashore to barter with a group of natives, but the barter did not go as planned, and a miscommunication led to an outbreak of hostilities in which two natives were injured. Subsequently, Columbus theorized that there were two in fact two groups of natives: the peaceful Tainos with whom he had met previously, and the hostile and violent Caribs, whom he claimed other natives had told him were man-eaters or "cannibals" (the term, coined in Columbus's diary, comes from the same uncertain indigenous lexeme as "Caribbean").

In La Navidad, the first European settlement in the Americas since Leif Ericsson's Norse colony in Newfoundland, things would go even worse. When Columbus returned on his second voyage in November, 1493, he found the village a charred ruin. The men, presumably as a result of their rapacious desire for gold and probable abuse of local women, eventually earned the hostility of nearby tribes, who promptly exterminated them. The consensual and peaceful colonization that Columbus had promised to undertake had been little more than a brief illusion.

By the time Columbus started setting east from the New World, he had explored San Salvador in the Bahamas (which he thought it was Japan, Cuba (which he thought was China), and Hispaniola, the source of gold. Due to the prevailing winds, Columbus took the Niña and the Pinta back to Spain by a completely different route, this time passing through the Portuguese-controlled Azores islands in the mid-Atlantic. Subsequently, storms at sea obliged him to dock in Lisbon before proceeding to Seville, and then on to Toledo and Barcelona, where he received a hero's welcome from a populace that had already received word of his supposed arrival in Asia. The Catholic Monarchs were currently holding court in Spain's great Mediterranean port of Barcelona, where a copy of Columbus's rhapsodic letter to Santángel had already been reproduced on a mechanical printing press (recently invented by Gutenberg) and circulated among the literate populace. Columbus also bore gifts of tobacco, pineapple, and a turkey, and he assured his hosts that gold as well as valuable spices would be forthcoming on his next expedition. They were evidently impressed, and fêted the "admiral and viceroy" at court for about five weeks.

In the meantime, Columbus and his sponsors were already scheming; they were concerned, particularly after his initial landfall in Portugal, that King John II might send his well-prepared fleets in pursuit of the lands Columbus had reached. In order to forestall further conflict with the rival Iberian kingdom, they sent an official request to the Pope for an official title to the new lands (as God's right-hand man, the Pope was understood to have jurisdiction over the entire globe). The result was a decree granting Spain sovereignty over the lands Columbus had reached and all territories to the West, while Portugal would obtain control over any territories to the East. This arrangement would ultimately result in the division of South America between the Spanish-speaking countries stretching from Argentina up the west coast of the continent to Venezuela and Portuguese-speaking Brazil occupying the eastern half of the land mass.

Chapter 5: The Second Voyage and the Beginnings of Colonization

On the heels of his apparent success and the approval of the Spanish crown, Columbus managed to assemble a much larger fleet for his second trip across the Atlantic, which began on September 24, 1492. His expeditionary force now consisted of 17 ships, including the *Niña* but neither of the other two vessels from the previous voyage. It is clear from the number of men and quantity of supplies carried over that Columbus now intended to establish more permanent settlements and pave the way for the establishment of full-scale colonies. He also brought with him a contingent of friars, who would be entrusted with the evangelization of the natives.

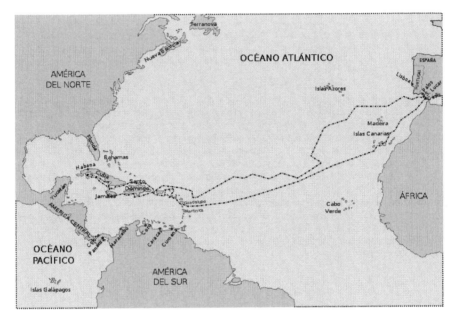

The route of Columbus's Second Voyage

Perhaps because he believed that he would reach the mainland (China) more directly, Columbus now tacked further to the south than he had on the first crossing. Instead, he found the long series of small islands that make up the Lesser Antilles. There, he found more of what he had found in the Bahamas: small-scale societies possessing no obvious material wealth. Having encountered and claimed several of these small islands for Spain, he proceeded back toward the Greater Antilles, the large islands he had repeatedly mistaken for the Asian coast.

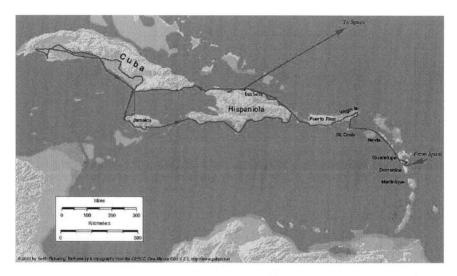

Columbus's exploration during his Second Voyage

One of the peculiarities of the second voyage is that Columbus succeeded in charting out most of what is now known as the Caribbean, but was unaware that this was what he was doing, so determined was he to find his way to the wealthy kingdoms of the East and so adept was he at fitting the geography he encountered into his schema. For instance, after he had proceeded along the southern coasts of the same islands whose northern coasts he explored on the previous trip, he still refused to consider that Cuba was an island. Instead, he assumed it was a peninsula jutting off the coast of Asia.

After skirting along the Lesser Antilles, Columbus and his crew passed first along the coast of what is now Puerto Rico, where they had another brief outbreak of hostilities with a group of natives. This skirmish set the far more violent tone for the rest of the trip. He soon proceeded to Hispaniola, where he found the ruins of La Navidad and began to investigate the causes of the falling out with the natives, deciding to blame a group of Tainos distinct from the band he had initially established an agreement with when the settlement was laid. He also took an expedition into the interior of the island, where he succeeded in finding gold deposits and established a fortress.

The two near-simultaneous discoveries – the ruined village of La Navidad and the definite presence of gold on Hispaniola – had nefarious consequences that would exercise a decisive impact on the nature of Spanish colonization and on the later history of the territories Columbus had encountered. The Spaniards established a new settlement, named La Isabela after the queen, but the conditions were harsh, and the men, disturbed by the evidence of massacre at La Navidad and by the lack of immediate enrichment, were restless and hostile to Columbus's authority. In the meantime, Columbus became increasingly concerned about further attacks from the local natives. In order to forestall what he perceived might be an impending disaster, he went on the offense, capturing well over 1,000 supposedly hostile Indians to sell into slavery. He sent a letter to the queen, whose piety made her morally uncomfortable with slavery, arguing that these particular Indians were cannibals prone to violence, and that they could only be reformed through forced servitude. She was unmoved by the argument, but Columbus proceeded with the plan against her orders anyway. Just as brutally, he now exacted a tribute from the remaining Indians of the island, demanding that they bring a certain quota of gold or cotton to the Spanish authorities every three months. The demands were impossible to fulfill given the modest deposits available, and the results on Spanish-Taino relations, and on Taino demography, would be disastrous.

Columbus's decision to resort to enslavement and a tribute system resulted in part from his own desperate circumstances. He had promised great things when last in Spain, and the many financiers who had invested in the expedition along with the king and queen would need to see a return on investment. Columbus had banked everything on success in his second voyage, and if he came up short, his credit and his contract with the crown would likely be ruined, so he resorted to the most efficient ways to extract wealth, placate his men and subdue the increasingly hostile natives.

Unfortunately, the entire enterprise was impossible, because the islands he had conquered simply did not have adequate resources to satisfy the demands his promises had created. The result of his tribute system was not a flood of wealth but the exhaustion of both the small gold deposits and the good will of the Tainos, who now understandably entered into open conflict with the invaders. Meanwhile, the Spanish settlers, who had come on the voyage expecting great and immediate material gain, were angry and nearly as hostile to the ostensible "viceroy" as the natives whose land he had appropriated. In order to escape the chaos that had consumed La Isabela, Columbus set out on another maritime expedition exploring the island of Jamaica and left his brother Diego in charge. Diego proved an even less popular leader, and the rage of the Spaniards continued to spill out onto the local natives, who fell victim to several massacres.

By 1496, Columbus became aware that negative reports about his leadership in Hispaniola had reached the Spanish king and queen. Partly in order to engage in damage control, and partly to solicit resources for a further expedition, he returned to Spain in March of that year. His brothers Diego and Bartholomew remained in charge, and he left instructions to build another town, since the location of La Isabela had proved unsustainable. The new settlement would be Santo Domingo, the only one of Columbus's settlements on Hispaniola to survive, but Bartholomew and Diego would prove incompetent leaders, and their failures would set the stage for the disasters of Columbus's third voyage.

For the moment, however, Columbus managed to persuade the monarchy to sponsor his next expedition. They had invested a great deal of effort in lobbying the Pope for control over the lands he found, and they were not willing to take a loss on the sum they had put into funding Columbus and in the process potentially lose control of the conquered territories.

Chapter 6: The Third and Fourth Voyages

- Disaster and Disgrace

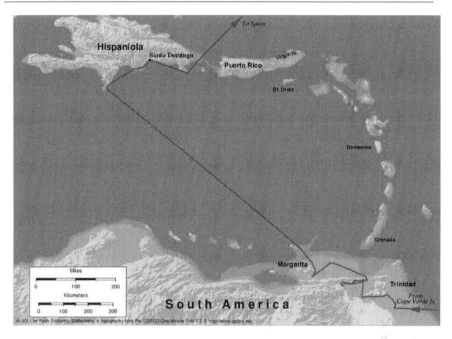

Columbus's exploration during the Third Voyage

Columbus's third expedition, which began in May of 1498, set out with fewer than half the number of ships he had taken five years earlier. Three of the six ships that set out for the Indies would proceed directly to Hispaniola, carrying provisions for the settlers, while Columbus took the other three ships on an expedition further south in the hope of finally reaching the Asian mainland. The ships passed through the southernmost Atlantic islands then colonized, the Portuguese-controlled Cape Verde islands, and then headed even further to the south, coming closer to the equator than he ever had before.

This time Columbus did reach terra firma, but not the terra firma he was expecting. He arrived in the Gulf of Paria in what is now Venezuela, where the vast Orinoco River, with its source in the Amazon, pours into the sea. From the abundance of fresh water he discovered, Columbus knew that what he had found could only be another continent – but certainly not the eastern coast of Asia, which he knew possessed no rivers spilling northward into the ocean. The resulting confusion gave birth to Columbus's most extravagant literary fantasy: in a letter back to Spain, he claimed that the new continent he had discovered was the Earthly Paradise. Conveniently, legend had it that great deposits of gold lay in the vicinity of this mythical place, which allowed him to maintain an optimistic tone.

Whatever degree of confidence the discovery of an indisputable mainland had produced in Columbus, it was severely counteracted in the next stage of his trip. He returned to Hispaniola in order to check on the settlement he had left in the care of his two brothers, only to find conditions even more catastrophic than when he had left. Bartholomew and Diego had managed to gain the undying enmity of both the Spanish colonists and of the Tainos, and both groups were in open and violent mutiny against their rule, while at the same time perpetrating increasingly merciless war against each other. Columbus retaliated against some of the most recalcitrant Spaniards, using his authority to prosecute them and send them to the gallows, but his harsh measures lost him the sympathy of even those in the colony who remained loyal, and several of them managed to convey a covert message to the crown demanding that it send an emissary to investigate the ineffectual rule of the Columbus brothers and restore order.

The result was catastrophic as far as Columbus's personal fortunes were concerned. The Spanish judge who arrived, Francisco de Bobadilla, issued a harsh repudiation of the Columbuses, stripped Christopher of his titles, and sent him back to Spain in shackles in October 1500. It was on his undoubtedly miserable voyage back across the Atlantic that Columbus composed the letter claiming that he had come close to the Earthly Paradise as well as to the great mines of King Solomon.

On one level, this outlandish claim looks to have been a clever strategy to persuade the king and queen that he was close to further and even more significant discoveries, in the hope that they would be merciful with him. It was effective, in so far as Columbus was released from prison and given the right to argue his case at court. On the other hand, the Book of Prophecies that Columbus began compiling in this period suggests that he did in fact believe that his was a divinely appointed mission that would bring the heathen world into Christendom and prepare the way for Christ's second coming. His feverish recourse to biblical citations may have reflected his true understanding of his appointed role.

Whatever, the case, he succeeded in regaining his admiralty but not his position as viceroy, and the crown permitted him to undertake a fourth (and ultimately final) voyage. It is unclear whether they acted out of pity, out of deep conviction, or out of fear that he might sell his nautical services and territorial knowledge to a rival like Genoa or Portugal. In any case, he was equipped with a relatively small fleet of four vessels. The newly appointed governor of Hispaniola, to which Columbus was now forbidden to return, set out around the same time with a fleet of thirty.

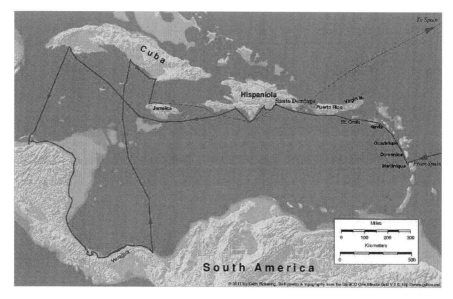

Columbus's exploration during his Fourth Voyage

Columbus's fourth journey was the most disastrous yet, and ended in career-destroying humiliation. He set out from Cádiz on May 9, 1502 and arrived in Hispaniola less than two months later, where he was promptly denied the right to dock his ships. He proceeded west and then south across the Caribbean, aiming to approach the continent he had skirted on his previous voyage from a different angle. He was successful in this endeavor, and by the end of July he and his crew had reached the coast of what is now Honduras, a terra firma continuous with the distant Venezuelan coast he had explored years back.

Columbus and his ships next proceeded southeast down the Central American coast, on the lookout for evidence of material wealth or a strait leading to India. Interestingly, had they proceeded inland in certain spots or made their way north toward the Yucatán, they would have encountered remnants of the great Mayan civilization, which had now been in decline for some time. It would, at least, have corresponded more to Columbus's presuppositions about the wealthy, urban civilizations of the East. Instead, they met more small-scale groups, a number of which showed a marked hostility to the newcomers. Off the coast of what is now Panama, they began to discover promising quantities of gold, and Columbus decreed that a settlement would be founded there. But it was not to be. Persistent native attacks ultimately drove the would-be colonists back in the direction they had come from, and on the attempted return to Hispaniola, they shipwrecked off the coast of Jamaica. There, the "Admiral of the Ocean Sea," again a castaway as he had been in Portugal at the beginning of his career, sent a desperate letter to Spain requesting reinforcements to assist in the colonization effort in Panama. He received no reply.

Chapter 7: Columbus's Final Years and Legacy

Despised as he was by the authorities in Hispaniola, the marooned Columbus had to wait nearly a year to be rescued and sent back to Spain, where he arrived near the end of 1504. At this point, both his health and his reputation were at a low point, and his situation was not helped by the death of his main sponsor, Queen Isabella, soon after his arrival.

With his chances at court as well as his own stamina so diminished, he settled in the port of Seville and used his remaining fortune to begin a litigation for the restoration of his titles and rights. He continued to insist, in his final years of life, that he had reached the far perimeter of the Indies, despite the lack of obvious correspondence between the lands he had discovered and the relatively accurate maps of Asia known to Europeans at the time, not to mention the lack of contact with any of the known peoples or products of the East. Confident of his accomplishments, he visited the court in several locations and attempted to gain a final audience, but to no avail. He went to his grave with his legacy and reputation highly uncertain.

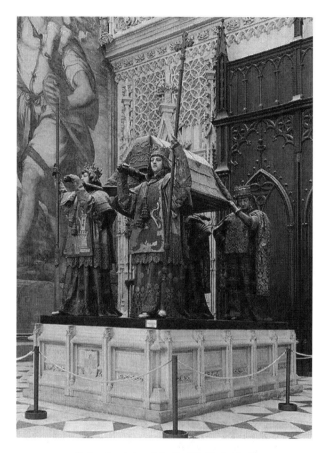

Columbus's tomb in Seville Cathedral

When Columbus died on May 20, 1506, his sons were forced to take up his case in order to establish what they regarded as their rightful inheritance. As part of this effort, his son Hernando, who had accompanied him on his final journey, began to compose the first biography of his father, which recapitulated Christopher's saintly self-image in attempt to redeem him in the eyes of the authorities and the public. Hernando's criticisms of the monarchy, however, made it difficult to publish, and the biography was still not in print by the time of his own death in 1539.

Meanwhile, the Dominican priest Bartolomé de las Casas, who edited and commented Columbus's log from his first voyage in preparation for the composition of his own *History of the Indies*, took a very different angle on the great admiral's life. A harsh critic of the cruelty of the Spaniards to the Indians, Las Casas shared Columbus's own conviction that his mission was divinely inspired, but he believed that the brutality and enslavement first unleashed by Columbus and perpetuated in more extreme forms by his successors had utterly derailed the true goal of the discovery: the evangelization of the natives, which he believed should have proceeded peacefully and consensually.

Las Casas waged an all-out battle against Spain's colonial enterprise and gained a sympathetic hearing at court, but the juggernaut of conquest had been unleashed, and the Spanish authorities proved either unwilling or unable to restrain most of the brutality unleashed by the conquistadors against the original inhabitants of the lands.

Bartolomé de las Casas

Among major historical figures, Christopher Columbus has held the rare distinction of being nearly all things to nearly all people. Since his death in Valladolid, Spain on May 20, 1506, his reputation has undergone an astonishing series of metamorphoses. At the time of his death, he had fallen into poverty and obscurity following the abject failures of his most recent expeditions across the ocean. He was only just beginning to acknowledge that he had not achieved the goal to which he had dedicated much of his life and fortune: the discovery of a westward maritime route to Asia. It would have surprised him, then, that his subsequent reputations, however varied, were all built on a very different accomplishment than the one he had sought for so long and ultimately fallen short of. Rather than the discoverer of new trade routes to China, India, and

Japan, Columbus became, for later generations, the discoverer of a new continent, "America," which some proposed naming "Columbia" in his honor.

It would have been just as surprising to Columbus, perhaps, that he later became a national hero for Spain, given that his origins were in Genoa (now part of Italy) and his relations with the Spanish crown, primarily commercial from the outset, had deteriorated by the time of his death. Perhaps more in line with his fervent religious inclinations would have been his later status as a hero of the Roman Catholic Church who had opened the path to evangelization for many thousands of new converts to the faith. But the unfolding of his many reputations would not end there. Columbus would also become a national hero of several of the republics of Spanish America, including one, Colombia, that would take his name as its own despite the fact that his historical relation to the place was highly tenuous: he had barely even skirted its coast during his several trajectories through the Caribbean Sea.

Perhaps most improbable of all, Columbus would also become a national hero, with a capital city and a national holiday in his honor, in the English-speaking republic to the north, whose territory he had never so much as glanced. There, he would be celebrated, with questionable accuracy, as a pioneer of science, entrepreneurialism, and individualism whose values anticipated those of the republic itself. In the meantime, he would also become a national and ethnic icon of the Italian nation and its various diasporic communities, despite the fact that such a thing as Italy did not exist until nearly four centuries after his death.

The story did not end, however, with Columbus's canonization as a patron saint of any number of nationalities, ethnicities, creeds, values, and ideals. In fact, when the 500th anniversary of his "discovery of America" arrived in 1992, something unexpected happened: people began to question whether it had in fact been a discovery at all. People had asked this question before, but it suddenly became the basis of a loud and emotional debate. After all, others had in fact discovered the land before him, and their descendants were living on it when he arrived. Shortly after his arrival, these inhabitants began to be massacred, enslaved, killed by imported diseases, and converted into second class citizens when they were allowed to remain on the land at all. Had not Columbus himself begun this process? Had he not begun the enslavement and killing on the first island where he established a settlement, which later, once the original inhabitants were all exterminated, became ground zero for the atrocities of African slavery? Was this a man whose deeds and legacy should be celebrated? Such questions led, in many quarters, to a devaluing of the previously sacrosanct reputation celebrated by the West, and thus was born the latest incarnation of Columbus: a villain and a racist, prototype of the colonialist warmonger, and ruthless capitalist exploiter of the Third World. This figure who once made people proud now, at best, makes them uncomfortable.

For a figure who has been subject to such remarkably diverse mythification, Columbus's actual life and career were in fact remarkably complex, mysterious, and equivocal. It is difficult, in light of the known facts of his life, to view him as an indisputable hero, as so many have done. The moral questions that have been raised about his celebrated activities and their consequences are surely both legitimate questions to ask of any historical figure and a valuable corrective to the lionization that had been prevalent for centuries. That they emerged was inevitable: for centuries, the lands opened up to European settlement by his explorations had been ruled mainly by white, Christian men like him, and it was only natural that they should see in him a forebear and a symbol of what they admired in themselves. But in the past half-century, people who were not white, not Christian, and/or not men have gained a great deal more influence on public debates, and it is not surprising that they might call into question the symbolism of a figure who played such a large role in allowing white, Christian men to rule over vast swaths of the earth, typically oppressing and marginalizing those were not like them.

On the other hand, it is somewhat unfair to convert Columbus into a scapegoat for the atrocities of the modern world. A more useful exercise is to attempt to situate Columbus within the larger processes that led to a world in which such things as colonialism and genocide became not only possible but in some periods routine. In doing so, it is possible to build a bridge between the world out of which Columbus emerged – a deeply religious late medieval world that is for the most part culturally and intellectually unfamiliar to contemporary readers – and the world that he helped create. For the world that he helped create is, simply put, today's world: a world of highly efficient communication and trade, but also one marked by perpetual conflict and rampant inequality, both driven in part by the legacies of conquest and colonialism. It makes no sense to selectively celebrate him for helping bring about the former or only blame him for the latter. Whatever today's world has of good and of bad, Columbus played an important role in making it that way.

Columbus's final legacy, then, was to have helped inaugurate one of the most momentous periods in world history, which would witness the rapid establishment of European power over two entire continents. Furthermore, his American exploration did open up new trade networks that ultimately (much as the explorer had hoped) gave Europe access to the riches of Asia, as well as those of the ruthlessly demolished empires of the Aztecs and the Incas. Further imperial enterprises, ultimately even more lucrative, would soon follow on the part of two of Spain's rivals, Britain and France, and the various regions of the world would become economically intertwined in way that few could have imagined in the 15th century. While debates over the exact nature of the man will continue to rage, by all estimates Columbus is a pivotal figure in the history of the ongoing phenomenon now known as globalization.

Extracts from Columbus's Journal of His First Voyage

This document is from the journal of Columbus in his voyage of 1492. The meaning of this voyage is highly contested. On the one hand, it is witness to the tremendous vitality and verve of late medieval and early modern Europe - which was on the verge of acquiring a world hegemony. On the other hand, the direct result of this and later voyages was the virtual extermination, by ill-treatment and disease, of the vast majority of the Native inhabitants, and the enormous growth of the transatlantic slave trade. It might not be fair to lay the blame at Columbus' feet, but since all sides treat him as a symbol, such questions cannot be avoided.

IN THE NAME OF OUR LORD JESUS CHRIST

Whereas, Most Christian, High, Excellent, and Powerful Princes, King and Queen of Spain and of the Islands of the Sea, our Sovereigns, this present year 1492, after your Highnesses had terminated the war with the Moors reigning in Europe, the same having been brought to an end in the great city of Granada, where on the second day of January, this present year, I saw the royal banners of your Highnesses planted by force of arms upon the towers of the Alhambra, which is the fortress of that city, and saw the Moorish king come out at the gate of the city and kiss the hands of your Highnesses, and of the Prince my Sovereign; and in the present month, in consequence of the information which I had given your Highnesses respecting the countries of India and of a Prince, called Great Can, which in our language signifies King of Kings, how, at many times he, and his predecessors had sent to Rome soliciting instructors who might teach him our holy faith, and the holy Father had never granted his request, whereby great numbers of people were lost, believing in idolatry and doctrines of perdition. Your Highnesses, as Catholic Christians, and princes who love and promote the holy Christian faith, and are enemies of the doctrine of Mahomet, and of all idolatry and heresy, determined to send me, Christopher Columbus, to the above-mentioned countries of India, to see the said princes, people, and' territories, and to learn their disposition and the proper method of converting them to our holy faith; and furthermore directed that I should not proceed by land to the East, as is customary, but by a Westerly route, in which direction we have hitherto no certain evidence that any one has gone. So after having expelled the Jews from your dominions, your Highnesses, in the same month of January, ordered me to proceed with a sufficient armament to the said regions of India, and for that purpose granted me great favors, and ennobled me that thenceforth I might call myself Don, and be High Admiral of the Sea, and perpetual Viceroy and Governor in all the islands and continents which I might discover and acquire, or which may hereafter be discovered and acquired in the ocean; and that this dignity should be inherited by my eldest son, and thus descend from degree to degree forever. Hereupon I left the city of Granada, on Saturday, the twelfth day of May, 1492, and proceeded to Palos, a seaport, where I armed three vessels, very fit for such an enterprise, and having provided myself with abundance of stores and seamen, I set sail from the port, on Friday, the third of August, half an hour before sunrise, and steered for the Canary Islands of your Highnesses which are in the said ocean, thence to take my departure and proceed till I arrived at the Indies, and perform the embassy of your Highnesses to the Princes there, and discharge the orders given me. For this purpose I determined to keep an account of the voyage, and to write down punctually every thing we performed or saw from day to day, as will hereafter appear. Moreover, Sovereign Princes, besides describing every night the occurrences of the day, and every day those of the preceding night, I intend to draw up a nautical chart, which shall contain the several parts of the ocean and land in their proper situations; and also to compose a book to represent the whole by picture with latitudes and longitudes, on all which accounts it behooves me to abstain from my sleep, and make many trials in navigation, which things will demand much labor.

Friday, 3 August 1492. Set sail from the bar of Saltes at 8 o'clock, and proceeded with a strong breeze till sunset, sixty miles or fifteen leagues south, afterwards southwest and south by west, which is the direction of the Canaries.

* * * * *

Monday, 6 August. The rudder of the caravel Pinta became loose, being broken or unshipped. It was believed that this happened by the contrivance of Gomez Rascon and Christopher Quintero, who were on board the caravel, because they disliked the voyage. The Admiral says he had found them in an unfavorable disposition before setting out. He was in much anxiety at not being able to afford any assistance in this case, but says that it somewhat quieted his apprehensions to know that Martin Alonzo Pinzon, Captain of the Pinta, was a man of courage and capacity. Made a progress, day and night, of twenty-nine leagues.

* * * * *

Thursday, 9 August. The Admiral did not succeed in reaching the island of Gomera till Sunday night. Martin Alonzo remained at Grand Canary by command of the Admiral, he being unable to keep the other vessels company. The Admiral afterwards returned to Grand Canary, and there with much labor repaired the Pinta, being assisted by Martin Alonzo and the others; finally they sailed to Gomera. They saw a great eruption of names from the Peak of Teneriffe, a lofty mountain. The Pinta, which before had carried latine sails, they altered and made her square-rigged. Returned to Gomera, Sunday, 2 September, with the Pinta repaired.

The Admiral says that he was assured by many respectable Spaniards, inhabitants of the island of Ferro, who were at Gomera with Dona Inez Peraza, mother of Guillen Peraza, afterwards first Count of Gomera, that every year they saw land to the west of the Canaries; and others of Gomera affirmed the same with the like assurances. The Admiral here says that he remembers, while he was in Portugal, in 1484, there came a person to the King from the island of Madeira, soliciting for a vessel to go in quest of land, which he affirmed he saw every year, and always of the same appearance. He also says that he remembers the same was said by the inhabitants of the Azores and described as in a similar direction, and of the same shape and size. Having taken in food, water, meat and other provisions, which had been provided by the men which he left ashore on departing for Grand Canary to repair the Pinta, the Admiral took his final departure from Gomera with the three vessels on Thursday, 6 September.

* * * * *

Sunday, 9 September. Sailed this day nineteen leagues, and determined to count less than the true number, that the crew might not be dismayed if the voyage should prove long. In the night sailed one hundred and twenty miles, at the rate of ten miles an hour, which make thirty leagues. The sailors steered badly, causing the vessels to fall to leeward toward the northeast, for which the Admiral reprimanded them repeatedly.

Monday, 10 September. This day and night sailed sixty leagues, at the rate of ten miles an hour, which are two leagues and a half. Reckoned only forty-eight leagues, that the men might not be terrified if they should be long upon the voyage.

Tuesday, 11 September. Steered their course west and sailed above twenty leagues; saw a large fragment of the mast of a vessel, apparently of a hundred and twenty tons, but could not pick it up. In the night sailed about twenty leagues, and reckoned only sixteen, for the cause above stated.

* * * * *

Friday, 14 September. Steered this day and night west twenty leagues; reckoned somewhat less. The crew of the Nina stated that they had seen a grajao, and a tropic bird, or water-wagtail, which birds never go farther than twenty-five leagues from the land.

* * * * *

Sunday, 16 September. Sailed day and night, west thirty-nine leagues, and reckoned only thirty-six. Some clouds arose and it drizzled. The Admiral here says that from this time they experienced very pleasant weather, and that the mornings were most delightful, wanting nothing but the melody of the nightingales. He compares the weather to that of Andalusia in April. Here they began to meet with large patches of weeds very green, and which appeared to have been recently washed away from the land; on which account they all judged themselves to be near some island, though not a continent, according to the opinion of the Admiral, who says, "the continent we shall find further ahead."

Monday, 17 September. Steered west and sailed, day and night, above fifty leagues; wrote down only forty-seven; the current favored them. They saw a great deal of weed which proved to be rockweed, it came from the west and they met with it very frequently. They were of opinion that land was near. The pilots took the sun's amplitude, and found that the needles varied to the northwest a whole point of the compass; the seamen were terrified, and dismayed without saying why. The Admiral discovered the cause, and ordered them to take the amplitude again the next morning, when they found that the needles were true; the cause was that the star moved from its place, while the needles remained stationary. At dawn they saw many more weeds, apparently river weeds, and among them a live crab, which the Admiral kept, and says that these are sure signs of land, being never found eighty leagues out at sea. They found the sea-water less salt since they left the Canaries, and the air more mild. They were all very cheerful, and strove which vessel should outsail the others, and be the first to discover land; they saw many tunnies, and the crew of the Nina killed one. The Admiral here says that these signs were from the west, "where I hope that high God in whose hand is all victory will speedily direct us to land." This morning he says he saw a white bird called a water- wagtail, or tropic bird, which does not sleep at sea.

* * * * *

19 September. Continued on, and sailed, day and night, twenty- five leagues, experiencing a calm. Wrote down twenty-two. This day at ten o'clock a pelican came on board, and in the evening another; these birds are not accustomed to go twenty leagues from land. It drizzled without wind, which is a sure sign of land. The Admiral was unwilling to remain here, beating about in search of land, but he held it for certain that there were islands to the north and south, which in fact was the case and he was sailing in the midst of them. His wish was to proceed on to the Indies, having such fair weather, for if it please God, as the Admiral says, we shall examine these parts upon our return. Here the pilots found their places upon the chart: the reckoning of the Nina made her four hundred and forty leagues distant from the Canaries, that of the Pinta four hundred and twenty, that of the Admiral four hundred.

Thursday, 20 September. Steered west by north, varying with alternate changes of the wind and calms; made seven or eight leagues' progress. Two pelicans came on board, and afterwards another,--a sign of the neighborhood of land. Saw large quantities of weeds today, though none was observed yesterday. Caught a bird similar to a grajao; it was a river and not a marine bird, with feet like those of a gull. Towards night two or three land birds came to the ship, singing; they disappeared before sunrise. Afterwards saw a pelican coming from west- northwest and flying to the southwest; an evidence of land to the westward, as these birds sleep on shore, and go to sea in the morning in search of food, never proceeding twenty leagues from the land.

Friday, 21 September. Most of the day calm, afterwards a little wind. Steered their course day and night, sailing less than thirteen leagues. In the morning found such abundance of weeds that the ocean seemed to be covered with them; they came from the west. Saw a pelican; the sea smooth as a river, and the finest air in the world. Saw a whale, an indication of land, as they always keep near the coast.

Saturday, 22 September. Steered about west-northwest varying their course, and making thirty leagues' progress. Saw few weeds. Some pardelas were seen, and another bird. The Admiral here says "this headwind was very necessary to me, for my crew had grown much alarmed, dreading that they never should meet in these seas with a fair wind to return to Spain." Part of the day saw no weeds, afterwards great plenty of it.

Sunday, 23 September. Sailed northwest and northwest by north and at times west nearly twenty-two leagues. Saw a turtle dove, a pelican, a river bird, and other white fowl;--weeds in abundance with crabs among them. The sea being smooth and tranquil, the sailors murmured, saying that they had got into smooth water, where it would never blow to carry them back to Spain; but afterwards the sea rose without wind, which astonished them. The Admiral says on this occasion "the rising of the sea was very favorable to me, as it happened formerly to Moses when he led the Jews from Egypt."

* * * * *

Tuesday, 25 September. Very calm this day; afterwards the wind rose. Continued their course west till night. The Admiral held a conversation with Martin Alonzo Pinzon, captain of the Pinta, respecting a chart which the Admiral had sent him three days before, in which it appears he had marked down certain islands in that sea; Martin Alonzo was of opinion that they were in their neighborhood, and the Admiral replied that he thought the same, but as they had not met with them, it must have been owing to the currents which had carried them to the northeast and that they had not made such progress as the pilots stated. The Admiral directed him to return the chart, when he traced their course upon it in presence of the pilot and sailors.

At sunset Martin Alonzo called out with great joy from his vessel that he saw land, and demanded of the Admiral a reward for his intelligence. The Admiral says, when he heard him declare this, he fell on his knees and returned thanks to God, and Martin Alonzo with his crew repeated Gloria in excelsis Deo, as did the crew of the Admiral. Those on board the Nina ascended the rigging, and all declared they saw land. The Admiral also thought it was land, and about twenty-five leagues distant. They remained all night repeating these affirmations, and the

Admiral ordered their course to be shifted from west to southwest where the land appeared to lie. They sailed that day four leagues and a half west and in the night seventeen leagues southwest, in all twenty-one and a half: told the crew thirteen leagues, making it a point to keep them from knowing how far they had sailed; in this manner two reckonings were kept, the shorter one falsified, and the other being the true account. The sea was very smooth and many of the sailors went in it to bathe, saw many dories and other fish.

Wednesday, 26 September. Continued their course west till the afternoon, then southwest and discovered that what they had taken for land was nothing but clouds. Sailed, day and night, thirty- one leagues; reckoned to the crew twenty-four. The sea was like a river, the air soft and mild.

* * * * *

Sunday, 30 September. Continued their course west and sailed day and night in calms, fourteen leagues; reckoned eleven.--Four tropic birds came to the ship, which is a very clear sign of land, for so many birds of one sort together show that they are not straying about, having lost themselves. Twice, saw two pelicans; many weeds. The constellation called Las Gallardias, which at evening appeared in a westerly direction, was seen in the northeast the next morning, making no more progress in a night of nine hours, this was the case every night, as says the Admiral. At night the needles varied a point towards the northwest, in the morning they were true, by which it appears that the polar star moves, like the others, and the needles are always right.

Monday, 1 October. Continued their course west and sailed twenty-five leagues; reckoned to the crew twenty. Experienced a heavy shower. The pilot of the Admiral began to fear this morning that they were five hundred and seventy-eight leagues west of the island of Ferro. The short reckoning which the Admiral showed his crew gave five hundred and eighty-four, but the true one which he kept to himself was seven hundred and seven leagues.

* * * * *

Saturday, 6 October. Continued their course west and sailed forty leagues day and night; reckoned to the crew thirty-three. This night Martin Alonzo gave it as his opinion that they had better steer from west to southwest. The Admiral thought from this that Martin Alonzo did not wish to proceed onward to Cipango; but he considered it best to keep on his course, as he should probably reach the land sooner in that direction, preferring to visit the continent first, and then the islands.

Sunday, 7 October. Continued their course west and sailed twelve miles an hour, for two hours, then eight miles an hour. Sailed till an hour after sunrise, twenty-three leagues; reckoned to the crew eighteen. At sunrise the caravel Nina, who kept ahead on account of her swiftness in sailing, while all the vessels were striving to outsail one another, and gain the reward promised by the King and Queen by first discovering land--hoisted a flag at her mast head, and fired a lombarda, as a signal that she had discovered land, for the Admiral had given orders to that effect. He had also ordered that the ships should keep in close company at sunrise and sunset, as the air was more favorable at those times for seeing at a distance. Towards evening seeing nothing of the land which the Nina had made signals for, and observing large flocks of birds coming from the North and making for the southwest, whereby it was rendered probable that they were either going to land to pass the night, or abandoning the countries of the north, on account of the approaching winter, he determined to alter his course, knowing also that the Portuguese had discovered most of the islands they possessed by attending to the flight of birds. The Admiral accordingly shifted his course from west to west-southwest, with a resolution to continue two days ill that direction. This was done about an hour after sunset. Sailed in the night nearly five leagues, and twenty-three in the day. In all twenty-eight.

8 October. Steered west-southwest and sailed day and night eleven or twelve leagues; at times during the night, fifteen miles an hour, if the account can be depended upon. Found the sea like the river at Seville, "thanks to God," says the Admiral. The air soft as that of Seville in April, and so fragrant that it was delicious to breathe it. The weeds appeared very fresh. Many land birds, one of which they took, flying towards the southwest; also grajaos, ducks, and a pelican were seen.

Tuesday, 9 October. Sailed southwest five leagues, when the wind changed, and they stood west by north four leagues. Sailed in the whole day and night, twenty leagues and a half; reckoned to the crew seventeen. All night heard birds passing.

Wednesday, 10 October. Steered west-southwest and sailed at times ten miles an hour, at others twelve, and at others, seven; day and night made fifty-nine leagues' progress; reckoned to the crew but forty-four. Here the men lost all patience, and complained of the length of the voyage, but the Admiral encouraged them in the best manner he could, representing the profits they were about to acquire, and adding that it was to no purpose to complain, having come so far, they had nothing to do but continue on to the Indies, till with the help of our Lord, they should arrive there.

Thursday, 11 October. Steered west-southwest; and encountered a heavier sea than they had met with before in the whole voyage. Saw pardelas and a green rush near the vessel. The crew of the Pinta saw a cane and a log; they also picked up a stick which appeared to have been carved with an iron tool, a piece of cane, a plant which grows on land, and a board. The crew of the Nina saw other signs of land, and a stalk loaded with rose berries. These signs encouraged them, and they all grew cheerful. Sailed this day till sunset, twenty-seven leagues.

After sunset steered their original course west and sailed twelve miles an hour till two hours after midnight, going ninety miles, which are twenty-two leagues and a half; and as the Pinta was the swiftest sailer, and kept ahead of the Admiral, she discovered land and made the signals which had been ordered. The land was first seen by a sailor called Rodrigo de Triana, although the Admiral at ten o'clock that evening standing on the quarter-deck saw a light, but so small a body that he could not affirm it to be land; calling to Pero Gutierrez, groom of the King's wardrobe, he told him he saw a light, and bid him look that way, which he did and saw it; he did the same to Rodrigo Sanchez of Segovia, whom the King and Queen had sent with the squadron as comptroller, but he was unable to see it from his situation. The Admiral again perceived it once or twice, appearing like the light of a wax candle moving up and down, which some thought an indication of land. But the Admiral held it for certain that land was near; for which reason, after they had said the Salve which the seamen are accustomed to repeat and chant after their fashion, the Admiral directed them to keep a strict watch upon the forecastle and look out diligently for land, and to him who should first discover it he promised a silken jacket, besides the reward which the King and Queen had offered, which was an annuity of ten thousand maravedis. At two o'clock in the morning the land was discovered, at two leagues' distance; they took in sail and remained under the square-sail lying to till day, which was Friday, when they found themselves near a small island, one of the Lucayos, called in the Indian language Guanahani. Presently they descried people, naked, and the Admiral landed in the boat, which was armed, along with Martin Alonzo Pinzon, and Vincent Yanez his brother, captain of the Nina. The Admiral bore the royal standard, and the two captains each a banner of the Green Cross, which all the ships had carried; this contained the initials of the names of the King and Queen each side of the cross, and a crown over each letter Arrived on shore, they saw trees very green many streams of water, and diverse sorts of fruits. The Admiral called upon the two Captains, and the rest of the crew who landed, as also to Rodrigo de Escovedo notary of the fleet, and Rodrigo Sanchez, of Segovia, to bear witness that he before all others took possession (as in fact he did) of that island for the King and Queen his sovereigns, making the requisite declarations, which are more at large set down here in writing. Numbers of the people of the island straightway collected together. Here follow the precise words of the Admiral: "As I saw that they were very friendly to us, and perceived that they could be much more easily converted to our holy faith by gentle means than by force, I presented them with some red caps, and strings of beads to wear upon the neck, and many other trifles of small value, wherewith they were much delighted, and became wonderfully attached to us. Afterwards they came swimming to the boats, bringing parrots, balls of cotton thread, javelins, and many other things which they exchanged for articles we gave them, such as glass beads, and hawk's bells; which trade was carried on with the utmost good will. But they seemed on the whole to me, to be a very poor people. They all go completely naked, even the women, though I saw but one girl. All whom I saw were young, not above thirty years of age, well made, with fine shapes and faces; their hair short, and coarse like that of a horse's tail, combed toward the forehead, except a small portion which they suffer to hang down behind, and never cut. Some paint themselves with black, which makes them appear like those of the Canaries, neither black nor white; others with white, others with red, and others with such colors as they can find. Some paint the face, and some the whole body; others only the eyes, and others the nose. Weapons they have none, nor are acquainted with them, for I showed them swords which they grasped by the blades, and cut themselves through ignorance. They have no iron, their javelins being without it, and nothing more than sticks, though some have fish-bones or other things at the ends. They are all of a good size and stature, and handsomely formed. I saw some with scars of wounds upon their bodies, and demanded by signs the of them; they answered me in the same way, that there came people from the other islands in the neighborhood who endeavored to make prisoners of them, and they defended themselves. I thought then, and still believe, that these were from the continent. It appears to me, that the people are ingenious, and would be good servants and I am of opinion that they would very readily become Christians, as they appear to have no religion. They very quickly learn such words as are spoken to them. If it please our Lord, I intend at my return to carry home six of them to your Highnesses, that they may learn our language. I saw no beasts in the island, nor any sort of animals except parrots." These are the words of the Admiral.

Saturday, 13 October. "At daybreak great multitudes of men came to the shore, all young and of fine shapes, very handsome; their hair not curled but straight and coarse like horse-hair, and all with foreheads and heads much broader than any people I had hitherto seen; their eyes were large and very beautiful; they were not black, but the color of the inhabitants of the Canaries, which is a very natural circumstance, they being in the same latitude with the island of Ferro in the Canaries. They were straight-limbed without exception, and not with prominent bellies but handsomely shaped. They came to the ship in canoes, made of a single trunk of a tree, wrought in a wonderful manner considering the country; some of them large enough to contain forty or forty-five men, others of different sizes down to those fitted to hold but a single person. They rowed with an oar like a baker's peel, and wonderfully swift. If they happen to upset, they all jump into the sea, and swim till they have righted their canoe and emptied it with the calabashes they carry with them. They came loaded with balls of cotton, parrots, javelins, and other things too numerous to mention; these they exchanged for whatever we chose to give them. I was very attentive to them, and strove to learn if they had any gold. Seeing some of them with little bits of this metal hanging at their noses, I gathered from them by signs that by going southward or steering round the island in that direction, there would be found a king who possessed large vessels of gold, and in great quantities. I endeavored to procure them to lead the way thither, but found they were unacquainted with the route. I determined to stay here till the evening of the next day, and then sail for the southwest; for according to what I could learn from them, there was land at the south as well as at the southwest and northwest and those from the northwest came many times and fought with them and proceeded on to the southwest in search of gold and precious stones. This is a large and level island, with trees extremely flourishing, and streams of water; there is a large lake in the middle of the island, but no mountains: the whole is completely covered with verdure and delightful to behold. The natives are an inoffensive people, and so desirous to possess any thing they saw with us, that they kept swimming off to the ships with whatever they could find, and readily bartered for any article we saw fit to give them in return, even such as broken platters and fragments of glass. I saw in this manner sixteen balls of cotton thread which weighed above twenty-five pounds, given for three Portuguese ceutis. This traffic I forbade, and suffered no one to take their cotton from them, unless I should order it to be procured for your Highnesses, if proper quantities could be met with. It grows in this island, but from my short stay here I could not satisfy myself fully concerning it; the gold, also, which they wear in their noses, is found here, but not to lose time, I am determined to proceed onward and ascertain whether I can reach Cipango. At night they all went on shore with their canoes.

Sunday, 14 October. In the morning, I ordered the boats to be got ready, and coasted along the island toward the north- northeast to examine that part of it, we having landed first at the eastern part. Presently we discovered two or three villages, and the people all came down to the shore, calling out to us, and giving thanks to God. Some brought us water, and others victuals: others seeing that I was not disposed to land, plunged into the sea and swam out to us, and we perceived that they interrogated us if we had come from heaven. An old man came on board my boat; the others, both men and women cried with loud voices--"Come and see the men who have come from heavens. Bring them victuals and drink." There came many of both sexes, every one bringing something, giving thanks to God, prostrating themselves on the earth, and lifting up their hands to heaven. They called out to us loudly to come to land, but I was apprehensive on account of a reef of rocks, which surrounds the whole island, although within there is depth of water and room sufficient for all the ships of Christendom, with a very narrow entrance. There are some shoals withinside, but the water is as smooth as a pond. It was to view these parts that I set out in the morning, for I wished to give a complete relation to your Highnesses, as also to find where a fort might be built. I discovered a tongue of land which appeared like an island though it was not, but might be cut through and made so in two days; it contained six houses. I do not, however, see the necessity of fortifying the place, as the people here are simple in war-like matters, as your Highnesses will see by those seven which I have ordered to be taken and carried to Spain in order to learn our language and return, unless your Highnesses should choose to have them all transported to Castile, or held captive in the island. I could conquer the whole of them with fifty men, and govern them as I pleased. Near the islet I have mentioned were groves of trees, the most beautiful I have ever seen, with their foliage as verdant as we see in Castile in April and May. There were also many streams. After having taken a survey of these parts, I returned to the ship, and setting sail, discovered such a number of islands that I knew not which first to visit; the natives whom I had taken on board informed me by signs that there were so many of them that they could not be numbered; they repeated the names of more than a hundred. I determined to steer for the largest, which is about five leagues from San Salvador; the others were some at a greater, and some at a less distance from that island. They are all very level, without mountains, exceedingly fertile and populous, the inhabitants living at war with one another, although a simple race, and with delicate bodies.

15 October. Stood off and on during the night, determining not to come to anchor till morning, fearing to meet with shoals; continued our course in the morning; and as the island was found to be six or seven leagues distant, and the tide was against us, it was noon when we arrived there. I found that part of it towards San Salvador extending from north to south five leagues, and the other side which we coasted along, ran from east to west more than ten leagues. From this island espying a still larger one to the west, I set sail in that direction and kept on till night without reaching the western extremity of the island, where I gave it the name of Santa Maria de la Concepcion. About sunset we anchored near the cape which terminates the island towards the west to enquire for gold, for the natives we had taken from San Salvador told me that the people here wore golden bracelets upon their arms and legs. I believed pretty confidently that they had invented this story in order to find means to escape from us, still I determined to pass none of these islands without taking possession, because being once taken, it would answer for all times. We anchored and remained till Tuesday, when at daybreak I went ashore with the boats armed. The people we found naked like those of San Salvador, and of the same disposition. They suffered us to traverse the island, and gave us what we asked of them. As the wind blew southeast upon the shore where the vessels lay, I determined not to remain, and set out for the ship. A large canoe being near the caravel Nina, one of the San Salvador natives leaped overboard and swam to her; (another had made his escape the night before,) the canoe being reached by the fugitive, the natives rowed for the land too swiftly to be overtaken; having landed, some of my men went ashore in pursuit of them, when they abandoned the canoe and fled with precipitation; the canoe which they had left was brought on board the Nina, where from another quarter had arrived a small canoe with a single man, who came to barter some cotton; some of the sailors finding him unwilling to go on board the vessel, jumped into the sea and took him. I was upon the quarter deck of my ship, and seeing the whole, sent for him, and gave him a red cap, put some glass beads upon his arms, and two hawk's bells upon his ears. I then ordered his canoe to be returned to him, and despatched him back to land.

I now set sail for the other large island to the west and gave orders for the canoe which the Nina had in tow to be set adrift. I had refused to receive the cotton from the native whom I sent on shore, although he pressed it upon me. I looked out after him and saw upon his landing that the others all ran to meet him with much wonder. It appeared to them that we were honest people, and that the man who had escaped from us had done us some injury, for which we kept him in custody. It was in order to favor this notion that I ordered the canoe to be set adrift, and gave the man the presents above mentioned, that when your Highnesses send another expedition to these parts it may meet with a friendly reception. All I gave the man was not worth four maravedis. We set sail about ten o'clock, with the wind southeast and stood southerly for the island I mentioned above, which is a very large one, and where according to the account of the natives on board, there is much gold, the inhabitants wearing it in bracelets upon their arms, legs, and necks, as well as in their ears and at their noses. This island is nine leagues distant from Santa Maria in a westerly direction. This part of it extends from northwest, to southeast and appears to be twenty-eight leagues long, very level, without any mountains, like San Salvador and Santa Maria, having a good shore and not rocky, except a few ledges under water, which renders it necessary to anchor at some distance, although the water is very clear, and the bottom may be seen. Two shots of a lombarda from the land, the water is so deep that it cannot be sounded; this is the case in all these islands. They are all extremely verdant and fertile, with the air agreeable, and probably contain many things of which I am ignorant, not inclining to stay here, but visit other islands in search of gold. And considering the indications of it among the natives who wear it upon their arms and legs, and having ascertained that it is the true metal by showing them some pieces of it which I have with me, I cannot fail, with the help of our Lord, to find the place which produces it.

Being at sea, about midway between Santa Maria and the large island, which I name Fernandina, we met a man in a canoe going from Santa Maria to Fernandina; he had with him a piece of the bread which the natives make, as big as one's fist, a calabash of water, a quantity of reddish earth, pulverized and afterwards kneaded up, and some dried leaves which are in high value among them, for a quantity of it was brought to me at San Salvador; he had besides a little basket made after their fashion, containing some glass beads, and two blancas by all which I knew he had come from San Salvador, and had passed from thence to Santa Maria. He came to the ship and I caused him to be taken on board, as he requested it; we took his canoe also on board and took care of his things. I ordered him to be presented with bread and honey, and drink, and shall carry him to Fernandina and give him his property, that he may carry a good report of us, so that if it please our Lord when your Highnesses shall send again to these regions, those who arrive here may receive honor, and procure what the natives may be found to possess.

Tuesday, 16 October. Set sail from Santa Maria about noon, for Fernandina which appeared very large in the west; sailed all the day with calms, and could not arrive soon enough to view the shore and select a good anchorage, for great care must be taken in this particular, lest the anchors be lost. Beat up and down all night, and in the morning arrived at a village and anchored. This was the place to which the man whom we had picked up at sea had gone, when we set him on shore. He had given such a favorable account of us, that all night there were great numbers of canoes coming off to us, who brought us water and other things. I ordered each man to be presented with something, as strings of ten or a dozen glass beads apiece, and thongs of leather, all which they estimated highly; those which came on board I directed should be fed with molasses. At three o'clock, I sent the boat on shore for water; the natives with great good will directed the men where to find it, assisted them in carrying the casks full of it to the boat, and seemed to take great pleasure in serving us. This is a very large island, and I have resolved to coast it about, for as I understand, in, or near the island, there is a mine of gold. It is eight leagues west of Santa Maria, and the cape where we have arrived, and all this coast extends from north-northwest to south-southeast. I have seen twenty leagues of it, but not the end. Now, writing this, I set sail with a southerly wind to circumnavigate the island, and search till we can find Samoet, which is the island or city where the gold is, according to the account of those who come on board the ship, to which the relation of those of San Salvador and Santa Maria corresponds. These people are similar to those of the islands just mentioned, and have the same language and customs; with the exception that they appear somewhat more civilized, showing themselves more subtle in their dealings with us, bartering their cotton and other articles with more profit than the others had experienced. Here we saw cotton cloth, and perceived the people more decent, the women wearing a slight covering of cotton over the nudities. The island is verdant, level and fertile to a high degree; and I doubt not that grain is sowed and reaped the whole year round, as well as all other productions of the place. I saw many trees, very dissimilar to those of our country, and many of them had branches of different sorts upon the same trunk; and such a diversity was among them that it was the greatest wonder in the world to behold. Thus, for instance, one branch of a tree bore leaves like those of a cane, another branch of the same tree, leaves similar to those of the lentisk. In this manner a single tree bears five or six different kinds. Nor is this done by grafting, for that is a work of art, whereas these trees grow wild, and the natives take no care about them. They have no religion, and I believe that they would very readily become Christians, as they have a good understanding. Here the fish are so dissimilar to ours that it is wonderful. Some are shaped like dories, of the finest hues in the world, blue, yellow, red, and every other color, some variegated with a thousand different tints, so beautiful that no one on beholding them could fail to express the highest wonder and admiration. Here are also whales. Beasts, we saw none, nor any creatures on land save parrots and lizards, but a boy told me he saw a large snake. No sheep nor goats were seen, and although our stay here has been short, it being now noon, yet were there any, I could hardly have failed of seeing them. The circumnavigation of the island I shall describe afterward.

Wednesday, 17 October. At noon set sail from the village where we had anchored and watered. Kept on our course to sail round the island; the wind southwest and south. My intention was to follow the coast of the island to the southeast as it runs in that direction, being informed by the Indians I have on board, besides another whom I met with here, that in such a course I should meet with the island which they call Samoet, where gold is found. I was further informed by Martin Alonzo Pinzon, captain of the Pinta, on board of which I had sent three of the Indians, that he had been assured by one of them I might sail round the island much sooner by the northwest. Seeing that the wind would not enable me to proceed in the direction I first contemplated, and finding it favorable for the one thus recommended me, I steered to the northwest and arriving at the extremity of the island at two leagues' distance, I discovered a remarkable haven with two entrances, formed by an island at its mouth, both very narrow, the inside capacious enough for a hundred ships, were there sufficient depth of water. I thought it advisable to examine it, and therefore anchored outside, and went with the boats to sound it, but found the water shallow. As I had first imagined it to be the mouth of a river, I had directed the casks to be carried ashore for water, which being done we discovered eight or ten men who straightway came up to us, and directed us to a village in the neighborhood; I accordingly dispatched the crews thither in quest of water, part of them armed, and the rest with the casks, and the place being at some distance it detained me here a couple of hours. In the meantime I strayed about among the groves, which present the most enchanting sight ever witnessed, a degree of verdure prevailing like that of May in Andalusia, the trees as different from those of our country as day is from night, and the same may be said of the fruit, the weeds, the stones and everything else. A few of the trees, however, seemed to be of a species similar to some that are to be found in Castile, though still with a great dissimilarity, but the others so unlike, that it is impossible to find any resemblance in them to those of our land. The natives we found like those already described, as to personal appearance and manners, and naked like the rest. Whatever they possessed, they bartered for what we chose to give them. I saw a boy of the crew purchasing javelins of them with bits of platters and broken glass. Those who went for water informed me that they had entered their houses and found them very clean and neat, with beds and coverings of cotton nets. Their houses are all built in the shape of tents, with very high chimneys. None of the villages which I saw contained more than twelve or fifteen of them. Here it was remarked that the married women wore cotton breeches, but the younger females were without them, except a few who were as old as eighteen years. Dogs were seen of a large and small size, and one of the men had hanging at his nose a piece of gold half as big as a castellailo, with letters upon it. I endeavored to purchase it of them in order to ascertain what sort of money it was but they refused to part with it. Having taken our water on board, I set sail and proceeded northwest till I had surveyed the coast to the point where it begins to run from east to west. Here the Indians gave me to understand that this island was smaller than that of Samoet, and that I had better return in order to reach it the sooner. The wind died away, and then sprang up from the west-northwest which was contrary to the course we were pursuing, we therefore hove about and steered various courses through the night from east to south standing off from the land, the weather being cloudy and thick. It rained violently from midnight till near day, and the sky still remains clouded; we remain off the southeast part of the island, where I expect to anchor and stay till the weather grows clear, when I shall steer for the other islands I am in quest of. Every day that I have been in these Indies it has rained more or less. I assure your Highnesses that these lands are the most fertile, temperate, level and beautiful countries in the world.

Thursday, 18 October. As soon as the sky grew clear, we set sail and went as far round the island as we could, anchoring when we found it inconvenient to proceed. I did not, however, land. In the morning set sail again.

Friday, 19 October. In the morning we got under weigh, and I ordered the Pinta to steer east and southeast and the Nina south- southeast; proceeding myself to the southeast the other vessels I directed to keep on the courses prescribed till noon, and then to rejoin me. Within three hours we descried an island to the east toward which we directed our course, and arrived all three, before noon, at the northern extremity, where a rocky islet and reef extend toward the North, with another between them and the main island. The Indians on board the ships called this island Saomete. I named it Isabela. It lies westerly from the island of Fernandina, and the coast extends from the islet twelve leagues, west, to a cape which I called Cabo Hermoso, it being a beautiful, round headland with a bold shore free from shoals. Part of the shore is rocky, but the rest of it, like most of the coast here, a sandy beach. Here we anchored till morning. This island is the most beautiful that I have yet seen, the trees in great number, flourishing and lofty; the land is higher than the other islands, and exhibits an eminence, which though it cannot be called a mountain, yet adds a beauty to its appearance, and gives an indication of streams of water in the interior. From this part toward the northeast is an extensive bay with many large and thick groves. I wished to anchor there, and land, that I might examine those delightful regions, but found the coast shoal, without a possibility of casting anchor except at a distance from the shore. The wind being favorable, I came to the Cape, which I named Hermoso, where I anchored today. This is so beautiful a place, as well as the neighboring regions, that I know not in which course to proceed first; my eyes are never tired with viewing such delightful verdure, and of a species so new and dissimilar to that of our country, and I have no doubt there are trees and herbs here which would be of great value in Spain, as dyeing materials, medicine, spicery, etc., but I am mortified that I have no acquaintance with them. Upon our arrival here we experienced the most sweet and delightful odor from the flowers or trees of the island. Tomorrow morning before we depart, I intend to land and see what can be found in the neighborhood. Here is no village, but farther within the island is one, where our Indians inform us we shall find the king, and that he has much gold. I shall penetrate so far as to reach the village and see or speak with the king, who, as they tell us, governs all these islands, and goes dressed, with a great deal of gold about him. I do not, however, give much credit to these accounts, as I understand the natives but imperfectly, and perceive them to be so poor that a trifling quantity of gold appears to them a great amount. This island appears to me to be a separate one from that of Saomete, and I even think there may be others between them. I am not solicitous to examine particularly everything here, which indeed could not be done in fifty years, because my desire is to make all possible discoveries, and return to your Highnesses, if it please our Lord, in April. But in truth, should I meet with gold or spices in great quantity, I shall remain till I collect as much as possible, and for this purpose I am proceeding solely in quest of them.

Saturday, 20 October. At sunrise we weighed anchor, and stood to the northeast and east along the south side of this island, which I named Isabela, and the cape where we anchored, Cabo de la Laguna; in this direction I expected from the account of our Indians to find the capital and king of the island. I found the coast very shallow, and offering every obstacle to our navigation, and perceiving that our course this way must be very circuitous, I determined to return to the westward. The wind failed us, and we were unable to get near the shore before night; and as it is very dangerous anchoring here in the dark, when it is impossible to discern among so many shoals and reefs whether the ground be suitable, I stood off and on all night. The other vessels came to anchor, having reached the shore in season. As was customary among us, they made signals to me to stand in and anchor, but I determined to remain at sea.

Sunday, 21 October. At 10 o'clock, we arrived at a cape of the island, and anchored, the other vessels in company. After having dispatched a meal, I went ashore, and found no habitation save a single house, and that without an occupant; we had no doubt that the people had fled in terror at our approach, as the house was completely furnished. I suffered nothing to be touched, and went with my captains and some of the crew to view the country. This island even exceeds the others in beauty and fertility. Groves of lofty and flourishing trees are abundant, as also large lakes, surrounded and overhung by the foliage, in a most enchanting manner. Everything looked as green as in April in Andalusia. The melody of the birds was so exquisite that one was never willing to part from the spot, and the flocks of parrots obscured the heavens. The diversity in the appearance of the feathered tribe from those of our country is extremely curious. A thousand different sorts of trees, with their fruit were to be met with, and of a wonderfully delicious odor. It was a great affliction to me to be ignorant of their natures, for I am very certain they are all valuable; specimens of them and of the plants I have preserved. Going round one of these lakes, I saw a snake, which we killed, and I have kept the skin for your Highnesses; upon being discovered he took to the water, whither we followed him, as it was not deep, and dispatched him with our lances; he was seven spans in length; I think there are many more such about here. I discovered also the aloe tree, and am determined to take on board the ship tomorrow, ten quintals of it, as I am told it is valuable. While we were in search of some good water, we came upon a village of the natives about half a league from the place where the ships lay; the inhabitants on discovering us abandoned their houses, and took to flight, carrying of their goods to the mountain. I ordered that nothing which they had left should be taken, not even the value of a pin. Presently we saw several of the natives advancing towards our party, and one of them came up to us, to whom we gave some hawk's bells and glass beads, with which he was delighted. We asked him in return, for water, and after I had gone on board the ship, the natives came down to the shore with their calabashes full, and showed great pleasure in presenting us with it. I ordered more glass beads to be given them, and they promised to return the next day. It is my wish to fill all the water casks of the ships at this place, which being executed, I shall depart immediately, if the weather serve, and sail round the island, till I succeed in meeting with the king, in order to see if I can acquire any of the gold, which I hear he possesses. Afterwards I shall set sail for another very large island which I believe to be Cipango, according to the indications I receive from the Indians on board. They call the Island Colba, and say there are many large ships, and sailors there. This other island they name Bosio, and inform me that it is very large; the others which lie in our course, I shall examine on the passage, and according as I find gold or spices in abundance, I shall determine what to do; at all events I am determined to proceed on to the continent, and visit the city of Guisay, where I shall deliver the letters of your Highnesses to the Great Can, and demand an answer, with which I shall return.

Hernan Cortés
Chapter 1: Origins and Background

Hernán Cortés was born on an uncertain date in 1485 in Medellín, in the Spanish province of Extremadura. A dry, dusty, and hot backwater in the southwest of Spain, Extremadura was the home of many families of noble descent who had fallen into poverty, and it would prove to be the breeding ground of a majority of the conquistadors, most of whom came from honorable lineages but had few viable prospects in their native country. Indeed, this was the case for Hernán, son of Martín Cortés de Monroy and Catalina Pizarro Altamarino (through his mother, Cortés was a distant cousin of the conqueror of Peru, Francisco Pizarro). Though he is commonly referred to as Hernán today, he called himself Hernando or Fernando during his life.

The Spanish nobility was traditionally a warrior caste forged in the *reconquista*, the slow but ultimately successful reincorporation of the Iberian peninsula into Christendom at the expense of the Arabic-speaking Muslims who had ruled it for centuries. Cortés's father, a captain in the military, had remained true to the martial vocation of his class, but it held little tangible reward now that the Moors had been finally driven back into North Africa in 1492, the same year that Christopher Columbus first arrived in the New World thinking it was Asia.

Apparently a bright and ambitious child, Hernán Cortés left home for the prestigious University of Salamanca at the age of 14 with the intention of studying law. His parents, like many today, probably saw the legal profession as a steady and promising career path for their son, one which might help him restore the family's diminished fortune. But Cortés only remained at the university for two years, thus falling short of earning a degree. His evident impatience with the need for prolonged, sustained study reveals the restlessness and impetuousness that would become one of his most prevalent character traits. On the other hand, his legal studies provided him with knowledge that would later prove valuable when he was attempting to justify his claims to the land he conquered across the ocean and negotiate with the Spanish crown over his share of its wealth.

Thus, two of the qualities that Cortés would share with later conquistadors are evident from his early choices. First, he did not wish to follow a slow, gradual route to wealth and prominence; he wanted to achieve these things in a dramatic and immediate fashion. Second, he was willing to use the most influential forms of knowledge of the time and place, especially law and theology, to pursue his own aims, but he had no real reverence for learning in itself. His departure from Salamanca set a pattern. As he would do again and again, he left behind the old, the familiar, and established for the new, the uncertain, and the adventurous.

Spain's great writer Miguel de Cervantes, in a story about a man from Extremadura, described the Americas as "the refuge of the despairing sons of Spain, the church of the homeless, the asylum of homicides, the haven of gamblers and cheats, the general receptacle for loose women, the common center of attraction for many, but effectual resource of very few." As a contemporary view of the conquistadors and other arrivistes in the new colonies, Cervantes's is not a flattering portrait of what motivated men like Cortés to make the dangerous crossing of the Atlantic. And yet from what we know of his personality and early life, it seems like an accurate enough characterization of the man and the circles he frequented. A restless, mischievous young man, he found employment as a notary in the port city of Seville, but he soon found himself attracted to the new lands to the West, for which ships were departing regularly from Seville's harbor, and from which new wealth was arriving and remaking the city's economy.

Cervantes

When he departed for the island of Hispaniola in 1504, the memory of Columbus's discoveries was still fresh in the minds of the Spanish public. Columbus himself was still alive, but as a result of his disastrous stint as governor of Hispaniola, he had been relieved of his title of Viceroy of the Indies, and the crown had moved to centralize control over the new colonies and ensure their profitability. And though Columbus's voyage to the New World is remembered as one of the seminal events of the last millennium, at the time it still represented a bit of a disappointment. After all, Columbus's goal had been to reach Asia and ensure Spain's access to the trade in luxurious commodities such as spices and silk, and he had also hoped, later in his career, to reach the legendary gold mines of King Solomon.

Instead, what he had actually achieved was now uncertain, but it was becoming clear that rather than reaching the eastern edge of Asia, Columbus had arrived at a different land mass altogether. Justifying himself by the claim that the natives were barbaric heathens who needed to be civilized and converted to Christianity, Columbus had initiated a treatment of the native inhabitants that was at best paternalistic and at worst horrifically brutal and exploitative.

Making matters worse, Columbus had attempted to exploit the islands of Hispaniola and Cuba for gold only to find that the deposits were scarce. In the meantime, a system of thinly disguised slave labor came into being under the name of the *encomienda*, or "entrustment." The notion was that Spanish settlers would be granted a piece of land and power over the natives who inhabited it; their responsibility would be to instruct the natives in religion, in return for which "service" they could exact tributes of gold or other valuables, or labor in extractive or agricultural activities. The system laid the ground for the plantation-slave economy that would later become prevalent in the Caribbean.

It was into this environment that Cortés arrived in 1504, still not yet 20. Although Columbus had met with a friendly reception from the inhabitants of the islands he first visited, the conflict between Spanish settlers and natives had now become implacable. Understandably, the natives were not fond of the *encomienda* system or of the extreme savagery and cruelty of many Spaniards, and some had taken up arms against the new arrivals. One of Cortés's first experiences in the New World was to participate in expeditions against the remaining groups of Indians who had not yet been subjugated. It was here that he got his first taste of the casual brutality of the colonial frontier culture, as well as of the rewards that military exploits could bring. Through his military involvement, Cortés was granted a large *encomienda* in Hispaniola, including control over several hundred subjugated natives. In the meantime, he also offered his services as a notary and clerk to other settlers, establishing a fruitful set of relationships with the colonial authorities. Just over five years after arriving in the Indies, Cortés would move on from Hispaniola and take part in an expedition to Cuba, a larger island with far more as yet unconquered land.

Cortés's services to the new governor of Cuba, Diego Velázquez, earned him a prominent position in the new colony. He became clerk and secretary to the governor himself, gained control of a large *encomienda*, and accumulated enough prestige to become mayor of the city of Santiago. However, he soon got ahead of himself, amassing debts through an extravagant lifestyle and gaining the hostility of the governor on account of his unapologetic ambition and his seduction of the governor's sister-in-law, Catalina Juárez, whom Cortés ultimately married. Furthermore, he proved not to be a model citizen of the colony. According to chronicler Bernal Díaz del Castillo, who would accompany Cortés on his expedition to Mexico, the soon-to-be conquistador was a dandy, a lover of fineries, and unrestrained spender; despite his apparent wealth, Cortés accumulated vast debts during his years in Cuba through his luxurious lifestyle. Such a predicament provides a relatively banal explanation for his desire to set off and conquer new lands. If he was ever going to repay his creditors, he would need a windfall much bigger than the *encomienda* he had already acquired. By obtaining the title of Captain General, necessary for leading further expeditions, Cortés also obtained a higher credit limit, so to speak, because his creditors would now be guaranteed a share of any further profits he obtained.

Diego Velázquez de Cuéllar

Chapter 2: Expedition to the Mainland

Once he had gained his commission in 1518, Cortés wasted no time in gathering a fleet of ships and an army of ambitious followers, to whom he promised riches and land. In addition to permanently defraying his debts, Cortés now aimed to establish a permanent presence on the *terra firma*, which no Spaniard had yet accomplished since Columbus's failed attempt to colonize what is now Panama nearly 20 years earlier.

Cortés had little clear sense of what he would find, but rumors had long circulated about the existence of great empires with enormous treasures of gold. A previous expedition to the coastal Yucatán region of what is now Mexico had ended in failure, with the Spanish ambushed by local Mayans and the leader of the Spanish group injured. Certainly never averse to risk, Cortés was happy to take his chances with re-attempting the same expedition. Governor Velázquez, uneasy about Cortés's ambitions, attempted to restrict the newly minted Captain General from actually conquering and settling any territory, mandating that he should establish trade relations with the local inhabitants instead.

Velázquez apparently had an inkling of the fame and wealth that Cortés would achieve if he did manage to colonize the mainland and certainly did not trust Cortés to follow the orders he was given. When the fleet was nearly organized and ready to depart, the governor attempted twice to intervene and relieve Cortés of his leadership. Velázquez first sent a messenger whom Cortés promptly ordered killed, showing perhaps for the first time the full extent of his ruthlessness, and by the time Velázquez intervened a second time, Cortés was already just about to set sail and simply departed in direct defiance of his superior. Thus, when his 11 ships departed with a crew of over 500 men, they did so in open mutiny, taking advantage of the automatic delay that would be required for the governor to gather another expedition to go after them. Given that Cortés had invested a great deal of his personal wealth and gone into considerable debt to finance his excursion, it is not entirely surprising that he would behave with this degree of audacity. He likely sensed that he had lost the good will of Velázquez and would not be given another opportunity after this. Had he remained, he would have been at the mercy of his creditors and without any obvious way of turning his situation around, since he had already risen about as high as he was likely to in Cuba. His future was by no means guaranteed at this point, but he could be sure that he had few other options than to stake everything on success.

Sailing from the southeastern end of the island of Cuba in early 1519, the closest stretch of coast Cortés and his crew would find on the mainland was the Yucatán peninsula, once home to the large and wealthy Mayan empire. The Mayas had in recent centuries fragmented into smaller sub-groups and city states, and their wealth was now diminished. Previous Spaniards had found little success in the region, and Cortés probably set his sights somewhere else even before he landed, but he did spend some time on the island of Cozumel, just off the Yucatán coast. Although he did not send a large land expedition into the peninsula, he acquired some of his most valuable assets there. First, he came across a Spaniard, survivor of a 1511 shipwreck, who had been living among the Mayas ever since. This man, Gerónimo de Aguilar, was now fluent in the Yucatec Mayan language, but he was also eager to return to his own people. Cortés took Aguilar in, and with that he had something that earlier conquistadors had lacked: a fully bilingual translator.

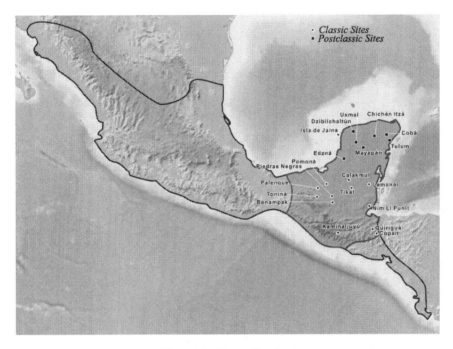

Map of the Mayan Empire

Aguilar's language skills, though, would have been of little use among the Nahuatl-speaking peoples further to the west had it not been for a second key encounter. On the other side of the Yucatán peninsula, Cortés was given possession of a young woman by the chief of another group of Mayas. This woman, it turned out, was a native of central Mexico and a fluent speaker of Nahuatl, as well as of Mayan and other languages. Cortés called her Doña Marina, but her original name was probably Malinalli, and she would later become known as Malintzin or Malinche to Mexicans. With the combined services of Aguilar and Doña Marina, Cortés now had the ability to communicate fluently with most of the peoples of Mexico, a capacity that gave him a crucial advantage in information gathering over earlier explorers such as Columbus, who proceeded with at-best rudimentary translation services, even in his later travels. Through the communicative chain he was able to establish, Cortés was able to find out not only the location of the great and wealthy Aztec empire, but also the resentment many neighboring tribes felt towards the Aztecs, a hostility he would make use of for his own purposes.

Hernan Cortes and La Malinche meet Moctezuma II in Tenochtitlan, November 8, 1519. Facsimile (c. 1890) of Lienzo de Tlaxcala.

Doña Marina, or Malinche, would play an outsized role in the conquest of Mexico. She ultimately became fluent in Spanish herself (diminishing Aguilar's importance), and was probably something of an advisor and confidant to Cortés. She was most certainly his mistress, and in 1522 she would bear him a son, Martín Cortés, often referred to as Mexico's first mestizo. The relationship would create tension with Cortés's Spanish wife, and Marina would be married off to another Spaniard. Still, her services earned her an *encomienda* and a relatively important status in the colony, and she was spoken of as a wise and graceful woman by Bernal Díaz and other chroniclers. Although the details of her later life are not known, she has become an iconic figure in Mexican history, sometimes a figure of pride, other times a figure of scorn and derision for her alleged betrayal of her native people and collaboration with the invading forces. However people choose to assess her actions, she was an extremely important figure whose participation in Cortés's expedition proved a crucial ingredient of its success.

Chapter 3: The Aztec Empire

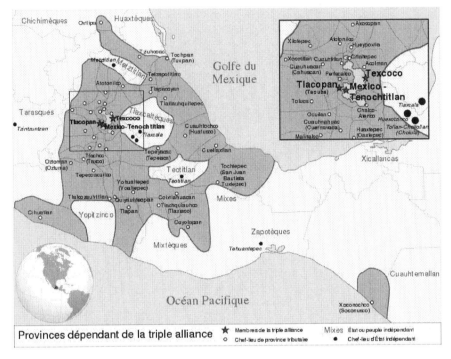

By the time he had made his way past the Yucatecan coast, Cortés seemed to know he wanted to reach what is to this day the Mexican heartland, the central valley of Mexico surrounding the city of Tenochtitlán. He had learned from many sources by now that this was the center of the region's most powerful and wealthy empire. If the reports proved true, Cortés knew, he would be able to accomplish something that had eluded previous Spanish explorers. When Columbus had set out in 1492, his goal was to establish contact with the great urban empires of Asia, places of immense wealth and sophistication. Instead, he had found a series of islands populated by people who were remarkable poor and simple by European standards. They did not live in cities or practice large-scale commerce or even possess more than small quantities of gold. If the Aztecs proved as wealthy as he had been told, Cortés would succeed where Columbus had failed. Within this context, his continued defiance of the orders of the colonial authorities makes sense: a conquest of the scale he was envisioning would so impress the Spanish crown that both his infractions and his debts would be instantly forgiven.

Cortés's reports were accurate: the Aztecs – also called the Mexica – did stand at the helm of an immense, sophisticated, and wealthy empire. Like the Spaniards, they had expanded their territories through a vertiginous process of territorial conquest. Surprisingly, given their vast power, the Aztecs had only risen to importance about a hundred years before Cortés arrived in their territory, but they had built on the architectural, religious, and military achievements of a sequence of earlier empires such as the Olmecs and Toltecs, and they had created a powerful network of alliances among the city states of the valley of Mexico. They now controlled a large portion of the central region of what is now Mexico, territories that stretched from the northern deserts to the southern rainforests and from the gulf of Mexico to the Pacific Ocean.

The territory over which the Aztecs held control expanded quickly under the rule of the all powerful kings. This was the period of what has been called the Aztec Empire, though calling it an empire is somewhat a misnomer. Unlike other historical empires, the Aztecs did not actually occupy or govern the people they conquered within their empire. When they conquered a city, the Aztecs acquired captives and the right to tribute, which was to be sent to Tenochtitlan according to a regular schedule. Since the Aztecs did not leave behind administrators or a garrison but merely went home with their captives, it was left up to the conquered city to render tribute when it was due. Those cities that reneged would be subject to a renewed attack in which more captives were taken and more tribute was demanded. Making this arrangement even more unique, the Aztecs did not maintain a standing army; their empire was controlled or policed by warriors assembled on an ad hoc basis. That they proved so successful and conquered such a large area is all the more remarkable.

The Aztecs' expansion was out of necessity. When Tenochtitlan suffered food shortages caused by increased population and/or crop failures, their warriors were dispatched to subjugate new territories and win more tribute. Of course, as time went on the new tribute cities were located further and further away from the capital, and the Aztecs found the land to the west and north was not productive enough to warrant imperial expansion. To the south, the tribute cities provided luxury goods but were too far distant to provide a source for food. So it was to the east that the Aztecs began expanding their empire. But the increasing distances of the tribute cities made the food distribution system less and less efficient as the empire expanded, because the Aztecs lacked wheeled vehicles and customary beasts of burden.

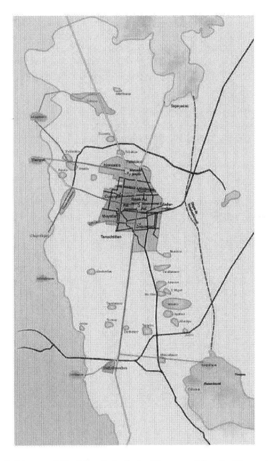

Tenochtitlan and the islands in Lake Texcoco. Map by Hanns Penn

As a result, the Aztecs had to rely on human porters to transport the incoming tribute, which posed a unique problem of its own. The further these human porters had to carry food, the more of it they consumed along the way. Thus, the most important cities within the empire that supplied food to the Aztecs were within easy reach of Lake Taxcoco.

Another important aspect of the transportation system was the fact that the Aztecs' capital was literally on an island, which required using water for travel and transportation. Plying the waters of lagoons or lakes in the Valley of Mexico, there were as many as 10,000 canoes, some as long as 50 feet. These vessels brought goods across Lake Texcoco from lakeshore farms and villages, as well as tribute carried from more distant vassal towns.

Perhaps most problematically, they demanded hundreds or even thousands of captives be sent every year to be sacrificed in the festivals of their patron deities. Such practices had earned the hostility of several of the neighboring regions. Since the Aztecs did not have a significant military presence outside of their immediate territory around the city of Tenochtitlán, this rendered them highly vulnerable to invasion if one of their tributary groups chose to take the side of the invader. That is precisely what would happen when Cortés and his men arrived.

Before that, however, Cortés had to ensure that he would have no further trouble from his superiors in Cuba. To achieve the autonomy he sought, he took two major steps. First, upon arriving to the stretch of the Gulf Coast nearest to the Aztec heartland, he established the city of Veracruz, complete with a mayor and city council drawn from among his men. By way of this legal slight of hand, Cortés could claim that he no longer needed to report to the governor of Cuba, since the legitimate authorities of an independent city reported directly to Charles V, the King of Spain. Cortés may not have finished studying the law, but he was clearly putting it to use here. Second, Cortés took the dramatic step of burning his ships in the harbor, signaling that he and his men would not be returning any time soon. Once again, the action suggests a remarkable impetuousness and willingness to gamble for high stakes.

In the meantime, Cortés began to establish contact both with local tribes, some of whom expressed to him their frustration with Aztec rule, and with emissaries of the Aztec emperor, Motecuhzoma (also known as Moctezuma or Montezuma). In the meantime, it was by no means certain that the ploy to elude Velázquez's authority would actually work, since it was possible that the Spanish crown would refuse to acknowledge Cortés's new settlement, but it would take months for news of Cortés's actions to reach Spain, and it would be several more before orders returned to Cortés himself.

The Spaniards bided their time on the coast for some weeks, exchanging messages with the Aztecs and attempting to glean more information before proceeding, since they still had little sense of the exact scale of the kingdom they were planning to take on. When Moctezuma became aware of the strangers in his territory, he responded in a mainly friendly and hospitable manner, repeatedly sending them gifts and inviting them to remain on the land if they were willing to move their settlement somewhat further away from the capital. Not surprisingly, the Spainards refused that offer.

Moctezuma II, from Historia de la conquista de México by Antonio de Solis

Historians have long speculated as to why Moctezuma was so generous and unsuspicious toward the invaders who would soon bring about his demise. One popular claim is that the arrival of Cortés and his men coincided with a long-prophesied return of the god Quetzalcoatl, said to be a light-haired and light-skinned being who would arrive from across the sea; Moctezuma's deference, in this account, would be the result of his fear that he was dealing with a god rather than a man. However, more recent analysis has suggested that the Quetzalcoatl legend was developed after the conquest, specifically as a way for the Aztec elite to explain the sudden and traumatic liquidation of their entire world. A more reasonable explanation may be based on local politics: Moctezuma knew that his rule was vulnerable and that he had many rivals in and out of Tenochtitlán, so he may have hoped to keep the strangers loyal to him lest they provide aid to his enemies.

If that was the case, Moctezuma actually proved quite prescient, because this is exactly the approach Cortés adopted. He made contact with several of the tribes that deeply resented Aztec rule and promised to support them in a war against their oppressors. What Moctezuma did not seem prepared for, though, was Cortés's endless capacity for treachery and duplicity. He remained in apparently friendly contact with Moctezuma for weeks, accepting gifts and sending more in exchange, even as he was steadily building up an army of indigenous allies who would help him take on the Aztecs. All evidence suggests that Moctezuma was a deeply honorable ruler who remained committed to basic rules and principles of decency and hospitality, and to his detriment he seemed to assume that these new arrivals would behave similarly. But Cortés, as his interactions with Velázquez have already demonstrated, had little use for deference to authority and did not consider customs worth much. His cynical act of establishing a city in order to circumvent the governor's authority suggests Cortés saw rules and laws as things to be manipulated in order to pursue his goals. He took the same approach in his interactions with the Aztec ruler.

Religion provided another fruitful area for Cortés's manipulations. While still on the Gulf Coast, he began attempting to evangelize the native inhabitants – essentially demanding that they accept Christianity or face the consequences. Given what is known of his unscrupulous character, it is difficult to imagine that the conquistador earnestly wished to bring these people to the true faith. But religion proved useful to him in several ways. For one, it allowed him to sanctify a mission that otherwise seemed transparently motivated by greed and egotism. This would prove particularly helpful in gaining royal support back in Spain, since the most widely accepted justification for conquests was that they were a way of spreading the faith. After all, this principle was at the basis of the *encomienda* system, since the holder of an encomienda was charged with instructing his subordinates in religion. Second, the natives understood from their own belief system that to accept a conqueror's rule also included accepting the conqueror's god. When Cortés and his men destroyed the native idols in a temple and replaced them with crucifixes and virgins, it was above all a gesture of power. Third, and even more cynically, religion provided a pretext for unleashing violence. When natives refused to accept the gospel and persisted in their allegedly satanic practices, Cortés used this recalcitrance as a justification for attacking and killing them, since rejection of Christ could be presented as an act of aggression equivalent to war. Several of the most brutal massacres against unarmed people he and his men carried out were performed in the midst of rituals, so that they could claim that they had used force to prevent their victims from carrying out their pagan rites. Cortés was adept at rhetorical displays of piety, but his behavior in war was so craven and so blatantly un-Christian that many contemporaries, including the king himself, had some trouble swallowing his protestations.

Having established alliances with several of the coastal peoples, while still remaining in contact with Aztec emissaries and holding out for a requested meeting with Moctezuma, Cortés eventually marched inland toward Tenochtitlán. He departed with about three hundred of his own men, plus several hundred Totonac allies, leaving another hundred or so Spaniards behind in Veracruz. Along the way he encountered another people which had long rejected the legitimacy of Aztec rule: the Tlaxcalans or Tlaxcaltecas. They were a particularly warlike people, as the Spaniards discovered in a series of skirmishes with them. It appears that both groups concluded, after a series of meetings between Spanish and Tlaxcalan emissaries, that each could make use of the other in a common war against the Aztecs.

Although it is not clear at this point that Cortés already intended to undertake an immediate war against Moctezuma and his people, the Tlaxcalan alliance would prove crucial in everything that followed. Indeed, by the time the Spaniards left Tlaxcala, they were accompanied by about 3,000 Tlaxcalan warriors, approximately three times the size of the Spanish force itself. This fact, as historian Matthew Restall has argued, puts to rest the myth of a tiny army of Spaniards defeating a great empire; in reality, the Spanish expedition would have almost certainly been routed without a massive contingent of allies.

With his large assembled forces in tow, Cortés proceeded onward to the city of Cholula, second only to the capital of Tenochtitlán in scale. Its inhabitants were traditionally close allies of the Aztecs and enemies of the Tlaxcalans, so the arrival of a large army of their rivals no doubt caused some unease. Nevertheless, the newcomers were welcomed into the city, and Cortés requested an audience with the king and other notables. What followed was a kind of rehearsal for the treachery and brutality that would then be practiced on a larger scale in the capital. Having invited the chief authorities of the city into a public square, they ambushed the crowd of hundreds of unarmed people gathered there, killing in one audacious stroke the entire leadership of the city as well as much of its warrior class. Cortés subsequently claimed that he had received word, through Doña Marina, that some of the Cholulans were plotting with a nearby Aztec regiment to massacre the Spaniards, and that they had acted in self-defense. Historians find this implausible, and have sought other explanations. One is that the massacre was carried out at the behest of the Tlaxcalans, who had their own agenda to pursue against their rivals. Another is that Cortés's main purpose was to instill fear in the local inhabitants in general and Moctezuma and his advisors in particular.

Chapter 4: Spaniards and Aztecs in Tenochtitlán

Today Tenochtitlan is mostly remembered for being a floating island city, made all the more ironic by the fact that it was essentially the forerunner of Mexico City, one of the biggest cities in the world today. Lake Texcoco was part of a closed river basin consisting of shallow lakes, lagoons and marshes that formed during the period of glaciation and received additional waters during the annual rainy season. It was on this lake that the floating city was created.

Because the existence of Tenochtitlan depended on water management for the safety of the city, the Aztecs developed ingenius waterworks to facilitate agriculture and the movement of goods. Aqueducts supplied the drinking water, while canals, wharves and flood control gates enabled reliable waterborne commerce. The Aztecs maintained control of the input of water into the lakes and marshes, keeping the salt content of the otherwise closed system under control. Though they accomplished this with hard labor, the Aztecs ensured that Tláloc, the god of water who controlled rain and storms, was content, with one of the two elevated sanctuaries on the great central pyramid of Tenochtitlan was dedicated to Tláloc.

Tlaloc, Codex Rios, after 1566. Vatican Library

Fresh water was first supplied to the city by means of two channels made of reeds and mud that ran from Chapultepec, and reservoirs were constructed in Tenochtitlan from which residents obtained their water for household use. The two channels also delivered water to underground aqueducts that supplied the palaces of the elite in the center of the city. The running water was used to supply the many baths in the palaces, as well as pools and irrigated gardens.

At the height of the Aztec empire, a more ambitious aqueduct was constructed between Chapultepec and the city, spanning nearly 10 miles. This aqueduct was over 20 feet wide. As the city grew further and more water was required, another elaborate aqueduct was constructed in 1499 to bring water from five springs that fed into a dammed basin in Coyoacán. Lacking a control mechanism to prevent exceptional water flow from coursing down the spill way into the city, the aqueduct actually proved to be a hazard to the inhabitants of Tenochtitlan. In 1500, when there were unprecedented rains, the city suffered a disastrous flood partly due to the rising water level in Lake Texcoco but more importantly from this unstoppable aqueduct.

The Aztecs used a considerable amount of water for bathing and washing their streets, with thousands of laborers watering and sweeping the streets daily. The elite classes also kept themselves clean by using soap to bathe, and according to the Spanish, Montezuma bathed twice a day in tubs in the royal palace. He apparently changed his clothes frequently as well.

The Aztecs were meticulous in the control of waste. No solid waste was disposed of through the drainage pipes that emptied into the lake. Care was taken to collect solid waste and what was appropriate was taken to the chiampas for use as fertilizer.

By the time Tenochtitlan was taken by the Spanish, it spanned some 1,000 hectares, the equivalent of 10 million square meters. The incredible size and organization of Tenochtitlan was so impressive to the conquistadors that some of them compared it to Venice. The population size also astonished the conquistadors, who found one well organized market in which 60,000 people were carrying on business. The market had a huge variety of goods for exchange, and nearby were a number of studios where highly skilled artisans worked and sold their goods.

Model of Temple Precinct at Tenochtitlan. Photo: Thelmadatter

The city centered on the walled square of the Great Temple and adjacent residences of the king, priests and elite warriors. The streets were laid out in a grid pattern interspersed by canals in each of the quarters and their constituent calpulli or wards. Causeways connected the city to the mainland, alongside which ran the aqueducts.

Ruins of Templo Mayor

In the center of Tenochtitlan was a walled precinct. The wall was decorated on the outside with snakes, earning it the name *coatepantli* or serpent wall. It contained a large square, the enormous pyramidal Templo Mayor. The Templo Mayor or Great Temple was rebuilt several times over, with the new and improved structure simply constructed over the previous and less elevated pyramid. The last version of the Templo Mayor was dedicated in 1487 and reached a height of about 130 feet.

Model of the Temple

The pyramid was capped by two temples, with one dedicated to Huizilopochtli and the other to Tláloc. The idea of capping a pyramid with twin temples was derived from earlier post classic construction at such sites as Tula and Teotihuacán. Though the Mayans are the ones remembered for their mastery of astronomy, the Aztecs' temples were oriented in such a way as to emphasize the seasonal movement of the sun. In the wetter season, the sun rose behind the Temple of Tláloc, and in the summer it rose behind the Temple of Huizilopochtli. On the two equinoctial days the sun rose between the two temples and shone on the Temple of Quetzalcoatl that faced the Templo Mayor.

In the walled central temple enclosure there were five other structures. Among them were the Temple of Xipe Totec and the Temple of Tezcatlipoca. Included in the central temple enclosure was also a ball court where it is presumed religiously based athletic competitions were held. The exact nature of the Aztec ball game is unknown, but it is likely that it was similar to that in other Mesoamerican cities and involved teams hitting a ball through a goal using their hips or chests or heads.

The common people of Tenochtitlan lived in houses that fronted on the streets of their calpulli. The adobe or wattle and daub houses were L-shaped, enclosing an interior courtyard in which most of the domestic activities were carried out. Here the women spun thread and wove fabric, ground corn, baked tortillas, prepared food and interacted with kin who came and went with little formality. The domestic court was the site of family festivals celebrating the birth or naming of a child, in which quantities of food were given to friends, neighbors and the hungry poor. The common men worked on their chinampas or fished in the lake.

Estimates of the population of Tenochtitlan vary considerably, but it is likely that the total population of the city was in the range of 200,000 to 300,000 most of which would have been of the common class. It is probable that the second largest segment of the population were slaves. The sheer number of people in Tenochtitlan amazed the conquistadors, who compared the size of the city to some of the largest municipalities at home in Spain. Incredibly, the city had amenities that were unthought of even in Europe. For example, there were schools for children of all classes, even commoners. Adjacent to the local temple the schools provided instruction for children from 7 to 14 years in age with boys and girls taught in separate rooms. Children were taught the history of the Aztecs, dancing, singing, public speaking and were even given religious instruction. The schools for children of the elite were located in the center of Tenochtitlan. There they were taught a broader curriculum that included astronomy, arithmetic, oratory, reading and writing.

Regardless of the precise population count, when Cortés and his men arrived in Tenochtitlán, it was probably larger than any European city of the era. Bernal Díaz, who accompanied Cortés, describes the reaction of the Spanish soldiers as they first approached the great city: "We saw so many cities and villages built both on the water and on dry land, and a straight, level causeway (to Tenochtitlan), we couldn't resist our admiration. It was like the enchantments in the book of Amadis (de Gaula, a popular Spanish chivalric romance of the late middle ages), because of the high towers, pyramids and other buildings, all of masonry, which rose from the water. Some of our soldiers asked if what we saw was not a dream."

This was the first great urban civilization that the Spaniards, who had initially come to the Americas seeking the rich and sophisticated kingdoms of Asia, encountered in the New World. It is a remarkable fact that within less than two years of their first arrival there, Tenochtitlán as they had found it would be in ruins. It is not entirely clear to what extent this outcome should be attributed to the ruthlessness and irreverence of the Spanish expedition's leader, but Cortés surely bears a great deal of responsibility for what occurred.

The combined Spanish and Tlaxcalan force of several thousand entered the Aztec capital on November 8, 1519. They were prepared for battle, but initially met a peaceful reception. Moctezuma, as he had previously done on several occasions through emissaries, presented the visitors with lavish gifts, including objects forged from gold, which surely whetted the Spaniards' appetite. They were welcomed into the city and brought into its central palace complex. Many have wondered why an apparently hostile army was treated with such hospitality, especially after the massacre at Cholula. One theory is that Moctezuma simply did not imagine that such a small force could be a threat to his enormous city. Once the strangers were ensconced in the city, he may have reasoned, they were trapped and would have great difficulty escaping. Once again, even if this was his intention, the Aztec ruler severely underestimated his opponent. Not long after arriving in Tenochtitlán, apparently prompted by a report that his men back in Veracuz had been attacked by the Aztecs, Cortés took Moctezuma hostage in his own palace. The ruler showed little resistance, and allowed the Spaniards to plunder the royal storehouses of gold. For several months, Cortés essentially ruled Tenochtitlán through the authority of his captive, not establishing decisive control there but biding his time until a more forceful move could be taken.

However, Cortés still had the authorities of his own government to deal with as well. In April 1520, a Spanish expedition of around 1,000 men under the command of Pánfilo de Narváez was sent out by Governor Velázquez from Cuba with orders to subdue Cortés. Here again Cortés was severely outnumbered, but his ruthlessness won out. Leaving Tenochtitlán and heading for the coast, Cortés feigned a desire to enter into peace talks, holding out a promise of consensual submission to the governor's authority. All the while, he was planning to attack and sending messengers to Narváez's camp with bribes and promises of rewards if they mutinied against their appointed leader. Narváez was unprepared when Cortés and his men descended on the encampment fully armed and ready to fight. He was forced to surrender and fell captive to his enemy, who left him imprisoned in Veracruz while leading off a large contingent of his soldiers back toward Tenochtitlán. It is an interesting fact that Cortés did not reserve his treacherous disregard for basic honesty for his interactions with the natives. He behaved with similar callousness toward his own people, albeit with much less brutality, but even that might have been only because he did not have to resort to brute force.

While Cortés was dealing with fellow Spaniards, the group of Spaniards in Tenochtitlán had meanwhile carried out a massacre as shocking and probably with more even bloodshed than the one in Cholula. Cortés's lieutenant Pedro de Alvarado was immediately responsible for planning and ordering the attack, but it is not clear whether he was acting under orders from his superior or on his own initiative. Some speculate that Cortés deliberately planned for it to occur during his absence so that he could claim to have been uninvolved. The occasion of the massacre was the festival of Toxatl, which celebrated the god Tezcatlipoca and was probably the largest and most important of all Aztec feast days. The nobles and priests of the city were gathered in the courtyard of the great Templo Mayor, which could only be accessed through four narrow entrances. With his small group of Spaniards, Alvarado sealed off the exits and in the midst of the celebration, entered into the courtyard and began slaughtering the gathered Aztecs, all of them unarmed. They are thought to have killed thousands, possibly as many as eight thousand, that day, primarily using swords, spears, and knives. As in Cholula, the perpetrators later claimed that they had gotten wind of a plot against them by the Aztecs; they also claimed that they were acting to prevent the participants in the festival from carrying out rituals involving human sacrifice and cannibalism.

Pedro de Alvarado

It's no surprise that the Spaniards would use the Aztec human sacrifice rituals as a pretext to justify their aggression. More is known about Aztec religious practices than any other aspect of their culture, mostly because the major element in the public ceremonies was focused on human sacrifice. The rituals were apparently so gruesome that they horrified even the Spanish, who were not exactly known for their gentility when it came to war and religious fervor.

Although some have suggested other theories to explain the large amount of human sacrifices, including political intimidation and even as a means of population control, it is still widely believed that they had religious symbolism. Thus, the Aztecs, either to please the gods or ensure their constant attention to earthly life, frequently bestowed on them the gift of sacrificial humans. This in itself was not unique to the region, as it was a well documented practice among other Mesoamerican civilizations. In fact, the Aztecs' enemy, the Tlaxcala, sacrificed captured Aztecs, and some of their accounts suggest it was considered an honor to die as a sacrifice. And human sacrifice in and of itself would not have been particularly upsetting to the Spanish, nor would it have been of great interest to generations of readers on the Aztecs.

However, the brutality, quantity and method of disposal of human remains as practiced by the Aztecs almost defy the imagination. An example of the rite of human sacrifice at its height was that performed for the dedication of the new Templo Mayor in 1487. The ceremony lasted four days, during which anywhere from 4,000 to 20,000 humans were sacrificed. As proof of their zeal, Aztec accounts themselves placed the number over 80,000, which would have required sacrificing over a dozen people a minute. Captives from the Huastec region to the east of

Tenochtitlan were paraded through the temple square joined by ropes threaded through their pierced noses. They climbed one by one up the steep steps of the pyramid to the temples at the top where they were laid over a stone. A priest wielding an obsidian-bladed ritual knife hacked open the victim's chest, tore out the still beating heart and placed it in a basin where it was incinerated. The body of the victim was kicked off the temple platform and rolled down to the square below. Here it was dismembered. The skull was installed on a rack and the limbs were distributed to the crowd assembled in the square.

A tzompantli or skull rack, Ramirez Codex, late 16th century. Museum of Anthropology, Mexico City

Temple Sacrifice. Codex Magliabechiano, mid 16th century based on an earlier codex. Biblioteca Nazionale Centrale, Florence

The ceremonial dedication of the Templo Mayor may have been on a grander scale than day to day ritual sacrifice, but the number of victims of Aztec religious practices was always high. When Cortés' men were shown into the temples of Tenochtitlan in 1519, they were nauseated by the stench of the burning hearts and the blood soaked walls. Bernal Diaz described what he saw in one of the temples. On these altars were idols, with evil looking bodies, he reported, and every night five captives were sacrificed before them. Their chests were cut open, and their arms and thighs were cut off. The walls of the temple were covered with blood. "We stood greatly amazed and gave the island the name *isleta de Sacrificios* (Island of the Sacrifices)."

Describing one sacrifice in detail, he wrote:

"They strike open the wretched Indian's chest with flint knives and hastily tear out the palpitating heart which, with the blood, they present to the idols [...]. They cut off the arms, thighs and head, eating the arms and thighs at ceremonial banquets. The head they hang up on a beam, and the body is [...] given to the beasts of prey."

The beasts of prey were the animals in Montequma's zoo. Diaz continues:

"They have a most horrid and abominable custom which truly ought to be punished and which until now we have seen in no other part, and this is that, whenever they wish to ask something of the idols, in order that their plea may find more acceptance, they take many girls and boys and even adults, and in the presence of these idols they open their chests while they are still alive and take out their hearts and entrails and burn them before the idols, offering the smoke as sacrifice. Some of us have seen this, and they say it is the most terrible and frightful thing they have ever witnessed."

Victim of Sacrificial Gladitorial Combat Holding a Feather Club, Codex Magliabechiano, mid 16th century. Biblioteca Nazionale Centrale, Florence

The victims taken to Tenochtitlan were well taken care of before suffering their fate. Warriors might claim a special victim that they had personally captured, and that captive would be well fed and tended in a cage. When he was dispatched by the priest, his limbs would be given to the warrior who had captured him. The warrior, who would have been among the 400 men put forth by each calpulli and who fought under a ward banner, celebrated his skill by inviting a number of people to join him in partaking of the special meal. The poor might also crowd into the party in the hopes that some scraps would be given to them.

The execution of captives varied depending on the god to which they were sacrificed. For example, in the temple dedicated to Mixocoatl, the god of hunting, a victim was shot full of arrows before his heart was removed and he was dismembered.

The festival of Tlacaxipehualiztli (flaying of men), celebrated annually just before the rainy season, was held at the temple of Xipe Totec, "our lord the flayed one", the sun god. The victims who had been well treated, perhaps even revered prior to the festival, were dressed in costumes to appear like Xipe Totec. They were tied to large stones and armed with feather encrusted weapons to fight off the advances of five warriors who were armed with spears and obsidian bladed clubs. The blood of the victims fed the earth and ensured a good planting season. The victims' bodies were flayed, and the priests of the temple wore their skins for 20 days.

The Aztecs clearly had a stomach for blood and death, but the massacre during a celebratory festival by the Spaniards definitively exhausted their toleration of the invaders, who despite the thousands they killed were still outnumbered and highly vulnerable under siege. Word of the massacre spread, and the city's inhabitants rose up against their would-be rulers, driving them back into Moctezuma's palace, where they were protected only by the presence of their venerated hostage. Meanwhile, Cortés was made aware by messengers of the latest events and made haste toward the capital with his enlarged force of Spaniards and a contingent of Tlaxcalan allies.

When they arrived, they found the city's streets deserted and the population openly hostile. What ensued was a kind of prototype of urban guerrilla warfare. In the tight, enclosed spaces of the city, the Spaniards' horses were of little advantage, and their weapons could not be fired effectively. Within a short period, it became clear that they had lost their advantage, and they were running low on food and artillery. Cortés's gambit was to have Moctezuma, still his captive, speak to his people, ostensibly in the hope of a further reconciliation. Having ascended to the roof of his palace to speak to the assembled Aztecs, Moctezuma was killed under circumstances that still remain uncertain. The Spaniards subsequently claimed that he was stoned to death by his own people, while the native accounts mainly assert that the Spaniards themselves killed the emperor, literally stabbing him in the back while he tried to speak. Both scenarios are relatively plausible, but the latter explanation certainly fits with Cortés's style.

The retreat that followed after Moctezuma's death has become known as the *Noche triste* ("sad night," "night of sorrow"), although the Aztecs were presumably not sorry to see the Spaniards go or even terribly sorry for the loss of their ineffectual ruler. Cortés and his men, knowing they were badly outnumbered and had little chance of surviving open combat in the city, chose to flee after sending a false message of truce to their enemies. They fled in the middle of the night, aiming for the most deserted causeway leading out of the city and across the lake, but the retreat still went disastrously. It began to rain heavily, thunderstorms added to their consternation, and all out chaos ensued when they were attacked by large numbers of their opponents, who had been alerted to their movements. Many of the Spaniards were weighted down with gold and other loot from the city and drowned when they tried to swim away from the causeway, while others were simply killed by the attackers. All in all, hundreds of them did not escape the city alive, leaving the force greatly diminished. By the time Cortés reached the shores of the lake, he had lost most of his army and much of the treasure he and his men had taken from Moctezuma's palace. His initial plan to take control of the Aztec empire by stealth, keeping Moctezuma on the throne as a nominal leader while ruling from behind the scenes, had failed disastrously. Now he would need to try a different and far more dramatic strategy.

Even after clearing the causeway, the retreating Spaniards were pursued by their Aztec enemies and engaged in repeated skirmishes as they fled toward Tlaxcala to reconvene with allies there. In the valley of Otumba, they were attacked by a large Aztec force and a bloody battle followed. Despite being outnumbered, the Spaniards ultimately beat back their opponents, partly because of the superior speed and agility provided by their horses, which had proved much less of an asset in the urban setting of Tenochtitlán. Their equivocal victory at Otumba allowed them to proceed on toward the east, but they lost many more men, both Spaniards and native allies, in the fighting. By the time they arrived in Tlaxcala, nearly 900 Spanish soldiers and more than a thousand native allies had perished. In their weakened position and having failed in their first campaign, the Spaniards were in a weaker bargaining position with their allies, who demanded further concessions in exchange for continued support. Cortés was willing to grant the Tlaxcalans much of what they requested, including control of previously held Aztec territories as tributary regions, and partial control of Tenochtitlán itself. In exchange, he obtained an army of allies who had even more stake in victory and thus higher morale.

Chapter 5: The Fall of Tenochtitlán

Tenochtitlán had been left in a chaotic state, and although Cuitláhuac had been appointed as a successor for Moctezuma, his authority was not yet fully consolidated. Traditionally Aztec rulers were required to demonstrate their prowess by leading an army into battle and taking captives, who would then be sacrificed to the gods upon his return. The military venture would also serve the purpose of confirming his effective leadership and obtaining the continued loyalty of tributary states. However appropriate it may have seemed to take an army to Tlaxcala to confront the Spaniards and their allies there, Cuitláhuac was formally prohibited from leading a full military campaign because the season for such activities had not yet arrived: most able-bodied men were supposed to be harvesting food rather than fighting. Only when the winter came would it be possible to assemble a large military force.

Cuitláhuac in the Primeros Memoriales.

On the other hand, there was a certain strategic advantage to remaining in Tenochtitlán, since it seemed an easy position to fortify and defend given its location on the lake: any advancing army would have to cross the narrow causeways, and as the Spaniards had already discovered, this would make them easy targets. For one of these reasons, or perhaps all of them, the Aztecs hung back for the moment, as did the Spaniards, who sent for reinforcements from Veracruz and Cuba and went about building support from several smaller cities in the Tlaxcalan sphere of influence.

By the time the Aztecs sent out expeditionary forces to attack the Spaniards in the Fall of 1520, the Spaniards had gathered an impressive array of support from native allied forces, and their own resources had augmented thanks to a growing trickle of soldiers, horses, and artillery arriving from the Gulf of Mexico. Still, the army that finally gathered to re-enter the Valley of Mexico toward the end of that same year was less than 5% Spanish, and it is unlikely that most of the native soldiers who participated regarded themselves as under Cortés's command. The traditional view of the "Spanish Conquest" thus needs to be revised. Although the Spaniards ultimately derived the most benefit from the war against the Aztecs, most of the participants in the successful campaign were neither Spanish nor conquerors: they were pursuing an agenda that would ostensibly increase their city's share of regional power. A further and equally crucial actor in the ultimate triumph of the Spaniards was one of the diseases they had brought with them from Europe: smallpox. By late 1520, a devastating outbreak of the illness had ravaged Tenochtitlán, killing perhaps 40% of its population. One of the victims was Cuitláhuac, who fell ill and died in early December, meaning that the Aztecs were without a leader at a time in which they should have been marshaling forces for war. The succession was controversial, and the next chosen king, Cuahtemoc, was not officially recognized until February of 1521. By this time, the Spaniards had returned and had a number of new advantages.

With a greatly enlarged contingent of native allies, hundreds of reinforcements from Cuba, and a refreshed stock of arquebuses, cannons, and gunpowder, Cortés now headed toward Tenochtitlán with a far superior force than he had previously. Even still, he did not proceed immediately to the city but set out to consolidate his control of the surrounding region, establishing alliances where possible and subduing cities and towns where necessary. The aim was to isolate the Aztecs, cut off their supplies of food and fresh water from neighboring territories, and prevent them from being able to summon reinforcements. The strategy was effective, and the result was a tightening noose around the already diminished, divided, and illness-ravaged Aztec populations. Cortés also arrived at Lake Texcoco with brigantines that allowed his forces to cross the lake and attack the city without needing to use the causeways. But for the most part, he and his allies waged a defensive war.

Once the supply chain had been cut off and food and water were scarce in the city, the Aztecs' only recourse was to go out and try to fend off the siege, thus leaving themselves vulnerable to attacks from their enemies. But despite mass starvation, the Aztecs held out and continued to prevent any major advances on their city for months.

Finally, in July, the Spaniards and their allies managed to gain a foothold on the island, and proceeded to make their way through the city, razing structures to the ground to prevent ambushes. Worn down by illness, starvation, thirst, and relentless arquebus and cannon attacks, the Aztecs held out until August 13, 1521, the day Cuahtemoc was captured. He reportedly surrendered directly to Cortés, but his surrender was not recognized and he was taken prisoner and ultimately executed. The total numbers are uncertain, but Aztec casualties from the siege, including the deaths of warriors in battle and deaths from illness, starvation, and massacres of civilians, reached the hundreds of thousands. In the latest stage of their campaign, the Spaniards had lost perhaps 500 and native allies had perished in the tens of thousands. Within less than two years, the Aztec empire had been destroyed, the population decimated, and the great capital left in ruins. Cortés proceeded to take credit for the entire enterprise, but in reality his success was highly dependent on the enormous assistance he received from his local allies. Perhaps more than a great military strategist, he had again shown himself to be a consummate politician.

Chapter 6: Cortés After the Conquest

Cortés would live more than 20 years after the conquest, and during those years his example would inspire many other Spaniards to seek their fortune in a similar way. The most successful of them was probably Francisco Pizarro, Cortés's second cousin, who would soon overcome an even larger empire to the south.

Pizarro

Cortés, on the other hand, would continue to reap benefits from his success, but his position would never again be quite as spectacular as it was in the wake of his defeat of the Aztecs. Although he had begun his campaign in a nearly treasonous manner, Charles V proved willing to forgive him his transgressions once he realized the wealth and scale of the newly subdued territory. He appointed Cortés governor of the entire Aztec empire, a position he was happy to assume since he no longer regarded his promises to allied native leaders as binding now once reinforcements were flooding in from Spain. The new name of the territory was to be New Spain. Cortés invited Franciscan friars to evangelize the population, and he began to establish the same *encomienda* system of labor practiced in the island territories. He continued the demolition of Aztec Tenochtitlán and began to build what would become Mexico City.

Once established firmly at the helm of the new colony, Cortés had no scruples about reneging on his promises to native allies, and he treated his own men nearly as poorly in some cases. They had come enticed by promises of wealth, but instead found themselves in debt to Cortés, who charged them for their use of weaponry he had supplied and for food, drink, and medical care. Meanwhile, merchants flooded in from Europe, selling goods at inflated prices. The disappointment suffered by many of those who fought with Cortés created a conflicted and tense environment and weakened the new governor's authority, even though it may have enriched him in the short term. Several of his former lieutenants set out on conquering expeditions on their own, hoping to recoup their losses and establish themselves independently as Cortés himself had done. One of them, Cristóbal de Olid, conspired with Cortés's old nemesis Diego Velázquez to take control of Honduras and rule it as his own territory. The attempt enraged Cortés, who had Olid captured and relieved of his command, but the conflict began a series of intrigues that pitted Cortés once more against Velázquez. Cortés clearly knew how to play the game, but Velázquez had far more influence in the Spanish court. The ultimate result was that Cortés was relieved of his governorship, exiled from the territory he had conquered, and sent back to Spain in 1528.

Cortés's remaining years were marked by repeated reversals of fortune. Sent back to Spain in a humiliating state, he was able to gain an audience with the crown. Successfully defending himself against various charges levelled by his enemies and rivals, he was honored by the king with a new title – Marquis of the Valley of Oaxaca – and a large *encomienda* in one of the wealthiest regions of New Spain. Despite these successes, he found himself with a reduced political stature when he returned to Mexico, not only because he was resented by many but because the crown, which was in the process of centralizing control over its American holdings, probably did not trust someone with his demonstrated ambitions to hold power responsibly. Already, the free-wheeling period of colonization in which he had taken part was giving way to the viceregal period, in which Spain would govern its overseas territories through a centralized and bureacratic administration in which individualists like Cortés would no longer thrive. In the late 1530s, perhaps attempting to relive his earlier triumphs, he set out on an expedition up the Pacific Coast, where he became among the first Europeans to reach Baja California.

Partly due to a conflict over his rights over the newly discovered territories and partly due to the lack of obvious wealth to be exploited there, Cortés eventually returned to central Mexico and then to Spain. His new exploratory mission had earned him a new crop of enemies in Mexico, and he probably hoped to obtain further support from the king. Instead, he received little recognition from Charles V, who was consumed with several wars in Europe and not terribly interested in his American holdings. In an attempt to win back the good grace of the sovereign, in 1541 he joined an expedition across the Mediterranean against the enemy Ottoman Empire, but a subsequent attack on Algiers led to a disastrous rout of the Spanish forces, and Cortés barely escaped with his life. He lived much of the rest of his life racked with debts and embittered about his lack of recognition. He attempted to return to Mexico in late 1547, but fell ill in the port of Seville, where he died on December 2, 1547.

Charles V

Chapter 7: The Legacy of Hernán Cortés

A curious myth that sprung up in the immediate aftermath of his death claimed that Hernán Cortés, the conqueror of Mexico, had both been born and died on the same day and hour as Martin Luther, the founder of Protestantism. Moreover, this myth asserted, Cortés and Luther had led precisely parallel careers: while Luther had led much of Europe away from the Roman Catholic Church, Cortés had brought the people of a new continent into the Catholic fold; while Luther's reforms had deprived the Church of much of its property in Northern Europe, Cortés's conquest had filled the Church's coffers with untold quantities of gold.

As bizarre as it may appear at first, it is clear why such a myth made sense to the embattled Catholic Church of the mid-sixteenth century, which had recently, with the Protestant

Reformation, felt its supremacy challenged from within for the first time in almost a thousand years. The parallel lives of Luther and Cortés proved that even though Satan was succeeding in undermining the Church through footsoldiers like Luther, God was counteracting the damage by way of appointed defenders of the faith such as Cortés. The latter's deeds were taken as proof of God's providential plan for human history, which would lead ultimately to universal salvation.

The Cortés-Luther legend provides a vivid index of the deeply theological worldview of Christian Europe in the Age of Exploration, the period in which Cortés played such a pivotal role. The new – in this case, in the form of the new lands being explored and conquered in the New World, and the new faiths springing up in a formerly united Christendom – had to be incorporated into traditional frameworks so that it would confirm the teleological and apocalyptic Christian narrative that had long been promulgated by the Church and accepted in some form by most Europeans. In his book *The Old World and the New*, historian J.H. Elliott argues that it took some centuries for the genuine newness and difference of the Americas to be registered by European culture, so intent were most observers on finding ways of incorporating all new data into familiar narrative structures. Similarly, it can obviously be pointed out that it took some time for Cortés's career to be assessed historically, rather than theologically and morally.

On the other hand, there are some striking continuities between the initial accounts of Cortés's life that sprung up in his time and modern views of him: Protestants, for the most part, saw him as a villain and a scoundrel, proof of the tyrannical and brutal ways of the Catholic world at large, while many Catholics saw him as a hero of the faith. A similar split persists to this day: he is greatly despised for his ruthlessness, cunning, and dishonesty in many quarters, but for many still remains a heroic figure and paragon of remarkable individual accomplishments. Although Cortés was in fact born two years later than Luther and died more than a year after the famous reformer, the strange legend of their parallel lives contains the seed of an insight that most historians would accept today. Both Luther and Cortés were undoubtedly pivotal figures in the making of the modern world. Both struck out decisively beyond the horizons of medieval Catholicism and did so with a disregard of traditional authorities and hierarchies that set them apart from many of their peers. Both played a significant role in begetting a new culture: Luther, the individualistic, literate, and anti-hierarchical culture of Protestant Northern Europe, and Cortés, the conflicted but vital cultural and racial blend that would ultimately become modern Mexico and Latin America. Both also propelled the development of modern global capitalism: Luther, by fomenting a religious culture more propitious to the ambitions of merchants, traders, and moneylenders, and Cortés, by injecting the precious metals of the New World into the world economy. All in all, while they may have been regarded as opposite figures in their time, any account of the birth of the modern, globalized world that exists today could regard their roles as complementary.

While Cortés was certainly one of the most important figures in the history of the last millennium, he remains a difficult figure to admire as an individual, even if his daring and defiance are impressive. His personality was essentially that of a gambler, with all of the greed, egotism, and unscrupulousness that that suggests. The scion of a Spanish culture that claimed to venerate honor above all things, Cortés was remarkably short on that quality, and his success as a conqueror must be attributed in part to his willingness to break even the most basic rules of decency to achieve political and military victory. Throughout his career, he cheated, deceived, and manipulated those he wished to gain advantage over, and showed himself repeatedly willing to use deadly force against unarmed, friendly interlocutors. He even ripped off his own men, who had loyally and bravely followed him on a highly dangerous expedition. Indeed, as one historian has asserted, "Cortés's actions embodied the political concepts developed by Machiavelli" (Pastor 83).

It is impossible that Cortés could have read Machiavelli's seminal political treatise *The Prince*, but he seemed to have developed a parallel understanding of politics as a ruthless game of deception and cunning all on his own. In fact, his disregard for traditional morality and lack of scruples about the pursuit of worldly power makes him a progenitor of what has later come to be called *Realpolitik*.

Cortes' Second Letter to Charles V

In his "Second Letter" to Charles V, dated October 30, 1520, Cortés provides perhaps the most descriptive firsthand account of Tenochtitlan and the Aztec people:

IN ORDER, most potent Sire, to convey to your Majesty a just conception of the great extent of this noble city of Temixtitlan, and of the many rare and wonderful objects it contains; of the government and dominions of Moctezuma, the sovereign: of the religious rights and customs that prevail, and the order that exists in this as well as the other cities appertaining to his realm: it would require the labor of many accomplished writers, and much time for the completion of the task. I shall not be able to relate an hundredth part of what could be told respecting these matters; but I will endeavor to describe, in the best manner in my power, what I have myself seen; and imperfectly as I may succeed in the attempt, I am fully aware that the account will appear so wonderful as to be deemed scarcely worthy of credit; since even we who have seen these things with our own eyes, are yet so amazed as to be unable to comprehend their reality. But your Majesty may be assured that if there is any fault in my relation, either in regard to the present subject, or to any other matters of which I shall give your Majesty an account, it will arise from too great brevity rather than extravagance or prolixity in the details; and it seems to me but just to my Prince and Sovereign to declare the truth in the clearest manner, without saying anything that would detract from it, or add to it.

Before I begin to describe this great city and the others already mentioned, it may be well for the better understanding of the subject to say something of the configuration of Mexico, in which they are situated, it being the principal seat of Moctezuma's power. This Province is in the form of a circle, surrounded on all sides by lofty and rugged mountains; its level surface comprises an area of about seventy leagues in circumference, including two lakes, that overspread nearly the whole valley, being navigated by boats more than fifty leagues round. One of these lakes contains fresh and the other, which is the larger of the two, salt water. On one side of the lakes, in the middle of the valley, a range of highlands divides them from one another, with the exception of a narrow strait which lies between the highlands and the lofty sierras. This strait is a bow-shot wide, and connects the two lakes; and by this means a trade is carried on between the cities and other settlements on the lakes in canoes without the necessity of traveling by land. As the salt lake rises and falls with its tides like the sea, during the time of high water it pours into the other lake with the rapidity of a powerful stream; and on the other hand, when the tide has ebbed, the water runs from the fresh into the salt lake.

This great city of Temixtitlan [Mexico] is situated in this salt lake, and from the main land to the denser parts of it, by whichever route one chooses to enter, the distance is two leagues. There are four avenues or entrances to the city, all of which are formed by artificial causeways, two spears' length in width. The city is as large as Seville or Cordova; its streets, I speak of the principal ones, are very wide and straight; some of these, and all the inferior ones, are half land and half water, and are navigated by canoes. All the streets at intervals have openings, through which the water flows, crossing from one street to another; and at these openings, some of which are very wide, there are also very wide bridges, composed of large pieces of timber, of great strength and well put together; on many of these bridges ten horses can go abreast. Foreseeing that if the inhabitants of the city should prove treacherous, they would possess great advantages from the manner in which the city is constructed, since by removing the bridges at the entrances, and abandoning the place, they could leave us to perish by famine without our being able to reach the main land, as soon as I had entered it, I made great haste to build four brigatines, which were soon finished, and were large enough to take ashore three hundred men and the horses, whenever it should become necessary.

This city has many public squares, in which are situated the markets and other places for buying and selling. There is one square twice as large as that of the city of Salamanca, surrounded by porticoes, where are daily assembled more than sixty thousand souls, engaged in buying and selling; and where are found all kinds of merchandise that the world affords, embracing the necessaries of life, as for instance articles of food, as well as jewels of gold and silver, lead, brass, copper, tin, precious stones, bones, shells, snails, and feathers. There are also exposed for sale wrought and unwrought stone, bricks burnt and unburnt, timber hewn and unhewn, of different sorts. There is a street for game, where every variety of birds in the country are sold, as fowls, partridges, quails, wild ducks, fly-catchers, widgeons, turtledoves, pigeons, reed-birds, parrots, sparrows, eagles, hawks, owls, and kestrels; they sell likewise the skins of some birds of prey, with their feathers, head, beak, and claws. There are also sold rabbits, hares, deer, and little dogs [i.e., the chihuahua], which are raised for eating. There is also an herb street, where may be obtained all sorts of roots and medicinal herbs that the country affords. There are apothecaries' shops, where prepared medicines, liquids, ointments, and plasters are sold; barbers' shops, where they wash and shave the head; and restaurateurs, that furnish food and drink at a certain price. There is also a class of men like those called in Castile porters, for carrying burdens. Wood and coal are seen in abundance, and braziers of earthenware for burning coals; mats of various kinds for beds, others of a lighter sort for seats, and for halls and bedrooms.

There are all kinds of green vegetables, especially onions, leeks, garlic, watercresses, nasturtium, borage, sorrel, artichokes, and golden thistle; fruits also of numerous descriptions, amongst which are cherries and plums, similar to those in Spain; honey and wax from bees, and from the stalks of maize, which are as sweet as the sugar-cane; honey is also extracted from the plant called maguey, which is superior to sweet or new wine; from the same plant they extract sugar and wine, which they also sell. Different kinds of cotton thread of all colors in skeins are exposed for sale in one quarter of the market, which has the appearance of the silk-market at Granada, although the former is supplied more abundantly. Painters' colors, as numerous as can be found in Spain, and as fine shades; deerskins dressed and undressed, dyed different colors; earthen-ware of a large size and excellent quality; large and small jars, jugs, pots, bricks, and endless variety of vessels, all made of fine clay, and all or most of them glazed and painted; maize or Indian corn, in the grain and in the form of bread, preferred in the grain for its flavor to that of the other islands and terra-firma; patés of birds and fish; great quantities of fish---fresh, salt, cooked and uncooked; the eggs of hens, geese, and of all the other birds I have mentioned, in great abundance, and cakes made of eggs; finally, everything that can be found throughout the whole country is sold in the markets, comprising articles so numerous that to avoid prolixity, and because their names are not retained in my memory, or are unknown to me, I shall not attempt to enumerate them.

Every kind of merchandise is sold in a particular street or quarter assigned to it exclusively, and thus the best order is preserved. They sell everything by number or measure; at least so far we have not observed them to sell anything by weight. There is a building in the great square that is used as an audience house, where ten or twelve persons, who are magistrates, sit and decide all controversies that arise in the market, and order delinquents to be punished. In the same square there are other persons who go constantly about among the people observing what is sold, and the measures used in selling; and they have been seen to break measures that were not true.

This great city contains a large number of temples, or houses, for their idols, very handsome edifices, which are situated in the different districts and the suburbs; in the principal ones religious persons of each particular sect are constantly residing, for whose use, besides the houses containing the idols, there are other convenient habitations. All these persons dress in black, and never cut or comb their hair from the time they enter the priesthood until they leave it; and all the sons of the principal inhabitants, both nobles and respectable citizens, are placed in the temples and wear the same dress from the age of seven or eight years until they are taken out to be married; which occurs more frequently with the first-born who inherit estates than with the others. The priests are debarred from female society, nor is any woman permitted to enter the religious houses. They also abstain from eating certain kinds of food, more at some seasons of the year than others.

Among these temples there is one which far surpasses all the rest, whose grandeur of architectural details no human tongue is able to describe; for within its precincts, surrounded by a lofty wall, there is room enough for a town of five hundred families.

Around the interior of the enclosure there are handsome edifices, containing large halls and corridors, in which the religious persons attached to the temple reside. There are fully forty towers, which are lofty and well built, the largest of which has fifty steps leading to its main body, and is higher than the tower of the principal tower of the church at Seville. The stone and wood of which they are constructed are so well wrought in every part, that nothing could be better done, for the interior of the chapels containing the idols consists of curious imagery, wrought in stone, with plaster ceilings, and wood-work carved in relief, and painted with figures of monsters and other objects. All these towers are the burial places of the nobles, and every chapel in them is dedicated to a particular idol, to which they pay their devotions.

Three halls are in this grand temple, which contain the principal idols; these are of wonderful extent and height, and admirable workmanship, adorned with figures sculptured in stone and wood; leading from the halls are chapels with very small doors, to which the light is not admitted, nor are any persons except the priests, and not all of them. In these chapels are the images of idols, although, as I have before said, many of them are also found on the outside; the principal ones, in which the people have greatest faith and confidence, I precipitated from their pedestals, and cast them down the steps of the temple, purifying the chapels in which they had stood, as they were all polluted with human blood, shed ill the sacrifices. In the place of these I put images of Our Lady and the Saints, which excited not a little feeling in Moctezuma and the inhabitants, who at first remonstrated, declaring that if my proceedings were known throughout the country, the people would rise against me; for they believed that their idols bestowed on them all temporal good, and if they permitted them to be ill-treated, they would be angry and without their gifts, and by this means the people would be deprived of the fruits of the earth and perish with famine. I answered, through the interpreters, that they were deceived in expecting any favors from idols, the work of their own hands, formed of unclean things; and that they must learn there was but one God, the universal Lord of all, who had created the heavens and earth, and all things else, and had made them and us; that He was without beginning and immortal, and they were bound to adore and believe Him, and no other creature or thing.

I said everything to them I could to divert them from their idolatries, and draw them to a knowledge of God our Lord. Moctezuma replied, the others assenting to what he said, That they had already informed me they were not the aborigines of the country, but that their ancestors had emigrated to it many years ago; and they fully believed that after so long an absence from their native land, they might have fallen into some errors; that I having more recently arrived must know better than themselves what they ought to believe; and that if I would instruct them in these matters, and make them understand the true faith, they would follow my directions, as being for the best.@ Afterwards, Moctezuma and many of the principal citizens remained with me until I had removed the idols, purified the chapels, and placed the images in them, manifesting apparent pleasure; and I forbade them sacrificing human beings to their idols as they had been accustomed to do; because, besides being abhorrent in the sight of God, your sacred Majesty had prohibited it by law, and commanded to put to death whoever should take the life of another. Thus, from that time, they refrained from the practice, and during the whole period of my abode in that city, they were never seen to kill or sacrifice a human being.

The figures of the idols in which these people believe surpass in stature a person of more than ordinary size; some of them are composed of a mass of seeds and leguminous plants, such as are used for food, ground and mixed together, and kneaded with the blood of human hearts taken from the breasts of living persons, from which a paste is formed in a sufficient quantity to form large statues. When these are completed they make them offerings of the hearts of other victims, which they sacrifice to them, and besmear their faces with the blood. For everything they have an idol, consecrated by the use of the nations that in ancient times honored the same gods. Thus they have an idol that they petition for victory in war; another for success in their labors; and so for everything in which they seek or desire prosperity, they have their idols, which they honor and serve.

This noble city contains many fine and magnificent houses; which may be accounted for from the fact, that all the nobility of the country, who are the vassals of Moctezuma, have houses in the city, in which they reside a certain part of the year; and besides, there are numerous wealthy citizens who also possess fine houses. All these persons, in addition to the large and spacious apartments for ordinary purposes, have others, both upper and lower, that contain conservatories of flowers. Along one of these causeways that lead into the city are laid two pipes, constructed of masonry, each of which is two paces in width, and about five feet in height. An abundant supply of excellent water, forming a volume equal in bulk to the human body, is conveyed by one of these pipes, and distributed about the city, where it is used by the inhabitants for drink and other purposes. The other pipe, in the meantime, is kept empty until the former requires to be cleansed, when the water is let into it and continues to be used till the cleaning is finished. As the water is necessarily carried over bridges on account of the salt water crossing its route, reservoirs resembling canals are constructed on the bridges, through which the fresh water is conveyed. These reservoirs are of the breadth of the body of an ox, and of the same length as the bridges. The whole city is thus served with water, which they carry in canoes through all the streets for sale, taking it from the aqueduct in the following manner: the canoes pass under the bridges on which the reservoirs are placed, when men stationed above fill them with water, for which service they are paid. At all the entrances of the city, and in those parts where the canoes are discharged, that is, where the greatest quantity of provisions is brought in, huts are erected, and persons stationed as guards, who receive a certain sum of everything that enters. I know not whether the sovereign receives this duty or the city, as I have not yet been informed; but I believe that it appertains to the sovereign, as in the markets of other provinces a tax is collected for the benefit of the cacique.

In all the markets and public places of this city are seen daily many laborers waiting for some one to hire them. The inhabitants of this city pay a greater regard to style in their mode of dress and politeness of manners than those of the other provinces and cities; since, as the Cacique Moctezuma has his residence in the capital, and all the nobility, his vassals, are in constant habit of meeting there, a general courtesy of demeanor necessarily prevails. But not to be prolix in describing what relates to the affairs of this great city, although it is with difficulty I refrain from proceeding, I will say no more than that the manners of the people, as shown in their intercourse with one another, are marked by as great an attention to the proprieties of life as in Spain, and good order is equally well observed; and considering that they are barbarous people, without the knowledge of God, having no intercourse with civilized nations, these traits of character are worthy of admiration.

In regard to the domestic appointments of Moctezuma, and the wonderful grandeur and state that he maintains, there is so much to be told, that I assure your Highness I know not where to begin my relation, so as to be able to finish any part of it. For, as I have already stated, what can be more wonderful than a barbarous monarch, as he is, should have every object found in his dominions imitated in gold, silver, precious stones, and feathers; the gold and silver being wrought so naturally as not to be surpassed by any smith in the world; the stone work executed with such perfection that it is difficult to conceive what instruments could have been used; and the feather work superior to the finest productions in wax or embroidery. The extent of Moctezuma's dominions has not been ascertained, since to whatever point he despatched his messengers, even two hundred leagues from his capital, his commands were obeyed, although some of his provinces were in the midst of countries with which he was at war. But as nearly as I have been able to learn, his territories are equal in extent to Spain itself, for he sent messengers to the inhabitants of a city called Cumatan (requiring them to become subjects of your Majesty), which is sixty leagues beyond that part of Putunchan watered by the river Grijalva, and two hundred and thirty leagues distant from the great city; and I sent some of our people a distance of one hundred and fifty leagues in the same direction.

All the principle chiefs of these provinces, especially those in the vicinity of the capital, reside, as I have already stated, the greater part of the year in that great city, and all or most of them have their oldest sons in the service of Moctezuma. There are fortified places in all the provinces, garrisoned with his own men, where are also stationed his governors and collectors of the rents and tribute, rendered him by every province; and an account is kept of what each is obliged to pay, as they have characters and figures made on paper that are used for this purpose. Each province renders a tribute of its own peculiar productions, so that the sovereign receives a great variety of articles from different quarters. No prince was ever more feared by his subjects, both in his presence and absence. He possessed out of the city as well as within numerous villas, each of which had its peculiar sources of amusement, and all were constructed in the best possible manner for the use of a great prince and lord. Within the city his palaces were so wonderful that it is hardly possible to describe their beauty and extent; I can only say that in Spain there is nothing equal to them.

There was one palace somewhat inferior to the rest, attached to which was a beautiful garden with balconies extending over it, supported by marble columns, and having a floor formed of jasper elegantly inlaid. There were apartments in this palace sufficient to lodge two princes of the highest rank with their retinues. There were likewise belonging to it ten pools of water, in which were kept the different species of water birds found in this country, of which there is a great variety, all of which are domesticated; for the sea birds there were pools of salt water, and for the river birds, of fresh water. The water is let off at certain times to keep it pure, and is replenished by means of pipes. Each specie of bird is supplied with the food natural to it, which it feeds upon when wild. Thus fish is given to the birds that usually eat it; worms, maize, and the finer seeds, to such as prefer them. And I assure your Highness, that to the birds accustomed to eat fish there is given the enormous quantity of ten arrobas every day, taken in the salt lake. The emperor has three hundred men whose sole employment is to take care of these birds; and there are others whose only business is to attend to the birds that are in bad health.

Over the polls for the birds there are corridors and galleries, to which Moctezuma resorts, and from which he can look out and amuse himself with the sight of them. There is an apartment in the same palace in which are men, women and children, whose faces, bodies, hair, eyebrows, and eyelashes are white from their birth. The emperor has another very beautiful palace, with a large court-yard, paved with handsome flags, in the style of a chess-board. There are also cages, about nine feet in height and six paces square, each of which was half covered with a roof of tiles, and the other half had over it a wooden grate, skillfully made. Every cage contained a bird of prey, of all the species found in Spain, from the kestrel to the eagle, and many unknown there. There was a great number of each kind; and in the covered part of the cages there was a perch, and another on the outside of the grating, the former of which the birds used in the night time, and when it rained; and the other enabled them to enjoy the sun and air. To all these birds fowls were daily given for food, and nothing else. There were in the same palace several large halls on the ground floor, filled with immense cages built of heavy pieces of timber, well put together, in all or most of which were kept lions, tigers, wolves, foxes, and a variety of animals of the cat kind, in great numbers, which were fed also on fowls. The care of these animals and birds was assigned to three hundred men. There was another palace that contained a number of men and women of monstrous size, and also dwarfs, and crooked and ill-formed persons, each of which had their separate apartments. These also had their respective keepers. As to the other remarkable things that the emperor had in his city for his amusement, I can only say that they were numerous and of various kinds.

He was served in the following manner: Every day as soon as it was light, six hundred nobles and men of rank were in attendance at the palace, who either sat, or walked about the halls and galleries, and passed their time in conversation, but without entering the apartment where his person was. The servants and attendants of these nobles remained in the court-yards, of which there were two or three of great extent, and in the adjoining street, which was also very spacious. They all remained in attendance from morning until night; and when his meals were served, the nobles were likewise served with equal profusion, and their servants and secretaries also had their allowance. Daily his larder and wine-cellar were open to all who wished to eat or drink. The meals were served by three or four hundred youths, who brought on an infinite variety of dishes; indeed, whenever he dined or supped, the table was loaded with every kind of flesh, fish, fruits, and vegetables that the country produced. As the climate is cold, they put a chafing-dish with live coals under every plate and dish, to keep them warm. The meals were served in a large hall, in which Moctezuma was accustomed to eat, and the dishes quite filled the room, which was covered with mats and kept very clean. He sat on a small cushion curiously wrought of leather. During the meals there were present, at a little distance from him, five or six elderly caciques, to whom he presented some of the food. And there was constantly in attendance one of the servants, who arranged and handed the dishes, and who received from others whatever was wanted for the supply of the table.

Both at the beginning and end of every meal, they furnished water for the hands; and the napkins used on these occasions were never used a second time; this was the case also with the plates and dishes, which were not brought again, but new ones in place of them; it was the same also with the chafing-dishes. He is also dressed every day in four different suits, entirely new, which he never wears a second time. None of the caciques who enter his palace have their feet covered, and when those for whom he sends enters his presence, they incline their heads and look down, bending their bodies; and when they address him, they do not look him in the face; this arises from excessive modesty and reverence. I am satisfied that it proceeds from respect, since certain caciques reproved the Spaniards for their boldness in addressing me, saying that it showed a want of becoming deference. Whenever Moctezuma appeared in public, which is seldom the case, all those who accompanied him, or whom he accidentally met in the streets, turned away without looking towards him, and others prostrated themselves until he had passed. One of the nobles always preceded him on these occasions, carrying three slender rods erect, which I suppose was to give notice of the approach of his person. And when they descended from the litters, he took one of them in his hand, and held it until he reached the place where he was going. So many and various were the ceremonies and customs observed by those in the service of Moctezuma, that more space than I can spare would be required for the details, as well as a better memory than I have to recollect them; since no sultan or other infidel lord, of whom any knowledge now exists; ever had so much ceremonial in his court.

Bibliography

Beezley, William, and Michael C. Meyer. *The Oxford History of Mexico*. Oxford: Oxford University Press, 2010.

Díaz del Castillo, Bernal. *True and Full Account of the Conquest of Mexico and New Spain*. Trans. James Lockhart. Gutenberg Project Ebook.

Elliott, J.H. *The Old World and the New*. Cambridge: Cambridge University Press, 1992.

Pastor, Beatriz. *The Armature of Conquest: Spanish Accounts of the Discovery of America 1492-1589*. Stanford: Stanford University Press, 1992.

Restall, Matthew. *Seven Myths of the Spanish Conquest*. Oxford: Oxford University Press, 2004.

Ferdinand Magellan
Chapter 1: The Portuguese Age of Exploration and Magellan's Origins

Today Ferdinand Magellan is remembered as the first man to circumnavigate the globe, an ironic legacy given that he died half a world away from completing that journey. But one of the things most overlooked is the fact that he was conducting his historic voyage at the same time as some of his most famous contemporaries.

Unlike Christopher Columbus, who was from an Italian mercantile background, and unlike Hernan Cortés, who came from an impoverished family of noble lineage in the remote province of Extremadura, Ferdinand Magellan was born into the heart of the Portuguese aristocracy. His father, Rui de Magalhães, was an official in the city of Aveiro, and the family of his mother, Alda de Mesquita, was well connected at court. As a result of this prestigious background, when his parents died while he was still a young boy, 10 year old Ferdinand became a page of Queen Leonor, whose husband King John II reigned from 1481-1495 and was then succeeded by her brother, King Manuel I. While such figures as Cortés and Pizarro were clearly motivated in part or entirely by the desire to enrich themselves and gain an improved social position through their foreign conquests, Magellan's motivations must have been quite different, as he could presumably have led a comfortable life of privilege in Portugal given his early background and connections. But given the cultural milieu of 15th century Portugal, it is not at all surprising that he chose the path he did.

Leonor

It's often forgotten centuries after the fact, but as far as maritime exploration was concerned, Portugal was far ahead of any other European country by the end of the 15th century. Though Columbus had made his historic voyage in 1492 for Spain, he had been motivated by previous Portugese explorers, and he had first offered his services to Portugal. Entering the 16th century, Portugal's nautical technology and knowledge was more advanced, its sailors were far more experienced on the high seas, and by the time of Magellan's birth its ships had already blazed a path down the west coast of Africa, as unknown to Europeans at the time as were the Americas.

The country's orientation towards the Atlantic provides a simple explanation of how all this came about. The oligarchic city states of Italy, closer to the points in the Levant where the trade routes radiating out of Asia terminated, had established lucrative trade through extensive naval control of the eastern Mediterranean. Merchants from Italy and other European countries had also created land-based trade routes with the East – the most famous being Marco Polo, whose descriptions of the riches of China provided inspiration for Columbus and many others. Portugal was excluded from all of this, but it attempted to turn its Atlantic location into an advantage by opening up new and more efficient routes to the East via the South. The enterprise was ultimately a spectacular success.

The imperative for Portuguese Atlantic expansion emerged out of the successful campaign to drive the Islamic Moors out of the southern reaches of the Iberian peninsula. Taking the form of a kind of local crusade, the Christian offensive against the Muslims led to territorial expansion as well as new riches for those who claimed the spoils of conquest in the newly Christian-controlled territories. Once the southward expansion was complete, religious, ideological and economic incentives made further offensives against the Muslims of North Africa a desirable prospect for Portugal's ruling class, and an expedition against the Muslim coastal stronghold of Ceuta in 1415 was successful, giving Portugal its first foothold on the African continent. Spain, meanwhile, was still decades away from conquering the kingdom of Granada from the Moors, and it was not until after that campaign that the Spanish monarchy would begin to look abroad for further conquests. Although Ceuta proved not to be a particularly lucrative territory for the Portuguese, it was a useful starting point for the far more expansive imperial and commercial project that would take shape in subsequent decades.

Portugal's head start in maritime expansion owed much to the efforts of Henry the Navigator, a prince born in 1394 who participated in the conquest of Ceuta as a young man. As the third son of King John I, Henry never ascended to the throne himself, but he marshaled much of his power and resources to fund exploration and colonization enterprises to the South and West. With his patronage and encouragement, ships pushed further and further down the African coast with several goals in mind. First, the Portuguese knew from trade with North Africa that the continent to the South had great stores of gold somewhere, and they hoped to find them. Second, they hoped to find an alternative passage to the Indian Ocean via Africa, since the inadequate cartography of the period nevertheless understood that part of the East African coast bordered the Indian Ocean. Finally, Henry and his contemporaries hoped to be the first Europeans to establish contact with the legendary Christian kingdom of Prester John – a mythical figure whom European Christians hoped to enlist as an ally in a crusade against the Muslims who controlled Jerusalem. In all probability, the legend of Prester John referred in a distorted way to the Christian kingdom of Abyssinia or Ethiopia.

Henry the Navigator

Portuguese explorers soon rounded Cape Bojador, a point in what is now Western Sahara beyond which no European had passed in centuries, and they established several settlements along the coast of what they called Guinea, reaching what is now Senegal by mid-century. They found lucrative alluvial gold deposits already being exploited in what is now Mauritania, and at the same time they began tapping into a trade that would decisively impact the economic history of the Atlantic zone: African slavery.

The Portuguese did not begin the African slave trade, which Arab and African merchants had already begun practicing some time before, but they were the first Europeans to become involved in what would now become a European-dominated trade, based around supplying labor to colonial agricultural enterprises. It began on a relatively small scale in a time when kidnapping, hostage-taking, and enslavement was rampant across the Mediterranean, but the Portuguese slave trade set the stage for what was to become possibly the most horrifyingly brutal of industries. In the meantime, Portuguese explorers also took control of islands in the Atlantic, including Madeira and the Azores, which they turned into plantation colonies, supplying wheat and other products to the mainland. All in all, Henry the Navigator and his contemporaries in the Portuguese elite helped foment a kind of laboratory for European imperialism, pioneering the major practices that other European empires would later adopt. In the course of a century, the small country of Portugal had transformed itself into a major world power.

Several decisive events in the history of Portuguese overseas expansion occurred during Ferdinand Magellan's childhood and youth. First, Bartholomew Diaz completed the expansion down the western coast of Africa by rounding the Cape of Good Hope in 1487. This put an end to the widespread European belief that the Indian Ocean was inaccessible by sea from the Atlantic; the Portuguese navigators themselves had initially assumed that they might find an overland passage across Africa to the Indian Ocean, but they had not hoped to reach it by sea. Around the same time, another less well-known explorer, Pêro de Covilhã, reached the Christian African kingdom of Ethiopia, which led the Portuguese to believe they were the first Europeans to establish relations with the famed kingdom of Prester John. The enterprise of Henry the Navigator (who had died in 1469) was finally paying dividends.

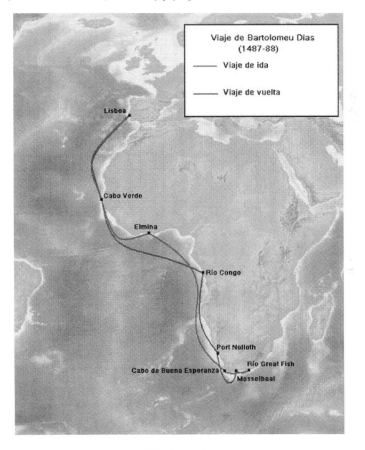

Diaz's voyage

Within this context, the news in 1493 that Columbus had reached the Indies by sailing to the West likely came as a shock, especially because the Portuguese crown had declined to support Columbus's proposed expedition several years earlier. Diplomatic wrangling ensued between

Portugal and Spain, which claimed the lands Columbus had reached, and the result was the Treaty of Tordesilhas, which granted Portugal jurisdiction over its African territories to the South and East and granted Spain control over territories to the West of a somewhat vaguely designated North-South meridian. Tordesilhas would ultimately lead to the division of South America into Portuguese Brazil and the Spanish Viceroyalty of Peru, and its precise terms would be disputed by the two kingdoms until the late 18th century. But for the moment it kept the Portuguese focused on the new route to the Indian Ocean opened up by Diaz.

Ten years after Diaz set out, a second expedition led by Vasco da Gama rounded the Cape of Good Hope, sailed up the East African coast, and ultimately reached the southern tip of India. Da Gama had arrived where Columbus had hoped to arrive, and within a few years the Portuguese had established trading posts and alliances with local Indian kingdoms.

Vasco da Gama

During Ferdinand Magellan's first 20 years of life in and around the Portuguese court, the commercial and military triumphs of maritime expansion were a major focus of political energy in a way that would not have been true in any other kingdom of the period. Even Spain, the other major expanding global power of the period, did not place such a great emphasis on this area of policy. When it sponsored Columbus, the Spanish crown was motivated less by its general ambitions than by its rivalry with Portugal, which had established such a clear maritime advantage over its much larger Iberian neighbor. It is thus interesting, ironic, and revealing that Columbus's and Magellan's careers both began in Portugal – though Genoese by origin, Columbus spent much of his early life as an apprentice navigator in Lisbon – but ended under the aegis of the Spanish monarchy. The reason is clear enough from the historical background just provided: Portugal's imperial ambitions passed by way of the South to the East, first out of convenience, but after Tordesilhas by necessity. This orientation was not congenial to Columbus and Magellan, whose enterprises involved westward routes of transit to Asia. Spain, never a maritime pioneer in its own right, was happy to use the nautical know-how of these two Portuguese defectors in order to maintain its own geopolitical parity with its rival.

Nevertheless, Magellan's early career unfolded in the newly established Portuguese Indies, where he first sailed around 1505 under the command of Francisco de Almeida, whom the Portuguese crown had appointed Viceroy of India. The available records do not make clear where he spent his first few years in the new territories of the Indian Ocean, but in addition to India, he is likely to have visited Malaysia and the African territory of Mozambique. Unlike in the Caribbean, where Columbus and his successors found for the most part small-scale societies with disappointingly low levels of trade and meager supplies of desirable commodities, Magellan and the other early Portuguese denizens of the Indian Ocean found themselves amidst a far more sophisticated network of commerce than any in Europe of the time. Arab, Indian, and Chinese merchants could be found around the entire perimeter of the Indian Ocean, and in cities of Malaysia dozens of African, Middle Eastern, and Asian languages could be heard. Furthermore, it was essentially a peaceful region, bound together by mutual economic interest and a religious unity fostered by centuries of Islamic dominance. While the "Indies" that Columbus reached proved a disappointment (at least initially), the Indian Ocean region was as wealthy and abundant in precious commodities as the Portuguese had hoped, and they soon took decisive measures to assure their control there.

In February 1509, the Portuguese won a crucial victory against the Ottoman Turks and their allied forces (including, curiously, the Italian Republic of Venice) at Diu in southwestern India. Within just over ten years of Vasco da Gama's expedition, the Portuguese had dealt a definitive blow to Muslim hegemony in the Indian Ocean. Although it was less a territorial conquest than an establishment of naval control over trade routes, it was as remarkable and unlikely a turn of events as Cortés's and Pizarro's overthrow of the great empires of the Americas. Magellan was present for the Battle of Diu, and also took part the following year in the conquest of the Indian city of Goa, which would remain a Portuguese colony until the 20th century. Having essentially extinguished Muslim power along the coasts of the African and Asian mainlands, the Portuguese turned their attention to the Malaysian city of Malacca. Malacca was an international port and trade center that stood on the Strait of Malacca, which separated the Asian continent from the archipelagos of present-day Malaysia and Indonesia. This meant control over Malacca would provide a gateway to the immense wealth of the Spice Islands to the South. A Portuguese force under Alonso de Alburquerque besieged Malacca for six weeks in 1511, and Magellan was among the conquerors who entered the city when it fell.

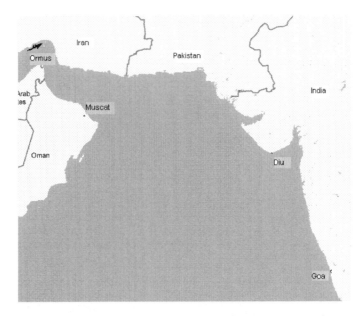

Points of Portugese control in the Indian Ocean during the early 16ᵗʰ century

Toward the end of 1511, Magellan may or may not have participated in a trade and reconnaissance expedition to the Spice Islands, but regardless of whether or not he actually went, he could have gleaned a great deal of intelligence about them in his new location. In the meantime, he was honored with promotion and awarded with a sizable share of the expedition's rich plunder. He also took a Malay man captive as a slave and baptized him with the Christian name Enrique. Enrique accompanied Magellan back to Portugal in 1512, and would return to his place of origin as a translator for Magellan's westward voyage back to the Indian Ocean some years later. In this sense, it was Enrique who may have been the first person to truly circumnavigate the globe, since it's presumed he would make it back to Malaysia during Magellan's voyage. In reality, it is uncertain what became of Enrique after Magellan's death, as his name drops from reliable historical records at this point. Whatever his ultimate fate, Enrique stands with Cortés's translator and consort Doña Marina and Pizarro's captive Felipillo as a remarkable non-European (and involuntary) participant in the Age of Exploration whose life has generally been overshadowed by that of his European captor.

Chapter 2: From Portugal to Morocco to Spain

Magellan returned to Portugal in 1513, having spent eight years in the Indies. It is not clear what motivated his return to his home country, but one theory is that he was hoping to find a way of gaining a greater fortune and more prestigious position in the new Portuguese colonies by utilizing his royal connections in Lisbon.

In the meantime, Magellan remained in contact with his friend (and possibly cousin) Francisco Serrão, with whom he had sailed in 1505 and who remained in Malucca. Serrão traveled around the Spice Islands on several occasions and his letters provided his friend with useful intelligence on the topography and politics of the region, which he would subsequently put to use when planning his return to the East. Had his career ended when he sailed back to Lisbon in 1513, Magellan's name would not be remembered. He would be only one of thousands who took part in the remarkably rapid and successful Portuguese expansion into the Indian Ocean, a process that, interestingly enough, produced no names that have gone down in history in the manner of Columbus, Cortés, Pizarro, Balboa, de Soto, or Coronado. Although the Portuguese had sacked a number of cities and slaughtered their inhabitants much like the Spaniards were doing in the New World, their fundamental approach differed in that they were far more concerned with controlling trade than with conquering vast territories. As it turned out, Magellan would end up making a name for himself by going into the service of Spain, Portugal's greatest imperial rival of the era.

Even after its successes in Asia, Portugal was still deeply involved militarily and commercially in the more proximate African continent, both because of ongoing conflicts with pirates from North Africa, because of religious enmity with Islam, and because of its involvement in the slave trade and other enterprises. Soon after his arrival back in Portugal, Magellan joined an expedition led by the Duke of Braganza against Azamor, a city in Morocco that had been conquered by the Portuguese in 1486. After the conquest, the inhabitants of Azamor were obliged to pay an annual tribute to the crown of Portugal, but in 1513 local ruler Moulay Zayam refused to pay the tribute and revolted against the Portuguese, gathering a sizable army to throw the invaders out. The king decided to respond with deadly force against this act of insubordination and sent a large expeditionary army of some 15,000 troops to put down the Moroccan rebels. There is some evidence to suggest that this strong resolve was motivated more by a desire not to show weakness than by genuine advantage; although the Portuguese would prove victorious, the victory would be somewhat Pyrrhic. They would ultimately be forced to abandon Azamor because the cost of maintaining their control there exceeded the revenues brought in by tribute payments and trade.

Magellan, by now an experienced veteran of several major sieges and battles, joined the Portuguese fleet that sailed down to Azamor, but it turned out to be one of the more ill-fated decisions of his career. During the hostilities there, he lost his horse and suffered a leg wound that left him with a pronounced limp for the rest of his life.

Even after the final victory over Zayam and his forces had been won, things continued not to go nearly as well for Magellan as they had in the East. As a participant in the successful conquest, he was given a share of the spoils of war, but he was then accused by superior officers of engaging in illegal trade with the Moroccans for selling some of the items he had been awarded back to inhabitants of Azamor at a profit. Although he was ultimately cleared of this accusation, it appears to have become something of a stain on his record, and the word of his supposed wrongdoing probably reached the Portuguese court relatively quickly. A continued aura of suspicion surrounding him seems to have worsened his standing with King Manuel, whose sister he had served as a page early in his life. When he returned to Lisbon in November 1415 and requested an increase in his pension as a reward for his service in Morocco, he was refused. Likewise, his requests to participate in various Portuguese expeditions were also refused. It was apparent the king and his advisors no longer trusted him.

King Manuel I of Portugal

It was around this period that Magellan began to hatch a plan to sail to the Spice Islands by sailing west across the Atlantic. The geography of the Americas was still only dimly understood at this point, but Magellan believed like Columbus before him that this would surely be the most efficient route to Asia. Unaware that Columbus had discovered a new continent, unaware of the scope of the Pacific Ocean, and unaware of how far south the South American continent stretched, Magellan imagined it would save the trouble of sailing all the way around the southern tip of Africa to reach the Indian Ocean. With these arguments, he petitioned the king to lead an expedition, also noting that the Spanish, now well-established in the islands to the East of the Indian Ocean (the Americas), might reach the Spice Islands from that direction and claim jurisdiction over them by invoking the Treaty of Tordesillas. Magellan was unsuccessful in his several petitions to the king, who seems to have permanently retracted his trust in him, and finally, in 1516, he requested and was given leave to present his petition to other rulers.

With that, he crossed the border into Spain. Here his path again closely follows that of Columbus, who had also repeatedly presented his plan for a westward journey to the Indies to the

Portuguese crown. Magellan first went to Seville in 1517, where he met with other Portuguese mariners and conferred with the Portuguese cosmographer Rui Faleiro. Based on Faleiro's geographical knowledge and the intelligence Magellan had gleaned from his time in the Indies and the letters of Serrão, they hatched a plan that must have seemed irresistible to the Spanish crown. Not only would a westward journey to the Spice Islands offer precisely what Columbus had promised (but not delivered) to Ferdinand and Isabella in the 1490s, it would avoid overt conflict with the Portuguese, who had already staked out the eastward route to the Indian Ocean. Furthermore, based on Faleiro's cartography and calculations, Magellan and Faleiro believed that their western location made the Spice Islands part of the territory granted to Spain as part of the Treaty of Tordesillas.

Magellan's decision to undercut the territorial gains of the country he had been born in and served has made him a less than heroic figure for Portuguese historians, who have branded him a traitor. Indeed, it seems quite likely that Magellan was trying to settle scores with the Portugese crown, at least to some extent. However, he had also first proposed his expedition to Porgual's King Manuel, and upon being rebuffed he simply did what what other explorers of his era, including Columbus, John Cabot, and Amerigo Vespucci, had also done: sought sponsorship for his enterprise, in whatever form it took, and whoever it came from.

Magellan's petition at the Spanish court in Valladolid met with more immediate success than Columbus's had 30 years before. He was, of course, proceeding from more solid information than his Genoese predecessor, having already spent eight years in the destination region himself, and his maps and proposed route were far less controversial. King Charles I, the grandson of Ferdinand and Isabella who would later become the Holy Roman Emperor and the most powerful ruler in Europe, did not hesitate long in granting Magellan and Faleiro most of their requests. They were appointed joint captains of the proposed expedition, made knights of the prestigious Order of Santiago, and granted a 10-year monopoly on all trade on their route and 5% of all profits from the route and the governorship of an island each. The crown would also cover the up-front costs of obtaining ships, recruiting crew, and gathering supplies. All in all, it amounted to one of the most successful petitions of the many that were put forward in this period of imperial expansion. By comparison, Columbus had had to wait years for his project to finally gain approval from the Spanish crown, and Cortés had carried out his initial expedition into Mexico in defiance of the orders of the governor of Cuba.

Charles I (later Charles V of the Holy Roman Empire)

Nevertheless, the two captains soon met with their share of hindrances. From the start, the Spanish seafaring community was enraged when it learned that two Portuguese mariners had been awarded with such a lucrative set of concessions, and powerful figures at court soon set out to sabotage the expedition. Enemies of Magellan and Faleiro managed to hold up their funding in the Casa de Contratación, the royal office that administered the financing and organization of all such enterprises, and the entire mission was delayed. In the meantime, the Portuguese king, Manuel I, became aware of the deal Magellan had cut with his Spanish counterpart, and evidently came to regret having turned down the petitions of his former subject. He sent agents to Spain to attempt to derail the Portuguese captains. On top of that, internal problems between Magellan and Faleiro began to surface, creating further tension in their preparations. The clash of personalities ultimately led to Faleiro being stripped of his captaincy and left out of the mission.

Magellan was also prevented from recruiting many of his Portuguese acquaintances, despite the fact that some of them were already familiar with the territories they were setting out for, because the anti-Magellan factions in Spain managed to ensure that a large proportion of the crew and officers recruited were Spanish. Nevertheless, Magellan managed to take his longtime companion Enrique with him, and the crew that was finally assembled included men from a wide array of national backgrounds, including some North Africans.

By the time he was ready to sail, Magellan had five ships: the Trinidad (his flagship), the Victoria, the Concepcion, the Santo Antonio, and the Santiago. 273 men manned the 5 ships, 80% of whom were Spanish.

A replica of Magellan's *Victoria*

Chapter 3: Magellan's Expedition

Of all the historic and famous expeditions made during the Age of Exploration, it's no exaggeration to say that Magellan's was the most unique and adventurous. Ironically, Magellan's expedition is taught to schoolchildren across the globe, but his fate during the voyage itself is not. As a result, much of what is known about the expedition came from the journal of one of the crew, Antonio Pigafetta:

"Finding myself in Spain in the year of the nativity of our Lord, 1519, at the court of the most serene King of the Romans (Charles V), and learning there of the great and awful things of the ocean world, I desired to make a voyage to unknown seas, and to see with my own eyes some of the wonderful things of which I had heard.

I heard that there was in the city of Seville an armada (armade) of five ships, which were ready to perform a long voyage in order to find the shortest way to the Islands of Moluco (Molucca) from whence came the spices. The Captain General of this armada was Ferdinand de Magagleanes (Magellan), a Portuguese gentleman, who had made several voyages on the ocean. He was an honorable man. So I set out from Barcelona, where the Emperor was, and traveled by land to the said city of Seville, and secured a place in the expedition.

The Captain General published ordinances for the guidance of the voyage.

He willed that the vessel on which he himself was should go before the other vessels, and that the others should keep in sight of it. Therefore he hung by night over the deck a torch or faggot of burning wood which he called a farol (lantern), which burned all night, so that the ships might not lose sight of his own.

He arranged to set other lights as signals in the night. When he wished to make a tack on account of a change of weather he set two lights. Three lights signified "faster." Four lights signified to stop and turn. When he discovered a rock or land, it was to be signalled by other lights.

He ordered that three watches should be kept at night.

On Monday, St. Lawrence Day, August 10th, the five ships with the crews to the number of two hundred and thirty-seven set sail from the noble city of Seville…"

Pigafetta

Thus, on August 10, 1519, two years and some months after being granted his petition by King Charles I, Magellan departed from Seville with five ships: the two larger vessels *Trinidad* and *San Antonio*, and the three smaller caravels *Concepción*, *Victoria*, and *Santiago*. They were older ships and not of the quality Magellan had hoped for, but they were what he was able to obtain in the face of widespread opposition to his mission among the Spanish maritime community. In Seville, he left behind a young wife, Beatriz Barbosa, the daughter of a Portuguese friend whom he had married not long after arriving in Seville in 1517. He also left behind his recently born son Rodrigo. Magellan would never see Beatriz or Rodrigo again, and all three of them would be dead within five years.

From Seville, they sailed down the Guadalquivir River to its mouth, where they anchored at the port of Sanlúcar de Barrameda, . It is from here, the same port Columbus departed from on his third voyage, that the five ships finally set out across the Atlantic about five weeks later, on September 20, 1519.

The first port of call was Tenerife, in the Canary Islands, an archipelago controlled by Spain for over a century. This first stretch of the journey was calm, but they met with severe storms after heading southwest from the Canaries and across the equator. Pigafetta, a clearly religious man, detailed some of the scares the crew had, writing:

> "During these storms the body of St. Anselm appeared to us several times. And among others on a night which was very dark, at a time of bad weather, the said saint appeared in the form of a lighted torch at the height of the maintop, and remained there more than two hours and a half, to the comfort of us all. For we were in tears, expecting only the hour of death."

He documented this "supernatural" phenomenon during other parts of the trip as well:

> "Here good St. Anseline met the ships; in the fancy of the mariners of the time, this airy saint appeared to favored ships in the night, and fair weather always followed the saintly apparition. He came in a robe of fire, and stood and shone on the top of the high masts or on the spars. The sailors hailed him with joy, as one sent from Heaven. Happy was the ship on the tropic sea upon whose rigging the form of good St. Anseline appeared in the night, and especially in the night of cloud and storm!

To the joy of all the ships good St. Anseline came down one night to the fleet of Magellan. The poetical Italian tells the story in this way:

"During these storms, the body of St. Anseline appeared to us several times.

One night among others he came when it was very dark on account of bad weather. He came in the form of a fire lighted at the summit of the main mast, and remained there near two hours and a half.

This comforted us greatly, for we were in tears, looking for the hour when we should perish.

When the holy light was going away from us it shed forth so great a brilliancy in our eyes that we were like people blinded for near a quarter of an hour. We called out for mercy.

Nobody expected to escape from the storm.

It is to be noted that all and as many times as the light which represents St. Anseline shows itself upon a vessel which is in a storm at sea, that vessel never is lost.

As soon as this light had departed the sea grew calmer and the wings of diverse kinds of birds appeared."

Clearly, the men were not familiar with "St. Elmo's Fire", the visible electrical discharge that often appears on the tall masts of ships during thunderstorms.

Weather wasn't the only thing giving Magellan's expedition difficulty early on. For a time, they were pursued by a fleet sent by King Manuel of Portugal, but as an initial testament to Magellan's navigational skill, the Spanish fleet successfully eluded its foes and set out for Brazil, stopping briefly in the Cape Verde islands. They were taking a risk by charting a course toward the Brazilian coast, since Brazil had already been claimed by Portugal almost 20 years earlier, and the Treaty of Tordesillas seemed to justify that claim. The Portuguese had not established much in the way of a settlement there, occupied as they were with their new Asian acquisitions in the Indian Ocean, but a violation of the agreement with his former employer Portugal could put Magellan's future claims at risk.

The fleet reached the South American coast by late November, passing by Cape St. Augustine and Cabo Frío along the Brazilian coast and heading further south to avoid lands already charted by previous Portuguese explorers. They ended up laying anchor in the bay of Río de Janeiro, not yet the major Portuguese settlement it would become.

At this point, Magellan had reached a turning point in his journey. He and Rui Faleiro had assured the Spanish crown that they would find a strait in the South American terra firma through which they could pass to what was then called the "South Sea" (the Pacific Ocean) and then to the East Indies. But the coast south from Brazil had not been accurately charted yet, so Magellan could not be genuinely certain that he would find such a passage. Furthermore, this uncertainty seems to have created an upswell of tension between him and the fellow officers and crew, no doubt exacerbated by the Spanish-Portuguese rivalries that had beset them even before they set sail.

The tensions came to a head as they sailed further to the South. After departing from Río de Janeiro, their next stop was in the Río de la Plata estuary. The expedition now stopped to replenish supplies and determine their next course of action, and the layover gave the crew time to familiarize themselves with some of the exotic surroundings. It was here that the crew met some cannibals for the first time, whom Pigafetta described as "giants" that were so tall the men of Magellan's crew were only as tall as their waists. Pigafetta explained, "They do not eat up the whole body of a man whom they take prisoner; they eat him bit by bit, and for fear that he should be spoiled, they cut him up into pieces, which they set to dry before the chimney. They eat this day by day, so as to keep in mind the memory of their enemy."

Pigafetta wasn't the only one fascinated by them; Magellan ordered that two of them be taken captive. According to Pigafetta, the crew tricked 4 of them into coming onboard and distracted them with trinkets. "Forthwith the captain had the fetters put on the feet of both of them. And when they saw the bolt across the fetters being struck with a hammer to rivet it and prevent them from being opened, these giants were afraid. But the captain made signs to them that they should suspect nothing. Nevertheless, perceiving the trick that had been played on them, they began to blow and foam at the mouth like bulls, loudly calling on Setebos (that is, the great devil) to help them."

The two others had their hands put in irons, but Magellan apparently decided to free them. Pigafetta continued, "The hands of the other two giants were bound, but it was with great difficulty; then the Captain sent them back on shore, with nine of his men to conduct them, and to bring the wife of one of those who had remained in irons, because he regretted her greatly."

As that incident suggests, the contact between Magellan's men and these "giants" was not friendly, and it soon devolved into combat. It was during this time that the expedition lost its first man after one of the crew was hit by a poisoned arrow and died shortly after. Somewhat fittingly, as Magellan's men were stopped here, Cortés was in the beginning stages of his conquest of the Aztec empire.

The Río de la Plata estuary appeared to be exactly the kind of massive portal into the South American continent that Magellan reasonably assumed to be the broad strait that would carry them across to the South Sea. However, once they sailed up the river, it was not difficult to determine that the great waters flowing southeast were in fact freshwater, meaning they could not possibly originate in an ocean on the other side of the continent. Recognizing his mistake, Magellan directed the fleet further south to what is now the Port of San Julián in Argentina, where they came to a stop in the days before Easter 1520. Magellan also made plans to spend the rest of the winter months there and set sail again in August.

It was in San Julián that a mutiny erupted against Magellan's authority, led by two Spanish captains who had always resented serving under Portuguese command. Magellan apparently managed to keep much of the crew on his side, however, and the mutinous sailors found themselves isolated and outflanked. Pigafetta described the conspiracy and its results:

"[A]s soon as we entered the port, the masters of the other four ships conspired against the captain-general to bring about his death. Whose names were Juan de Cartagena, overseer of the fleet, the treasurer Luis de Mendoza, the overseer Antonio de Coca, and Gaspar Quesada. But the treachery was discovered, because the treasurer was killed by dagger blows, then quartered. This Gaspar Quesada had his head cut off, and then he was quartered. And the overseer Juan de Cartagena, who several days later tried to commit treachery, was banished with a priest, and put in exile on that land named Patagoni."

Magellan's leadership abilities had now been thoroughly tested, but he had come out of the trial with the loyalty of his crew intact. In the weeks that followed, the resolve of the mission's participants would continue to be tested. In a reconnaissance mission to the South, the *Santiago* was wrecked near the mouth of the Santa Cruz River in what is now Southern Argentina. Of the 37 crewmen, one died and the rest were rescued, but the expedition was now down to 4 ships.

In addition to the loss of the *Santiago*, the Santa Cruz River itself was another disappointment; a brief survey demonstrated that it was clearly not the strait the expedition was seeking. After rescuing the castaways from the *Santiago*, the four remaining ships continued south along the South American coast, reaching Cape Vírgenes, which juts dramatically out to the East just above a strait separating the South American mainland from the large island of the Tierra del Fuego. This was the strait they were looking for, and the one that would later be named the Strait of Magellan, though Pigafetta's comments suggest someone else may have discovered it before them. "But the captain-general said that there was another strait which led out, saying that he knew it well and had seen it in a marine chart of the King of Portugal, which a great pilot and sailor named Martin of Bohemia had made."

Either way, an expedition sent to explore the waterway was able to confirm that the saltwater did not give way to freshwater as they proceeded inland. However, since the strait had a southeast and a southwest channel, Magellan had the *Concepcion* and the *Santo Antonio* explore the southeast while the *Trinidad* and *Victoria* went southwest. During this exploration, the *Santo Antonio* became separated from the *Concepcion*, and its men decided to mutiny. With that, the *Santo Antonio* turned around to head back to Spain without informing the other ships.

The reduced fleet of three ships set off westward along the strait on November 1, 1520. Because of this date, the original name given the waterway was the *Estrecho de Todos los Santos* or Strait of All Saints; only after Magellan's death would it become the *Estrecho de Magallanes*. By the end of the month, they had reached the South Sea, which Magellan, impressed by the initial stillness of the waters they encountered on the other end of the strait, renamed the *Mar Pacífico* or Pacific Ocean. By some accounts, the Portuguese captain wept upon first passing through the western end of the strait into the sea. Although Vasco Núñez de Balboa had reached the Pacific traveling westward by land across Panama some seven years earlier, Magellan's crew were the first Europeans to reach the great ocean travelling westward by sea, an accomplishment that had been sought for decades by Columbus and many after him. Successfully sailing through the previously uncharted strait, which cuts a tortuous path along the Tierra del Fuego and then through an intricate archipelago to the west of it, was undoubtedly one of the more impressive feats among the many performed by European mariners in the Age of Exploration.

Despite the triumph of Magellan's enterprise in achieving its basic goal, many more challenges were to follow. The most fundamental was that the crew had run desperately low on supplies because the anticipated passage had required a much greater southern detour than had been projected by Magellan and Faleiro before setting out. While they might have tarried somewhere along the South American coast to gather what food supplies and fresh water they could, such a stop would entail risks, particularly because the territories were at that point totally unknown and uncharted by Europeans. An encounter with hostile indigenous groups could even further reduce the already diminished crew, and going ashore under uncertain conditions risked a repetition of the kind of shipwreck that had befallen the *Santiago* on the other side of the South American continent. Thus, pressed on by the strong Humboldt or Peru current that runs northward along the western shores of South America, the fleet continued onwards, first some leagues to the north up the coast of what is now Chile. Then, around the middle of December, they headed back out into open ocean, not knowing when they would reach land again.

Had Magellan's crew known the expanse of the Pacific Ocean, it's safe to say they would not have sailed west. It would be more than 3 months before they would see land again, and they had nowhere near enough supplies for such a journey. Pigafetta described just how dire their straits became. "We only ate old biscuit reduced to powder, and full of grubs, and we drank water that had turned yellow and smelled." When that failed, the crew started eating "ox hides that were under the main yard." Rats were eventually consumed, and some even took to eating leather, cloth, sawdust, and anything else they could scrounge from the ship.

Not surprisingly, many of the sailors onboard came down with scurvy and other diseases. The gums of some men swelled so much that they simply could not eat at all. Pigafetta passed some of his time trying to learn the language of one of the captive "giants", at least until that giant died. Both of the captives died during this part of the trip, as did nearly 30 of the crew. Another 30 were on the verge of death before they would see meaningful land.

Not surprisingly, morale reached a desperate level. Although Magellan's leadership was apparently effective at keeping many of the men on the crew loyal, mutiny was probably only avoided because everyone on the ships knew that turning back to Spain would at this point be a longer journey than reaching the intended destination of the Spice Islands, and that they would be unlikely to survive such an effort.

Around the end of January, several small islands were sighted, somewhere in what is now French Polynesia, but they were inhabited only by birds. It was not until over a month later that they arrived, and laid anchor, at the island of Guam in the Mariana Islands on March 6, 1521, which they nicknamed "Island of Thieves" because some of the natives came onboard and stole whatever they could get their hands on. Nevertheless, Magellan's crew was certainly more than happy to be there, and they were able to obtain food and supplies for the first time in over three months before continuing their journey. Guam would later be successively conquered by Spain, the United States, and Japan, as it was regarded by all three powers as a crucial eastern gateway to the Pacific, but Magellan and his fleet did not remain for long, and Spain would not actually establish control over the island for another century or so.

Magellan's communications with the King of Spain suggest that he was oriented well enough to know how to reach the Spice Islands from Guam and the Marianas, but he chose to direct the fleet southwest toward the islands that would later become known as the Philippines. Less than two weeks after its landing in Guam, the Spanish flotilla had reached the island of Homonhon. It seems that Magellan was eager to make friendly contact with natives in this group of islands to assure he had a place to establish a safe haven in case of any hostile encounters with the Portuguese in the Spice Islands. The Philippines had apparently been visited by Portuguese sailors already at this point, but they had not yet been brought into the Portuguese sphere of influence in the East.

The diplomatic efforts in the Philippines initially bore fruit for Magellan, thanks in part to the translation efforts of his longtime Malay slave and companion Enrique. Through an exchange of gifts, he was able to forge an alliance with the chieftain of Limasawa Island, who then directed him to the larger island of Cebu nearby. Pigafetta described their contact with the natives:

"That people became very familiar and friendly, and explained many things in their language, and told the names of some islands which they beheld. The island where they dwelt was called Zuluam, and it was not large. As they were sufficiently agreeable and conversible the crews had great pleasure with them. The Captain seeing that they were of this good spirit, conducted them to the ship and showed them specimens of all his goods—that he most desired—cloves, cinnamon, pepper, ginger, nutmeg, mace, and gold.

He also had shots fired with his artillery, at which they were so much afraid that they wished to jump from the ship into the sea. They made signs that the things which the Captain had shown them grew there.

When they wished to go they took leave of the Captain and of the crew with very good manners and gracefulness, promising to come back.

Friday, the 22d of March, the above-mentioned people, who had promised to return, came about midday with two boats laden with the said fruit, cochi, sweet oranges, a vessel of palm wine, and a cock, to give us to understand that they had poultry in their country.

The lord of these people was old, and had his face painted, and had gold rings suspended to his ears, which they name 'schione,' and the others had many bracelets and rings of gold on their arms, with a wrapper of linen round their head. We remained at this place eight days; the Captain went there every day to see his sick men, whom he had placed on this island to refresh them; and he gave them himself every day the water of this said fruit, the cocho, which comforted them much."

Location of the Philippines

However, this alliance set off the fateful chain of events that would deprive Magellan of achieving his final goal of reaching the Spice Islands. Magellan had been directed to go to Cebu, but he was still a little weary about the kind of greeting his crew would receive there. Pigafetta explains how Magellan ensured they would be safe upon their arrival: "On Sunday the seventh of April, about noon, we entered the port of Zzubu, having passed by many villages, where we saw some houses which were built on trees. And nearing the principal town the captain-general ordered all the ships to put out their flags. Then we lowered the sails as is done when one is about to fight, and fired all the artillery, at which the people of those places were in great fear."

As it turned out, the artillery barrage was unnecessary because the alliance with Limasawa ensured the sailors were greeted hospitably in Cebu, where the chieftain, Rajah Humabon, and his consort and top advisors all accepted baptism as Christians. Pigafetta described the conversion of the natives. "And the captain told them that they should not become Christians for fear of us, or in order to please us, but that if they wished to become Christians, it should be with a good heart and for the love of God. For that, if they did not become Christians, we should show them no displeasure. But that those who became Christians would be more regarded and better treated than the others. Then all cried out together with one voice that they wished to become Christians not for fear, nor to please us, but of their own free will. Then the captain said that if they became Christians he would leave them weapons which Christians use..."

Based on their contact, Magellan apparently mistakenly believed Rajah Humabon to be king over all of the neighboring islands, and therefore believed he had secured the loyalty of the remaining population of the archipelago. In fact, the local politics were far more complicated; local chieftains operated in varying degrees of alliance with one another, and there was no particular one who had power over the others. It may have been this mistake that sealed Magellan's fate when he proceeded to the island of Mactan, where he hoped the ruler would also accept Christianity, perhaps believing him to be subordinate to Humabon. It has also been widely speculated that Rajah Humabon had a score to settle with Mactan's chieftain, Lapu Lapu, and manipulated Magellan by sending him to Mactan. According to this viewpoint, Humabon expected hostilities to ensue between Lapu Lapu and Magellan's crew in the hope that the Europeans' firepower would propel them to victory over his rival.

Whatever the case may be, Lapu Lapu refused to submit to Magellan and did not accept the offer of baptism. In general, this kind of supposed "insubordination" was regarded among conquistadors as sufficient justification for waging war, and in this instance Magellan also hoped that subduing Mactan would strengthen his alliance with Cebu, which he believed to be the superior kingdom. It is also believed that Humabon assured Magellan that he would not need a large force to subdue Lapu Lapu.

On April 27, 1521, a force of about 60 men, including crewmen and an uncertain number of native allies from Cebu headed toward Mactan, armed and ready to fight the inhabitants. As it turned out, Magellan was leading his men ashore against upwards of 1,500-3,000 warriors under Lapu Lapu's command. On other occasions during their era of global conquest, Spanish forces were able to eke out victory despite comparable odds out of a mixture of audacity, spectacular firepower, and sheer brutality and ruthlessness, but the coral reefs surrounding Mactan foiled the initial strategy of assaulting the enemy warriors with the cannons on board ship. Instead, they were forced to anchor the ships far from shore and make their way ashore swimming and wading, all the while being pelted by thousands of arrows and spears.

The crew were certainly equipped with better weapons, but their muskets and crossbows were awkward, inaccurate, and slow to reload, which made it hard for them to inflict casualties on the more mobile combatants on shore. Magellan sent some Spaniards to set fire to some of the thatched structures near the shore, in the hope of creating confusion and fear, but apparently this only heightened the resolve of Lapu Lapu and his men, who quickly killed the arsonists.

Pigafetta was present and described the attack, explaining how Magellan's men were forced to conduct their fight while still wading in the water off shore. "Our large pieces of artillery which were in the ships could not help us, because they were firing at too long range, so that we continued to retreat for more than a good crossbow flight from the shore, still fighting, and in water up to our knees. And they followed us, hurling poisoned arrows four or six times; while, recognizing the captain, they turned toward him inasmuch they hurled arrows very close to his head."

Pigafetta described the chaotic climax of the failed assault:

So many of them charged down upon us that they shot the captain through the right leg with a poisoned arrow. On that account, he ordered us to retire slowly, but the men took to flight, except six or eight of us who remained with the captain. The natives shot only at our legs, for the latter were bare; and so many were the spears and stones that they hurled at us, that we could offer no resistance. The mortars in the boats could not aid us as they were too far away. So we continued to retire for more than a good crossbow flight from the shore always fighting up to our knees in the water. The natives continued to pursue us, and picking up the same spear four or six times, hurled it at us again and again. Recognizing the captain, so many turned upon him that they knocked his helmet off his head twice, but he always stood firmly like a good knight, together with some others. Thus did we fight for more than one hour, refusing to retire farther. An Indian hurled a bamboo spear into the captain's face, but the latter immediately killed him with his lance, which he left in the Indian's body. Then, trying to lay hand on sword, he could draw it out but halfway, because he had been wounded in the arm with a bamboo spear. When the natives saw that, they all hurled themselves upon him. One of them wounded him on the left leg with a large cutlass, which resembles a scimitar, only being larger. That caused the captain to fall face downward, when immediately they rushed upon him with iron and bamboo spears and with their cutlasses, until they killed our mirror, our light, our comfort, and our true guide. When they wounded him, he turned back many times to see whether we were all in the boats. Thereupon, beholding him dead, we, wounded, retreated, as best we could, to the boats, which were already pulling off."

Upon Magellan's death, the remaining Spaniards turned back and retreated toward the ships. Shocked, disoriented, and outnumbered, the remaining forces that had stayed on board the ship retreated to Cebu, leaving Magellan's body behind. Centuries later, the victorious Lapu Lapu was proclaimed a national hero in the Philippines as the first to successfully drive off imperialist invaders from the nation's shores.

After this disaster, only 120 of the original crew were still alive, and the expedition had lost its leader, leaving the fleet and its crew in disarray. Making matters worse, Humabon ended up reconsidering his alliance with the Europeans for reasons that are not entirely clear. He may have simply felt that they had ceded any advantage they might have had for his own power by failing to defeat Lapu Lapu, but he also may also have plotted against them with Enrique, Magellan's interpreter. Magellan had declared in his will that Enrique should be freed from servitude upon his death, but Magellan's successor, Juan Sebastián Elcano, refused to do so. Back in Cebu, about thirty of the Spaniards were poisoned at Humabon's command during a large feast to which they had been invited, and at this point Enrique managed to escape with help from Humabon.

Elcano

Realizing the danger, the remaining members of the crew now needed to flee, as they might easily be massacred by a much larger native force. Without enough men to command all three ships, so the *Concepción* was taken out to sea and burned, and the two remaining ships sailed onward to the Spice Islands, where they made several trading stops on Brunei (which Pigafetta described as "a collection of houses built on piles over the water, where were twenty-five thousand fires or families") and other islands. Maximilianus Transylvanus described their stop here after interviewing survivors from the *Victoria*:

> "They came to the shores of the Island of Solo, where they heard that there were pearls as big as dove's eggs, and sometimes as hen's eggs, but which can only be fished up from the very deepest sea. Our men brought no large pearl, because the season of the year did not allow of the fishery. But they testify that they had taken an oyster in that

region, the flesh of which weighed forty-seven pounds. For which reason I could easily believe that pearls of that great size are found there; for it is clearly proved that pearls are the product of shellfish. And to omit nothing, our men constantly affirm that the islanders of Porne told him that the King wore in his crown two pearls of the size of a goose's egg.

Hence they went to the Island of Gilo, where they saw men with ears so long and pendulous that they reached to their shoulders. When our men were mightily astonished at this, they learnt from the natives that there was another island not far off where the men had ears not only pendulous, but so long and broad that one of them would cover the whole head if they wanted it (cum exusu esset). But our men, who sought not monsters but spices, neglecting this nonsense, went straight to the Moluccas, and they discovered them eight months after their Admiral, Magellan, had fallen in Matan. The islands are five in number, and are called Tarante, Muthil, Thidore, Mare, and Matthien; some on this side some on the other, and some upon the equinoctial line.

One produces cloves, another nutmegs, and another cinnamon. All are near to each other, but small and rather narrow."

Magellan's expedition had successfully reached the Spice Islands by sailing west, albeit with considerably more difficulty than anticipated. But now there was disagreement about how to return to Spain, and the remaining two ships parted ways, with the *Trinidad* attempting to sail back across the Pacific and the *Victoria* taking the risk of traveling the Portuguese route around the Cape of Good Hope. Strangely enough, it would be the *Trinidad* that was halted by Portuguese officials, even as it sailed away from territories most closely held by Portugal, and its captain and crew arrested.

Meanwhile, the *Victoria*, under the command of Elcano, sailed across the Indian Ocean and around Africa. On May 19, 1522, the *Victoria* passed by the Cape of Good Hope, but by now the crew was starving and their ship was literally falling apart. Their plight was so desperate that when they reached the Portugese-held Cape Verde islands on July 9, 1522, some of the men went ashore to try to obtain supplies. Suspicious, the Portugese detained 13 of them, leaving the *Victoria* to make a speedy exit.

On September 6, 1522, the *Victoria* arrived back in Seville, Spain. One of the most intriguing anecdotes about their return was that they discovered they had lost a day because they had sailed west while the Earth rotated the other way, so despite keeping an accurate daily log, their date was still inaccurate. This would lead to the creation of an International Date Line.

Though the ship was laden with valuable spices, when the *Victoria* pulled into port she was manned by a desperate and starving crew. The survivors onboard the *Victoria* had traveled nearly 38,000 miles, and of the 237 that had set sail with Magellan in August 1519, only 18 had made it back to the original port from which they had set sail over 3 years earlier. 4 of the 55 men who had been arrested onboard the *Trinidad* made it back to Spain in 1525 (the other 51 having died from disease or battle). More than 90% of the men who sailed with Magellan fell victim to the voyage, as did the captain himself.

The *Victoria* was the only of the five ships that succeeded in circumnavigating the globe, and so it was that Elcano rather than Magellan was awarded with a medal by Charles I in honor of this achievement. Although the trip had ended catastrophically for Magellan and the vast majority of his crew, it had essentially achieved what he had proposed. It would take some decades for the Spanish colonization of the Philippines to succeed in earnest, but the reconnaissance achieved by the mission had laid the groundwork for that enterprise and for the lucrative trade routes across the Pacific that would be developed over the next century. Its main achievement was to forge a vital link between two processes of imperial expansion and commercial expansion that until then had proceeded separately: the Spanish colonization of the American continent and the Portuguese incursions into the Indian Ocean.

Furthermore, until the construction of the Panama Canal in the early 20th century, the Strait of Magellan would remain the principal sea route between the Atlantic and Pacific, and the challenge of its navigation would be taken up by many generations of later sailors. Magellan and the diverse crew that accompanied him suffered and died en masse, but they became some of the earliest pioneers of the age of globalization.

Sir Francis Drake
Chapter 1: Drake's Early Years

The future courtier, captain, privateer and pirate Sir Francis Drake was born during the early 1540s in the small village of Tavistock in Devon, England, the oldest of twelve sons born to Edmund and Mary Mylwaye Drake. Edmund was a farmer and one of the earliest members of the Protestant Reformation, and he named his first son after Francis Russell, Earl of Bedford. Bedford also stood as the boy's godfather.

Drakes godfather

Ironically, the boy who would grow up to become one of the national heroes of his day was subjected to such religious persecution by fellow countrymen that he and his family were forced to leave their home in Devon because of disagreements over the new English Prayer Book. They sided with the Crown's version of the new Book of Common Prayer and thus settled in Kent, where most of the Protestants agreed with their views. Edmund was so erstwhile about his religion that he was ordained a deacon in the local church and given the pastorate of Upnor Church. In recognition of his loyalty to the Protestant Crown, the senior Drake was later made a chaplain in the Royal Navy. As biographer William Wood would colorfully describe it, "[Edmund's] friends at court then made him a sort of naval chaplain to the men who took care of His Majesty's ships laid up in Gillingham Reach on the River Medway, just below where Chatham Dockyard stands to-day. Here, in a vessel too old for service, most of Drake's eleven brothers were born to a life as nearly amphibious as the life of any boy could be. The tide runs in with a rush from the sea at Sheerness, only ten miles away; and so, among the creeks and marshes, points and bends, through tortuous channels and hurrying waters lashed by the keen east wind of England, Drake reveled in the kind of playground that a sea-dog's son should have."

Given a childhood that included so much time spent at sea, it was only natural that Edmund eventually sent young Francis to apprentice with the captain of a small type of boat called a barque. Used primarily to traverse the English Channel, these boats were popular with both French and English merchants. Despite being just 10 years old, Francis proved up to the physical challenges, and contemporary accounts claim that the boy "so pleased the old man by his industry that, being a bachelor, at his death he bequeathed his bark unto him by will and testament."

In 1563, when he was still in his early 20s, Drake left the safety of the English Channel and sailed with his cousin, Sir John Hawkins, to the newly founded English colonies in America. This voyage remains a stain on Drake's record to this day, as it was one of the first slave-trading expeditions to North America. Though two other ships had previously brought slaves to America, Hawkins is considered to be the first captain to take the business of trafficking in human beings seriously and establishing the triangular route from Africa to Europe to the New World.

Sir John Hawkins

The first trip that Drake made with Hawkins was to what was then known as the Spanish Main. They were carrying a load of people that the Spanish were willing to "buy" to work on their plantations. According to Hawkins's own records, they obtained some of the slaves from African warlords who were only too willing to sell their captured rivals in order to get rid of them. Not having enough to make a full load, they also captured a human cargo from Portuguese traders who were on their way to the New World from Africa. Once they had their ships full, Hawkins and Drake sailed to South America, where they exchanged the newly enslaved peoples for barrels of tobacco and other goods from the New World.

Pleased with their success, the two returned to the New World again the following year, but things did not go nearly as well the second time around. While resupplying at the port of San Juan de Ulúa in 1568, Drake and Hawkins were attacked by a fleet of Spanish warships, losing all but two of their ships and almost all of their crew. Drake and Hawkins personally escaped by swimming away during the chaos and making their way back to England. At the time, several European nations were on the brink of war, including England, France, and Spain, and news of what happened at Ulúa caused Queen Elizabeth I some serious consternation. William Wood explained:

"Just as the winter night was closing in, on the 20th of January, 1569, the *Judith* sailed into Plymouth. Drake landed. William Hawkins, John's brother, wrote a petition to the Queen-in-Council for letters-of-marque in reprisal for Ulua, and Drake dashed off for London with the missive almost before the ink was dry. Now it happened that a Spanish treasure fleet, carrying money from Italy and bound for Antwerp, had been driven into Plymouth and neighboring ports by Huguenot privateers. This money was urgently needed by Alva, the very capable but ruthless governor of the Spanish Netherlands, who, having just drowned the rebellious Dutch in blood, was now erecting a colossal statue to himself for having 'extinguished sedition, chastised rebellion, restored religion, secured justice, and established peace.' The Spanish ambassador therefore obtained leave to bring it overland to Dover.

But no sooner had Elizabeth signed the order of safe conduct than in came Drake with the news of San Juan de Ulua. Elizabeth at once saw that all the English sea-dogs would be flaming for revenge. Everyone saw that the treasure would be safer now in England than aboard any Spanish vessel in the Channel. So, on the ground that the gold, though payable to Philip's representative in Antwerp, was still the property of the Italian bankers who advanced it, Elizabeth sent orders down post-haste to commandeer it. The enraged ambassador advised Alva to seize everything English in the Netherlands. Elizabeth in turn seized everything Spanish in England. Elizabeth now held the diplomatic trumps; for existing treaties provided that there should be no reprisals without a reasonable delay; and Alva had seized English property before giving Elizabeth the customary time to explain."

Queen Elizabeth I

As Elizabeth was mulling over what to do next concerning the hostilities, it turned out that Drake's career as a slaver was already finished. These initial three trips as a slaver proved to be the only such trips that Drake would participate in, and while it is possible that he had some sort of attack of conscience, it is more likely that he came to believe that there was more money to be made elsewhere. At the time, the slave trade was technically illegal in England, though it was not typically seriously enforced. Also, it is only fair to note that Drake's involvement in the slave trade was not necessarily out of any sense of racism so much as it was simply a profitable proposition. He would later recruit African slaves (known as Maroons) who escaped from Spanish owners and add them to his crew, depending on them during battles and praising their efforts.

While Drake was done with the slave trade, he was far from done with the Spanish. He and Hawkins began plotting their revenge against the Spanish, who they hated not only for what they perceived to be personal slights but because they were Catholic. Raised by a devout Protestant, Edmund's influence clearly rubbed off on Francis, who had been taught from an early age that Papists were at best ignorant and superstitious and at worst heretics. Not long after his marriage to Mary Newman in 1569, Drake returned to the West Indies in search of his former captors.

Chapter 2: The Captain

Though it is unclear whether or not Drake found the revenge he was seeking, his trips to America did solidify his reputation as skilled seaman. This led, in 1572, to his first trip as an independent captain of his own ship. Never one to shy away from a challenge, Drake chose to attack England's most serious enemy at that time, Spain, near the infamous Spanish Main.

In the mid-16th century, Spain had colonized much of present-day Central America, South America and parts of North America, giving them control over the Gulf of Mexico and the Caribbean Sea. At the center of it was the Isthmus of Panama, which provided the center of the gold and silver trade from Peru. Ships coming from South America landed on the western coast of this narrow strip of land and unloaded their cargo, which then had to be carried overland to the eastern shore of the isthmus and loaded into other ships that would take it on to Spain. Several hundred years later, this process would be eliminated by the construction of the Panama Canal, but at the time this allowed he Spanish to avoid having to sail their ships south and around South America. It also happened to provide an excellent opportunity for theft and piracy.

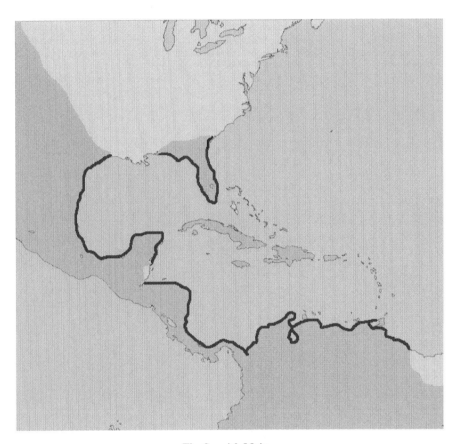

The Spanish Main

Drake sailed from Plymouth, England, on May 24, 1572, headed for Nombre de Dios, where he planned to capture the town and as much Spanish gold as he could get his hands on. With him he took 73 men and the *Pascha* and the *Swan*, two small ships built for speed and maneuverability rather than fighting. He began his attack on the town in late July of that year, and soon took possession of it and its treasure, but he was gravely wounded in battle and forced to withdraw to a safer location where he and his crew could fully recover. Wood described the audacious and chaotic attack:

"Springing eagerly ashore the Englishmen tumbled the Spanish guns off their platforms while the astonished sentry ran for dear life. In five minutes the church bells were pealing out their wild alarms, trumpet calls were sounding, drums were beating round the general parade, and the civilians of the place, expecting massacre at the hands of the Maroons, were rushing about in agonized confusion. Drake's men fell in—they were all well-drilled—and were quickly told off into three detachments. The largest under Drake, the next under Oxenham—the hero of Kingsley's Westward Ho!—and the third, of twelve men only, to guard the pinnaces. Having found that the new fort on the hill commanding the town was not yet occupied, Drake and Oxenham marched against the town at the head of their sixty men, Oxenham by a flank, Drake straight up the main street, each with a trumpet sounding, a drum rolling, fire-pikes blazing, swords flashing, and all ranks yelling like fiends. Drake was only of medium stature. But he had the strength of a giant, the pluck of a bulldog, the spring of a tiger, and the cut of a man that is born to command. Broad-browed, with steel-blue eyes and close-cropped auburn hair and beard, he was all kindliness of countenance to friends, but a very 'Dragon' to his Spanish foes.

As Drake's men reached the Plaza, his trumpeter blew one blast of defiance and then fell dead. Drake returned the Spanish volley and charged immediately, the drummer beating furiously, pikes levelled, and swords brandished. The Spaniards did not wait for him to close; for Oxenham's party, fire-pikes blazing, were taking them in flank. Out went the Spaniards through the Panama gate, with screaming townsfolk scurrying before them. Bang went the gate, now under English guard, as Drake made for the Governor's house. There lay a pile of silver bars such as his men had never dreamt of: in all, about four hundred tons of silver ready for the homeward fleet—enough not only to fill but sink the Pascha, Swan, and pinnaces. But silver was then no more to Drake than it was once to Solomon. What he wanted were the diamonds and pearls and gold, which were stored, he learned, in the King's Treasure House beside the bay.

A terrific storm now burst. The fire-pikes and arquebuses had to be taken under cover. The wall of the King's Treasure House defied all efforts to breach it. And the Spaniards who had been shut into the town, discovering how few the English were, reformed for attack. Some of Drake's men began to lose heart. But in a moment he stepped to the front and ordered Oxenham to go round and smash in the Treasure House gate while he held the Plaza himself. Just as the men stepped off, however, he reeled aside and fell. He had fainted from loss of blood caused by a wound he had managed to conceal. There was no holding the men now. They gave him a cordial, after which he bound up his leg, for he was a first-rate surgeon, and repeated his orders as before. But there were a good many wounded; and, with Drake no longer able to lead, the rest all begged to go back. So back to their boats they went, and over to the Bastimentos or Victualling Islands, which contained the gardens and poultry runs of the Nombre de Dios citizens."

Drake and his men stayed in and around the Isthmus for the next year, attacking Spanish galleons periodically and continuing to gather any booty they could. After a year of acting on his own, Drake teamed up with French privateer Guillaume Le Testu (who may have been working for Italy) to go after a load of gold being transported overland on the isthmus. They sailed into a port near Darien in modern day Panama and followed the famous Spanish Silver Train to Nombre de Dios. There they attacked the mule train in March of 1573 and captured more than 20 tons of gold and silver, a prize so rich that it proved to be more than they could carry away with them. Instead, they took the more valuable gold and buried buried the silver in a secret site known only to them, one of the first known incidents involving pirates and buried treasure.

Prior to leaving the site of his victory, Drake, in typically dramatic style, climbed a tall palm tree and looked to the west, and from that high vantage point he became the first Englishman to see the Pacific Ocean. He also began to make plans in the back of his mind to someday sail it. However, at that moment he had more pressing concerns.

During the attack on the mule train, Le Testu was wounded and subsequently captured by their Spanish victims, and he was later tried and convicted of piracy and beheaded. This left Drake completely in charge of the expedition, so he ordered his men to drag and carry as much of the treasure as they could back to the cove where their boats were anchored. The grueling trip across 18 miles of mountainous jungle took several days and left the men exhausted, but the worst was yet to come. This exhaustion turned to rage when they arrived at the cove to find that their boats had been taken by the Spanish.

Knowing that his men were starving and that the Spanish would no doubt soon return, Drake instructed his crew to bury the rest of the treasure right there on the beach. He then sent two of his best sailors aboard a makeshift raft ten miles up the coast to where he had left his flagship. Thankfully for Drake and his crew, the two sailors made it there and soon returned for the rest of the men.

When the flagship arrived, the crew that had been left behind was shocked by Drake's worn out appearance. They immediately assumed that the raid had been a failure and were reluctant to ask how the others had fared. In a moment more suited to a Hollywood movie than real life, Drake allowed them to worry for a few minutes before pulling out a solid gold necklace from under his shirt and crying, "Our voyage is made, lads!" He then had them dig up the gold buried on the beach and set sail back to England. A crewman later recounted the journey home:

"'Within 23 days we passed from the Cape of Florida to the Isles of Scilly, and so arrived at Plymouth on Sunday about sermon time, August 9, 1573, at what time the news of our Captain's return, brought unto his friends, did so speedily pass over all the church, and surpass their minds with desire to see him, that very few or none remained with the preacher, all hastening to see the evidence of God's love and blessing towards our Gracious Queen and country, by the fruit of our Captain's labour and success. Soli Deo Gloria."

They arrived in Plymouth to a hero's welcome in August of 1573, though the Queen was not at that time able to publicly acknowledge his success, since a treaty recently signed with Philip II of Spain technically made Drake's activities illegal.

Perhaps because of this change in the political atmosphere, Elizabeth assigned Drake to a handle a more domestic crisis upon his return. In 1575, he sailed with a group of English soldiers to Rathlin Island in Ulster, Ireland, where they were ordered to put down a rebellion of the Irish against the English plantation owners. While Drake remained at sea safeguarding the English contingent, the soldiers brutally put down the rebellion. More than 600 men, women and children surrendered to the English, and while it was traditional at that time to execute the leaders of such an incident, the English instead killed everyone they had captured, including the women and children. It is unclear how involved Drake actually was in this incident. Records show that he was in charge of the ships transporting the British troops, under the command of John Norreys, to the Island. At the time of the actual massacre, he may very well have been patrolling the coast, searching for Scottish troops who had threatened to reinforce the Irish.

Chapter 3: The Pirate

While pirates are traditionally considered to be outlaws, such was not the case with Francis Drake. While the Spanish considered him a thief and a criminal, the English considered him a hero, and he was a very public presence when he was home. In fact, his exploits made him a favorite courtier of Elizabeth I of England, and the Queen met with him regularly to congratulate him of his attacks on the Spanish. She also made sure that he was present at every major court event, where he could very conspicuously entertain the lords and ladies with his tails of sailing, fighting and treasure hunting.

Though he was popular at home, Drake was much too valuable an asset to the crown to keep on land for very long. Despite having signed a treaty earlier in the 1570s, Spain and England were back at each other's throats just a few years later, and in 1577 Elizabeth sent him to the Pacific coast of North America to hunt and harass Spanish vessels plying those waters. Drake later described being summoned and given orders to hunt Spanish ships: "Secretary Walsingham declared that Her Majesty had received divers[e] injuries of the King of Spain, for which she desired revenge. He showed me a plot [map] willing me to note down where he might be most annoyed. But I refused to set my hand to anything, affirming that Her Majesty was mortal, and that if it should please God to take Her Majesty away that some prince might reign that might be in league with the King of Spain, and then would my own hand be a witness against myself." It was Drake who suggested that he be allowed to raid the Pacific Ocean, which was incredibly daring because the waters around the southern tip of South America were so treacherous that the Spanish had long avoided them whenever possible.

In a mistake unusual for such a skilled seaman, Drake departed during the early winter in November of 1577. Because of the cold and rough seas, he did not get very far before having to dock at the port of Falmouth, in Cornwall. There they rested for a few days before returning to Plymouth to make repairs to the battered ships.

Still determined to leave as soon as possible, Drake sailed again on December 13th. This time he took the *Pelican* and the *Christopher,* as well as the *Swan,* the *Pascha* and one other ship with him. With about 165 crewmen, the 5 boats were so crowded that they were forced to add a sixth ship, the *Mary,* which Drake purchased cheaply from a captain who had previously captured it off the coast of the Cape Verde Islands in Africa. With the additional ship came another captain, the Italian Nuno da Silva, whose knowledge of South American seas would prove to be an invaluable asset to Drake.

As it turned out, Drake would not have a problem with overcrowding for long. He lost many of his crew in the Atlantic crossing. By the time he reach San Julian, located in modern day Argentina, he no longer had enough men to continue to man all his ships. As a result, he was forced to leave behind both the *Christopher* and the *Swan* on the coast. They also burned the *Mary* after they discovered that her hull was beginning to rot and would no longer be seaworthy.

Upon arriving in San Julian, the remaining crew were met with a grim reminder of the task before them. There, on the sandy shore, were the weathered skeletons of the crew members of Ferdinand Magellan. A mere 50 years before, these men had made the ill-fated decision to mutiny against their captain while he himself was looking for treasure and glory. He had had them killed there on the beach and left the unburied bodies hanging on display as a gruesome reminder to any other sailors that might think they knew better than their leader how to run an expedition

Ironically, Drake found himself facing an issue related to mutiny at this same juncture. He heard rumors that Thomas Doughty, his own co-commander on the expedition, was practicing witchcraft. Like most people of that era, and especially those with a devoutly Protestant background, Drake both abhored and feared anything related to the occult. He charged Doughty with both treason and mutiny, though there was little evidence of either. Doughty replied by asking to review Drake's commission from the Queen to see if he was authorized to act on such charges. Drake refused his request to see the documents, and also his request to be transported to England for trial. Instead, he proceeded to try the case himself, there on the shores of South America.

What most of the men present that day did not know was that Drake had long been concerned about Doughty's role in the expedition. While the public story was that Drake was simply going exploring, the back story was that Elizabeth herself had instructed him to attack and plunder as many Spanish ships as possible. This could not be made public because England and Spain were not technically at war with each other. However, prior to leaving, Drake had confided their secret orders to Doughty.

Doughty had made it clear both initially and later that he was not comfortable with attacking ships without some sort of provocation. He even went as far as to approach a member of Parliament with his concerns. When he was encouraged to go along with the plan anyway, he did so, but not without often voicing his concerns about both Drake's commission and his methods in carrying it out.

During the trial, evidence came to light from several sources, all of whom accused Doughty of speaking badly about both the ships and their captain. He also appears to have been very critical of the men aboard and made many enemies. However, there appears to have been little evidence of behavior that would rise to the level of mutiny. Still, within the context of an unknown land and a still rather young captain, there was little room for error. Those hearing the charges, nudged along no doubt by Drake himself, found Doughty guilty and agreed to his execution.

What follow is perhaps one of the strangest scenes in the history of the seas. Doughty asked to receive Holy Communion prior to his execution. Not only did Drake agree to his request, but he also joined him in the sacred rite. According to the ship's chaplain, Francis Fletcher:

"The general himself communicated at this Sacred ordinance, with this condemned penitent gentleman, who showed great tokens of a contrite and repentant heart, as who was more deeply displeased with his own act than any man else. And after this holy repast, they dined also at the same table together, as cheerfully, in sobriety, as ever in their lives they had done aforetime, each cheering up the other, and taking their leave, by drinking each to other, as if some journey only had been in hand.

After dinner, all things being brought in a readiness, by him that supplied the room of the provost-marshal; without any dallying, or delaying the time, he came forth and knelt down, preparing at once his neck for the ax, and his spirit for heaven; which having done without long ceremony, as who had before digest this whole tragedy, he desired all the rest to pray for him, and willed the executioner to do his office, not to fear nor spare."

Biographer William Wood described the Doughty affair in a similar manner:

"[W]itchcraft was not Thomas Doughty's real offence. Even before leaving England, and after betraying Elizabeth and Drake to Burleigh, who wished to curry favor with the Spanish traders rather than provoke the Spanish power, Doughty was busy tampering with the men. A storekeeper had to be sent back for peculation designed to curtail Drake's range of action. Then Doughty tempted officers and men: talked up the terrors of Magellan's Strait, ran down his friend's authority, and finally tried to encourage downright desertion by underhand means. This was too much for Drake. Doughty was arrested, tied to the mast, and threatened with dire punishment if he did not mend his ways. But he would not mend his ways. He had a brother on board and a friend, a 'very craftie lawyer'; so stern measures were soon required. Drake held a sort of court-martial which condemned Doughty to death. Then Doughty, having played his last card and lost, determined to die 'like an officer and gentleman.'

Drake solemnly 'pronounced him the child of Death and persuaded him that he would by these means make him the servant of God.' Doughty fell in with the idea and the former friends took the Sacrament together, 'for which Master Doughty gave him hearty thanks, never otherwise terming him than "My good Captaine."' Chaplain Fletcher having ended with the absolution, Drake and Doughty sat down together 'as cheerfully as ever in their lives, each cheering up the other and taking their leave by drinking to each other, as if some journey had been in hand.' Then Drake and Doughty went aside for a private conversation of which no record has remained. After this Doughty walked to the place of execution, where, like King Charles I,

'He nothing common did or mean
Upon that memorable scene.'

'Lo! this is the end of traitors!' said Drake as the executioner raised the head aloft."

With the Doughty affair behind him, Drake decided to weather the rest of the winter in San Julian before moving one in his expedition. Prior to leaving for the next phase of his mission, he made a rousing speech before his men, saying in part:

"For by the life of God, it doth even take my wits from me to think on it. Here is such controversy between the sailors and gentlemen, and such stomaching between the gentlemen and sailors, it doth make me mad to hear it. But, my masters, I must have it left. For I must have the gentleman to haul and draw with the mariner, and the mariner with the gentleman. What! let us show ourselves to be of a company and let us not give occasion to the enemy to rejoice at our decay and overthrow. I would know him that would refuse to set his hand to a rope, but I know there is not any such here…"

With that, Drake took his remaining crew and three remaining ships around the Magellan Strait off the southern tip of South America during the summer of 1578 and arrived in the Pacific Ocean that September. However, the Straits took their toll, and Drake lost two more ships, with one sinking and the other returning to England. This left him only his flagship in which to continue his journey. Wood described the harrowing ordeal:

"Drake sailed for the much dreaded Straits, before entering which he changed Pelican's name to the Golden Hind, which was the crest of Sir Christopher Hatton, one of the chief promoters of the enterprise and also one of Doughty's patrons. Then every vessel struck her topsail to the bunt in honor of the Queen as well as to show that all discoveries and captures were to be made in her sole name. Seventeen days of appalling dangers saw them through the Straits, where icy squalls came rushing down from every quarter of the baffling channels. But the Pacific was still worse. For no less than fifty-two consecutive days a furious gale kept driving them about like so many bits of driftwood. 'The like of it no traveller hath felt, neither hath there ever been such a tempest since Noah's flood.' The little English vessels fought for their very lives in that devouring hell of waters, the loneliest and most stupendous in the world. The Marigold went down with all hands, and Parson Fletcher, who heard their dying call, thought it was a judgment. At last the gale abated near Cape Horn, where Drake landed with a compass, while Parson Fletcher set up a stone engraved with the Queen's name and the date of the discovery."

A modern replica of Drake's *Golden Hind*

Like other explorers before him, Drake had continued to sail south, reaching a previously undiscovered island that he named Elizabeth Island in honor of his Queen and patroness. He remained close to the South American coast while turning north in his only remaining ship, the *Golden Hind*. From this sturdy craft he engaged in one attack after another of Spanish sea towns and coastal villages, while also capturing Spanish ships and stealing their more accurate nautical charts. He also pressed those that he could into service within his own fleet. Just as importantly, Drake moved onto the next target before word of his whereabouts could spread widely.

While on his way to Peru, Drake stopped in at the port at Mocha Island, which proved to be a mistake because the local natives had already developed a distrust of European visitors. According to the records of the voyage:

"When Frances Drake had passed the Straits of Magellan, the first land he fell with was an island named Mocha, where he came to an anchor, and hoisting out his boat, he, with ten of his company, went on shore, thinking there to have taken in fresh water. Two of the company, going far into the island were intercepted and cut of by the Indians that inhabit the island, who, as some as then saw our men come to anchor, thought they would come on land (as they did indeed), and laid an ambush of about 100 Indians; and where our boat was fast on ground and all the men gone on land, the ambush broke out and set upon them, and before they could recover their boat and get her on float, they hurt all our men very sore with their arrows.

More died of their wounds, the rest escaped their wounds and were cured. They stayed here but one day, but set sail toward the coast of Chile, where arriving they met with an Indian in a canoe near the shore, who thinking them to have been Spaniards, told them that behind there, at a place called St. Yago, there was a Spanish ship, for which good news they gave him diverse trifles. The Indian being joyful thereof went on shore and brought them … sheep and a small quantity of fish, and so they returned back again to St. Yago to seek the Spanish ship (for they had overshot the place before they were where); and when they came thither, they found the same ship."

Once he was situated off the coast of Lima, Drake and his men captured 25,000 pesos worth of Peruvian gold, the equivalent of about $10 million today. He also heard rumors that another ship, the *Nuestra Señora de la Concepción*, had recently departed, full of treasure and headed for Manila. Drake decided to go after the ship and managed to capture it. Its hold proved to be the most valuable one to date and included eighty pounds of gold, as well as a large, solid gold crucifix and twenty-six tons of silver. The chests also contained a wide variety of jewels and 13 chests of royal plate.

One Spanish letter described Drake's passage through the Straits and their attempts to capture him:

"A ship belonging to English raiders passed through the Strait of Magellan into the Pacific Ocean and reached the port of Santiago in the province of Chile on 6th December last year, 1578. This ship plundered one laden with a large quantity of gold that was in port there, and also other ships in ports along this coast, and did other damage. On the 13th February it arrived off the port of this city [i.e., Callao, port of Lima] and we were taken entirely unawares by so surprising an event, for, although there had been so much time for me to be warned from Chile of the presence of this ship, nothing was done. The excuse for this was that the Governor was away at the front in the region of the Araucanians, and neither the royal officials nor the city council were willing to take responsibility for chartering a ship to bring me the news, which, if it had arrived, would have saved so much loss and avoided the expense to His Majesty and to private citizens.

This has grown considerable because of the loss of a ship that the raider plundered which was carrying a large sum in silver dispatched from this country to the kingdom of Tierra Firme. We have taken a great deal of trouble to capture this raider and have sent two armed ships in search of him."

In the summer of 1579, Drake made landfall somewhere north of Spain's colonial borders, where he found a safe harbor and anchored his ships for long term repairs. While some of his men devoted themselves to making repairs to the ships' hulls and rigging, Drake sent others into the surrounding jungle to obtain fresh food and water. Having learned his lesson from his earlier encounter on Mocha Island, he worked hard to make sure that there was no trouble with the local peoples. Scholar Robert F. Heizer, who wrote a short book discussing the debates over where Drake landed in present-day California, noted what was written by Drake's chaplain in a diary that summer:

'June 21.—On this day the ship was brought near shore and anchored. Goods were landed, and some sort of stone fortification was erected for defense. The Indians made their appearance in increasing numbers until there was a 'great number both of men and women.' It is clearly apparent that the natives were not simply curious, but acted, as Fletcher points out, 'as men rauished in their mindes' and 'their errand being rather with submission and feare to worship vs as Gods, then to haue any warre with vs as with mortall men.' It would seem that the natives demonstrated clearly their fear and wonderment at the English, and it is certain that they behaved as no other natives had done in the experience of the chronicler. The English gave their visitors shirts and linen cloth, in return for which (as Fletcher thought) the Indians presented to Drake and some of the English such things as feathers, net caps, quivers for arrows, and animal skins which the women wore. Then, having visited for a time, the natives left for their homes about three-quarters of a mile away. As soon as they were home, the Indians began to lament, 'extending their voices, in a most miserable and dolefull manner of shreeking.' Inserted between the passages dealing with the departure of the Indians to their homes and their lamenting is a description of their houses and dress. The houses are described as 'digged round within the earth, and haue from the vppermost brimmes of the circle, clefts of wood set vp, and ioyned close together at the top, like our spires on the steeple of a church: which being couered with earth, suffer no water to enter, and are very warme, the doore in the most part of them, performes the office of a chimney, to let out the smoake: its made in bignesse and fashion, like to an ordinary scuttle in a ship, and standing slopewise: their beds are the hard ground, onely with rushes strewed vpon it, and lying round about the house, haue their fire in the middest....' The men for the most part were naked, and the women wore a shredded bulrush (tule? Scirpus sp.) skirt which hung around the hips. Women also wore a shoulder cape of deerskin with the hair upon it."

Drake's cousin John would later discuss some of their interactions with the Native Americans after being captured by the Spanish and forced to give a deposition:

"There he [Francis Drake] landed and built huts and remained a month and a half, caulking his vessel. The victuals they found were mussels and sea-lions. During that time many Indians came there and when they saw the Englishmen they wept and scratched their faces with their nails until they drew blood, as though this were an act of homage or adoration. By signs Captain Francis told them not to do that, for the Englishmen were not God. These people were peaceful and did no harm to the English, but gave them no food. They are of the colour of the Indians here [Peru] and are comely. They carry bows and arrows and go naked. The climate is temperate, more cold than hot. To all appearance it is a very good country. Here he caulked his large ship and left the ship he had taken in Nicaragua. He departed, leaving the Indians, to all appearances, sad."

Prior to leaving, Drake claimed the land on behalf of England and in honor of the Holy Trinity. He gave it the name Nova Albion, meaning "New Britain." He also appears to have left behind some of hims own men to try to establish a colony there, though this remains unclear due to the secret nature of the voyage and the colony itself. Drake is believed to have altered his own records in order to keep the Spanish from discovering the exact location of the colony.

Controversy had long surrounded the exact location of Nova Albion. Drake's own records of its establishment, as well as those of his men, were destroyed in a fire in the late 17th century. A bronze plaque that was found in Marin County, California, was for years believed to have been the marker of the village's original location. However, it was later proven to be a hoax. Today, historians believe that the most likely location of Nova Albion was actually as far north as present day Drakes Bay on the coast of California. One scholar who has advocated that site noted an old Native American legend from the region that was supposed to have been about Drake:

"First of all comes an old Indian legend which comes down through the Nicasios to the effect that Drake did land at this place [Drake's Bay]. Although they have been an interior tribe ever since the occupation by the Spaniards and doubtless were at that time, it still stands to reason that they would know all about the matter. If the ship remained in the bay thirty-six days it is reasonable to suppose that a knowledge of its presence reached every tribe within an area of one hundred miles and that the major portion of them paid a visit to the bay to see the 'envoys of the Great Spirit,' as they regarded the white seamen. One of these Indians named Theognis who is reputed to have been one hundred and thirty years old when he made the statement, says that Drake presented the Indians with a dog, some young pigs, and seeds of several species of grain.... The Indians also state that some of Drake's men deserted him here, and, making their way into the country, became amalgamated with the aboriginals to such an extent that all traces of them were lost, except possibly a few names [Nicasio, Novato] which are to be found among the Indians."

Given that the Spanish were now all too aware that Drake was in the area, sailing back south along South America would have been suicidal. Thus, upon leaving the western coast of North America, Drake sailed across the Pacific to what is now the eastern coast of Indonesia. There he experienced another bit of bad luck when the Golden Hind was trapped for three days on a coral reef. At first, Drake was concerned that he might not be able to save his favorite ship, but his crew worked non-stop for three days to remove all the cargo and lighten its load. When the next tide came in, they were able to shift it off the reef and get it sailing again.

While in Indonesia, Drake became friends with the leader of the local people, the sultan of the Moluccas, and by the time he made his way from there to Africa, he had acquired significant knowledge related to the ways and means of Portuguese trade. Wood explained:

"From California Drake sailed to the Philippines; and then to the Moluccas, where the Portuguese had, if such a thing were possible, outdone even the Spaniards in their fiendish dealings with the natives. Lopez de Mosquito—viler than his pestilential name—had murdered the Sultan, who was then his guest, chopped up the body, and thrown it into the sea. Baber, the Sultan's son, had driven out the Portuguese from the island of Ternate and was preparing to do likewise from the island of Tidore, when Drake arrived. Baber then offered Drake, for Queen Elizabeth, the complete monopoly of the trade in spices if only Drake would use the Golden Hind as the flagship against the Portuguese. Drake's reception was full of Oriental state; and Sultan Baber was so entranced by Drake's musicians that he sat all afternoon among them in a boat towed by the Golden Hind. But it was too great a risk to take a hand in this new war with only fifty-six men left. So Drake traded for all the spices he could stow away and concluded a sort of understanding which formed the sheet anchor of English diplomacy in Eastern seas for another century to come. Elizabeth was so delighted with this result that she gave Drake a cup (still at the family seat of Nutwell Court in Devonshire) engraved with a picture of his reception by the Sultan Baber of Ternate."

Drake's trip around the African coast was less eventful, with him rounding the Cape of Good Hope safely and with little trouble. He reached Sierra Leone in late July 1580 before turning his ship north toward Plymouth and home. When he arrived back home on September 26, 1580, Drake had only about one third of his original crew still with him, but he also had a large cargo of spices and Spanish treasure with him. The Queen's 50% share of his fortune comprised more than half of her entire income for that year.

Chapter 4: The Knight

Though Spain still considered him a pirate, the English people considered him a hero. He was hailed upon his homecoming as the first Englishman to circumnavigate the globe, and his crew had completed the second circumnavigation after Magellan's crew. Elizabeth herself insisted that she and her most trusted ministers alone should review the records of his journey, and any member of the crew who shared any information about the specifics of their trip risked execution. She was determined that nothing Drake learned on his voyage should fall into Spanish hands.

With his substantial share of the fortune he had acquired, Drake purchase a large manor called Buckland Abbey in Devon, near Yelverton, where he would live for most of the rest of his life when not at sea, and he was only too happy to bask in the fame of being a sea hero. He presented Elizabeth with a special jewel that he chose just for her from his treasure, a jewel pendant made from gold he captured off the coast of Mexico and set with a diamond mined in Africa. At the bottom was a tiny ship carved out of ebony.

Not to be outdone, Elizabeth gave Drake her own miniature portrait, set in a jeweled frame. Unlike most pins of this nature this one was reversible. On the back was a cameo of twin busts. One was of an obviously royal woman, perhaps meant to be Elizabeth herself. The other was of an African man. Known throughout the court as the "Drake Jewel," it became one of Drake's most prized possessions.

The "Drake Jewel" given to Drake by the Queen

While it was a common practice for a sovereign to give elaborate gifts to the nobility, it was practically unheard of for a monarch to bestow such a gift on a commoner. Naturally, Drake wore the pin regularly at court. Elizabeth did not stop with just a gift of jewelry, however. On April 4, 1581, she made a very special visit to the *Golden Hind*. There, on decks embedded with everything from gold dust to their captain's blood, she knighted Drake, creating him Sir Francis Drake. Always the shrewd politician, Elizabeth did not do the dubbing herself but instead handed the job off to the French ambassador, who was only to happy to oblige since he wanted to please the Queen and persuade her to marry his own king's brother. However, by participating in the knighting, the diplomat was also giving tacit approval of the French crown to Drake's exploits against the Spaniards.

A plaque depicting Drake's knighthood

With the knighthood came a coat of arms. At first, he claimed the right to the arms of the well-known sailor, Sir Bernard Drake, who Sir Francis claimed was a distant relative Sir Bernard, however, took issue with this claim. Though his family, the Drakes of Ash, had also lived in Devon for generations, he assured both the queen and her council that they knew nothing of the Drakes that had moved to Kent. He also confronted Sir Francis about the matter while the two were at court and is said to have boxed the younger man's ears.

In order to smooth out matters between her two courtiers, the queen authorized a new coat of arms for Sir Francis Drake himself. Drake chose a simple pattern the represented his professional exploits and accomplishments. It is an ocean wave with a star above, representing the Arctic Pole, and another below, representing Antarctica. This simple design is surrounded by heraldic feathers and a banner with the motto *"Sic Parvis Magna"* ("Thus great things from small things come"). To the upper left a hand reaches to heaven, holding another banner that reads "With Divine Help."

While Drake was nearing the apex of his career, he suffered a setback in his personal life. His wife of twelve years died in 1581, possibly as the result of pregnancy complications. She was never able to successfully bear a child. Busy with his new life at court, Drake showed little interest in remarrying and instead turned his sight to politics. That September, he was made Mayor of Plymouth, and he also won a seat in parliament, possibly from Camelford. He was reelected a few years later, this time to Bossiney, in 1584.

The following year, Drake made a politically and financially advantageous marriage to Elizabeth Sydenham. 12 years his junior, she was the only living child of Sir George Sydenham, the High Sheriff of Somerset. The two would remain married until Drake's death, but they also never had any children together.

Chapter 5: The Armada

Shortly after Drake's marriage to Sydenham, war finally broke out between England and Spain. Elizabeth immediately dispatched Drake and his fleet to the New World to attack the Spanish ports at Santo Domingo and Cartagena. On his way home in June of 1586, he attacked the Spanish fort at Saint Augustine in Florida. His actions, along with those of other British sailors, provoked Philip II of Spain to begin planning to invade England.

Philip II of Spain

Upon hearing of Philip's plan, Drake decided strike first. Planning to "singe the beard of the King of Spain," he sailed a fleet of British ships into Spanish ports at Cadiz and Corunna. He quickly defeated the naval vessels that were supposed to be defending the ports and completely occupied the harbors. In the process, he sunk more than 35 military and merchant ships, a daring and decisive victory that forced Spain's timeline for attack by a full year.

To make sure that the Spanish navy remained off-kilter, Drake continued to sail up and down the coasts of Iberia between Cape St. Vincent and Lisbon. Over the next month, he destroyed dozens of Spanish ships and thoroughly tangled up his enemy's supply lines, capturing enough barrel-making supplies to prevent the Spaniards from making more than 25,000 barrels. In recognition of these efforts, Drake was made vice admiral of the British fleet, serving directly under Lord Howard of Effingham. This would put him at the forefront of the naval battle against the Spanish Armada during their attempted invasion of England in 1588.

16th century depiction of the Spanish Armada

On July 12, 1588, the legendary Armada started for the English channel. The Spanish plan was to take this invasion, led by the Duke of Parma, to the coast of southeast England, where they would be released to conquer Elizabethan England for the Spanish monarch and Catholic Christendom. The Armada included over 150 ships, 8,000 sailors and 18,000 soldiers, and it boasted a firepower of 1,500 brass guns and 1,000 iron guns. Just leaving port itself took the entire Armada two days.

Always the rogue, Drake broke off from the English fleet as they chased the Armada into the English Channel. As darkness fell around him, he captured the galleon *Rosario*, taking the ship's captain, Admiral Pedro de Valdes, and his entire crew prisoner. In addition to the ship and its personnel, Drake also found a hull full of gold and silver designated for paying the Spanish forces opposing the English.

The actual capture of the *Rosario* was not exactly Drake's finest hour. The fleet was sailing at night, using lamplight to designate where each ship was. When Drake spotted the Spanish ships, he ordered the lamps put out so that they would not give away their positions. While this kept the Spanish from seeing them, it also prevented the English ships from seeing each other. While there were no actual collisions, there were enough near misses to thoroughly aggravate the captains of the other vessels. It took them most of the rest of the night to regain their proper positions.

In spite of this minor glitch, Drake remained firm in his belief that the British Navy would ultimately triumph over Spain. It appears that he spent much of the war on land, resting and waiting for the best time to attack. There is a legend that he was one day lawn bowling in Plymouth when a rider came with the urgent news that the Spanish were approaching. Rather than panic and rush to his ship, Drake merely laughed and assured those around him that he had time to defeat both his bowling opponent and the Spanish fleet. While this story is likely apocryphal, it is also true that the weather kept the English fleet from launching as early as some thought it should. Drake may well have been merely waiting for the most opportune time to take his ships to sea.

A plaque depicting Drake bowling while receiving news about the Armada

As always, Drake was alert to any chance to try a new technique to attack the enemy. During a night time battle fought on July 29, 1588, Drake set fire to a number of captured Spanish ships and sent them floating into the massed Spanish ships along the shores of Calais. Terrified, most of the ships broke formation and sailed for the open seas, which led to a major English victory the next day at the Battle of Gravelines. Writing from his position aboard the Revenge a few days later, Drake described their fight against the Spanish fleet:

> "Coming up unto them, there has passed some cannon shot between some of our fleet and some of them, and so far as we perceive they are determined to sell their lives with blows. ... This letter honorable good Lord, is sent in haste. The fleet of Spaniards is somewhat above a hundred sails, many great ships; but truly, I think

not half of them men-of-war. Haste.

As everyone who has been taught history now knows, the Armada was one of the most famous military debacles in history. Whether it was simple mathematical miscalculation or plain bad luck, coupled with English fire ships assailing the Spanish Armada, the Aramada was defeated – decisively so. By the time the Armada found its reluctant way home in awful conditions, it had permanently lost over one third of the ships. On the Irish coast, the Armada had suffered further losses. Drake's biographer Wood would summarize the debacle: "In those ten days the gallant Armada had lost all chance of winning the overlordship of the sea and shaking the sea-dog grip off both Americas. A rising gale now forced it to choose between getting pounded to death on the shoals of Dunkirk or running north, through that North Sea in which the British Grand Fleet of the twentieth century fought against the fourth attempt in modern times to win a world-dominion."

Chapter 6: The Final Voyages

Following the defeat of the Spanish Armada in 1588, Elizabeth gave Drake a new assignment. This time she asked him to team up with Sir John Norreys and take on a lengthy mission to tie up the loose ends of the war. They were to patrol the shores of England and Spain and destroy any remaining Spanish ships.

Unfortunately, this final mission of the war did not go very well. While the English fleet was able to destroy a few ships in the Spanish harbor at La Coruna, they did so at a high cost in both life and property. Drake and Norreys lost more than 12,000 men, as well as 20 of the ships that had thus far survived the war. The high losses slowed down the seeking and destroying process to the point that Drake finally abandoned the mission altogether.

Elizabeth then wanted Drake and Norreys to provide nautical support for the rebels in Lisbon who were fighting for their independence from Spain. Elizabeth rightly believed that so long as Portugal was separate from Spain, both countries would be weaker. Also, by backing Portugal in the revolution, she could win a new ally for England against the Spaniards. Elizabeth also instructed Drake and Norreys to try to capture the Azores, a group of islands off the coast of Portugal, which would strengthen England's position against Spain while at the same time obtaining a useful pawn against the Spanish.

Once again, Drake met with failure:

"Lisbon was a failure. The troops landed and marched over the ground north of Lisbon where Wellington in a later day made works whose fame has caused their memory to become an allusion in English literature for any impregnable base—the Lines of Torres Vedras. The fleet and the army now lost touch with each other; and that was the ruin of them all. Norreys was persuaded by Don Antonio, pretender to the throne of Portugal which Philip had seized, to march farther inland, where Portuguese patriots were said to be ready to rise en masse. This Antonio was a great talker and a first-rate fighter with his tongue. But his Portuguese followers, also great talkers, wanted to see a victory won by arms before they rose.

Before leaving Lisbon Drake had one stroke of good luck. A Spanish convoy brought in a Hanseatic Dutch and German fleet of merchantmen loaded down with contraband of war destined for Philip's new Armada. Drake swooped on it immediately and took sixty well-found ships. Then he went west to the Azores, looking for what he called 'some comfortable little dew of Heaven,' that is, of course, more prizes of a richer kind. But sickness broke out. The men died off like flies. Storms completed the discomfiture. And the expedition got home with a great deal less than half its strength in men and not enough in value to pay for its expenses. It was held to have failed; and Drake lost favor."

Following mixed success with these last two assignments, Drake attacked the Spanish port of Las Palmas on Grand Canary Island in 1595, which did not go well. They had originally hoped to make it to Puerto Rico but then decided to attack Las Palmas because they believed it would be an easy target. Instead, it proved to be a well established fort with excellent arms and men. The English were soundly beaten and forced to leave the area.

Following that defeat, Drake returned to the Americas, perhaps in the hopes a regaining some of his former glory. This also proved to be a mistake, as he suffered one defeat after another. In a final push for success, he attacked San Juan, Puerto Rico. On November 22, 1595, he and John Hawkins tried to land in San Juan with 2,500 men in 27 canoes. They first tried to land at the eastern end of the island, at Ensenada del Escambron, but when that failed they returned to their ships and attempted to sail into San Juan bay. This plan also failed, and Hawkins was killed. A Spanish account reported:

"Everybody was surprised and overjoyed at this happy outcome, when two sail came in sight. We gave them chase until three in the afternoon, when our vice-admiral brought one of them by the lee, grappled with her and took her, leaving the Santa Isabel to keep her company. The flagship and the remaining vessels of the squadron continued in chase of the other ship. About then--that is to say, around four o'clock in the afternoon--the vice-admiral shot off three guns, as a warning to the flagship. Ordered to search the sea, the lookouts sighted nine sail coasting along the island of Guadeloupe. We thereupon abandoned the chase: the flagship returned to the convoy to pick up the frigates and spoke with [Vice-]Admiral Gonzalo Méndez, who transmitted the report he had extracted from the prisoners he had taken, as follows:

First, that they had de parted from Plymouth on 8th September in the year aforesaid, in company with a fleet commanded by the generals Francis Drake and [Sir] John Hawkins. The prize and her companion had lost company with the fleet in rough weather, four days earlier. Ships that might lose company had been ordered to rendezvous with the main body either at Bayona [in Galicia, on the north coast of Spain] or at Puerto Santo [in the Canary Islands] or off Guadeloupe [as might be requisite according to the stage of the voyage reached]. If they did not fall in with the fleet at those roadsteads they were to proceed to Puerto Rico where they were told the expedition would spend ten days. They had fallen with the island on the previous afternoon, and had sighted and counted nineteen sail, but had not succeeded in fetching them to speak with them; then they had taken our frigates for ships of their own squadron, and that was why they had fallen in with our flotilla.

Asked how strong their fleet was, they said that it consisted of 26 sail. Of these six were Queen's ships: five of them ranged from 800 down to 500 tons, and the other was of 300. Among the remaining 20 vessels, which were adventured by private persons, some were comparable to them in strength and burthen. All of them were under orders from the Queen.

Asked what effect the fleet was intended to accomplish when it left England, witness said that he knew no more than that it was to proceed to Puerto Rico and there take the silver; but that it was so well victualled and stored that the men believed that they were expected to spend a long time in the Indies."

Drake then left for Potobello, Panama, and his final battle. During the battle for El Morro Castle in December of 1595, the Spanish shot a cannon ball through the hull of his flagship and into his own cabin. The blast should have killed him but he survived and lived through Christmas.

Wood summed up the sentiments of Drake and his crew after that defeat:

"'Since our return from Panama he never carried mirth nor joy in his face,' wrote one of Baskerville's officers who was constantly near Drake. A council of war was called and Drake, making the best of it, asked which they would have, Truxillo, the port of Honduras, or the 'golden towns' round about Lake Nicaragua. 'Both,' answered Baskerville, 'one after the other.' So the course was laid for San Juan on the Nicaragua coast. A head wind forced Drake to anchor under the island of Veragua, a hundred and twenty-five miles west of Nombre de Dios Bay and right in the deadliest part of that fever-stricken coast. The men began to sicken and die off. Drake complained at table that the place had changed for the worse. His earlier memories of New Spain were of a land like a 'pleasant and delicious arbour' very different from the 'vast and desert wilderness' he felt all round him now. The wind held foul. More and more men lay dead or dying. At last Drake himself, the man of iron constitution and steel nerves, fell ill and had to keep his cabin. Then reports were handed in to say the stores were running low and that there would soon be too few hands to man the ships. On this he gave the order to weigh and 'take the wind as God had sent it.'"

In the end, Drake did not even have the dignity of a hero's death. During the first part of January he met a foe he could not defeat: dysentery. As the illness took its toll, Drake sensed that he was dying and asked to be dressed in his best set of armor. One of his crewmen kept a diary of the events of January 28, 1596:

"The 28 at 4 of the clocke in the morning our Generall sir Francis Drake departed this life, having bene extremely sicke of a fluxe, which began the night before to stop on him. He used some speeches at or a little before his death, rising and apparelling himselfe, but being brought to bed againe within one houre died. He made his brother Thomas Drake and captaine Jonas Bodenham executors, and M. Thomas Drakes sonne [the later Sir Francis Drake, first baronet] his heire to all his lands except one manor which he gave to captain Bodenham.

The same day we ankered at Puerto Bello, being the best harbour we found along the maine both for great ships and small...After our comming hither to anker, and the solemne buriall of our Generall sir Francis in the sea"

The 55 year old Drake was entombed in a lead coffin and lowered into the sea off the coast of Portobelo, Panama. To this day, people still search for the coffin.

A plaque depicting Drake's burial at sea

At the time of his death, Drake's fleet was anchored off the coast of Panama hoping to capture some Spanish ships that were rumored to be carrying treasure. However, without Drake's leadership, the other captains lost interest in the expedition and returned to England.

Because Drake died without children, his title and fortune passed to his nephew and namesake. His real legacy, however, belongs to the world. The state of California has honored him with a bay, a Boulevard, a hotel and even a high school named after him. On the other side of the Atlantic, there are also a number of streets and squares that bear his name across Britain. Finally, there is the Sir Francis Drake Channel in the British Virgin Islands. Even 400 years after his death, there are contemporary video games like *Drake's Fortune*, which follows the adventures of Nathan Drake, a treasure hunter who claims to be descended from Drake himself.

Drake continues to be a well known figure in the West today, often viewed as a cross between pirates like Blackbeard and adventurers like Sir Walter Raleigh. While he was an important figure of the Elizabethan Era, scholarly debate focuses on the various aspects of his historic circumnavigation of the globe, which was an inadvertent byproduct of his piracy more than anything else. It was also due in part to Drake's travels and naval career that England was positioned to establish colonies in North America by the early 17th century. In that sense, it's somewhat fitting that his career as a privateer and pirate are also obscured by his other accomplishments.

Sir Francis Drake's Famous Voyage Round the World

After Drake's famous circumnavigation of the world, one of his crewmen, Francis Pretty, wrote a brief account of the historic voyage that was subsequently published in 1910. The following is Pretty's account of the trip:

"The 15th day of November, in the year of our Lord 1577, Master Francis Drake, with a fleet of five ships and barks, and to the number of 164 men, gentlemen and sailors, departed from Plymouth, giving out his pretended voyage for Alexandria. But the wind falling contrary, he was forced the next morning to put into Falmouth Haven, in Cornwall, where such and so terrible a tempest took us, as few men have seen the like, and was indeed so vehement that all our ships were like to have gone to wrack. But it pleased God to preserve us from that extremity and to afflict us only for that present with these two particulars: the mast of our Admiral, which was the Pelican, was cut overboard for the safeguard of the ship, and the Marigold was driven ashore, and somewhat bruised. For the repairing of which damages we returned again to Plymouth; and having recovered those harms, and brought the ships again to good state, we set forth the second time from Plymouth, and set sail the 13th day of December following.

The 25th day of the same month we fell with the Cape Cantin, upon the coast of Barbary; and coasting along, the 27th day we found an island called Mogador, lying one mile distant from the main. Between which island and the main we found a very good and safe harbour for our ships to ride in, as also very good entrance, and void of any danger. On this island our General erected a pinnace, whereof he brought out of England with him four already framed. While these things were in doing, there came to the water's side some of the inhabitants of the country, shewing forth their flags of truce; which being seen of our General, he sent his ship's boat to the shore to know what they would. They being willing to come aboard, our men left there one man of our company for a pledge, and brought two of theirs aboard our ship; which by signs shewed our General that the next day they would bring some provision, as sheep, capons, and hens, and such like. Whereupon our General bestowed amongst them some linen cloth and shoes, and a javelin, which they very joyfully received, and departed for that time. The next morning they failed not to come again to the water's side. And our General again setting out our boat, one of our men leaping over-rashly ashore, and offering friendly to embrace them, they set violent hands on him, offering a dagger to his throat if he had made any resistance; and so laying him on a horse carried him away. So that a man cannot be too circumspect and wary of himself among such miscreants. Our pinnace being finished, we departed from this place the 30th and last day of

December, and coasting along the shore we did descry, not contrary to our expectation, certain canters, which were Spanish fishermen; to whom we gave chase and took three of them. And proceeding further we met with three carvels, and took them also.

The 17th day of January we arrived at Cape Blanco, where we found a ship riding at anchor, within the Cape, and but two simple mariners in her. Which ship we took and carried her further into the harbour, where we remained four days; and in that space our General mustered and trained his men on land in warlike manner, to make them fit for all occasions. In this place we took of the fishermen such necessaries as we wanted, and they could yield us; and leaving here one of our little barks, called the Benedict, we took with us one of theirs which they called canters, being of the burden of 40 tons or thereabouts. All these things being finished we departed this harbour the 22nd of January, carrying along with us one of the Portugal carvels, which was bound to the islands of Cape Verde for salt, whereof good store is made in one of those islands. The master or pilot of that carvel did advertise our General that upon one of those islands, called Mayo, there was great store of dried cabritos (goats), which a few inhabitants there dwelling did yearly make ready for such of the king's ships as did there touch, being bound for his country of Brazil or elsewhere. We fell with this island the 27th of January, but the inhabitants would in no case traffic with us, being thereof forbidden by the king's edict. Yet the next day our General sent to view the island, and the likelihoods that might be there of the provision of victuals, about threescore and two men under the conduct and government of Master Winter and Master Doughty. And marching towards the chief place of habitation in this island (as by the Portugal we were informed), having travelled to the mountains the space of three miles, and arriving there somewhat before the daybreak, we arrested ourselves, to see day before us. Which appearing, we found the inhabitants to be fled; but the place, by reason that it was manured, we found to be more fruitful than the other part, especially the valleys among the hills.

Here we gave ourselves a little refreshing, as by very ripe and sweet grapes, which the fruitfulness of the earth at that season of winter, it may seems strange that those fruits were then there growing. But the reason thereof is this, because they being between the tropic and the equinoctial, the sun passeth twice in the year through their zenith over their heads, by means whereof they have two summers; and being so near the heat of the line they never lose the heat of the sun so much, but the fruits have their increase and continuance in the midst of winter. The island is wonderfully stored with goats and wild hens; and it hath salt also, without labour, save only that the people gather it into heaps; which continually in greater quantity is increased upon the sands by the flowing of the sea, and the receiving heat of the sun kerning the same. So that of the increase thereof they keep a continual traffic with their neighbours.

Amongst other things we found here a kind of fruit called cocos, which because it is not commonly known with us in England, I thought good to make some description of it. The tree beareth no leaves nor branches, but at the very top the fruit groweth in clusters, hard at the top of the stem of the tree, as big every several fruit as a man's head; but having taken off the uttermost bark, which you shall find to be very full of strings or sinews, as I may term them, you shall come to a hard shell, which may hold a quantity of liquor a pint commonly, or some a quart, and some less. Within that shell, of the thickness of half-an-inch good, you shall have a kind of hard substance and very white, no less good and sweet than almonds; within that again, a certain clear liquor which being drunk, you shall not only find it very delicate and sweet, but most comfortable and cordial.

After we had satisfied ourselves with some of these fruits, we marched further into the island, and saw great store of cabritos alive, which were so chased by the inhabitants that we could do no good towards our provision; but they had laid out, as it were to stop our mouths withal, certain old dried cabritos, which being but ill, and small and few, we made no account of. Being returned to our ships, our General departed hence the 31st of this month, and sailed by the island of Santiago, but far enough from the danger of the inhabitants, who shot and discharged at us three pieces; but they all fell short of us, and did us no harm. The island is fair and large, and, as it seemeth, rich and fruitful, and inhabited by the Portugals; but the mountains and high places of the island are said to be possessed by the Moors, who having been slaves to the Portugals, to ease themselves, made escape to the desert places of the island, where they abide with great strength. Being before this island, we espied two ships under sail, to the one of which we gave chase, and in the end boarded her with a ship-boat without resistance; which we found to be a good prize, and she yielded unto us good store of wine. Which prize our General committed to the custody of Master Doughty; and retaining the pilot, sent the rest away with his pinnace, giving them a butt of wine and some victuals, and their wearing clothes, and so they departed. The same night we came with the island called by the Portugals Ilha do Fogo, that is, the burning island; in the north side whereof is a consuming fire. The matter is said to be of sulphur, but, notwithstanding, it is like to be a commodious island, because the Portugals have built, and do inhabit there. Upon the south side thereof lieth a most pleasant and sweet island, the trees whereof are always green and fair to look upon; in respect whereof they call it Ilha Brava, that is, the brave island. From the banks thereof into the sea do run in many places reasonable streams of fresh water easy to come by, but there was no convenient road for our ships; for such was the depth that no ground could be had for anchoring. And it is reported that ground was never found in that place; so that the tops of Fogo burn not so high in the air, but the roots of Brava are quenched as low in the sea.

Being departed from these islands, we drew towards the line, where we were becalmed the space of three weeks, but yet subject to divers great storms, terrible lightnings and much thunder. But with this misery we had the commodity of great store of fish, as dolphins, bonitos, and flying-fishes, whereof some fell into our ships; wherehence they could not rise again for want of moisture, for when their wings are dry they cannot fly.

From the first day of our departure from the islands of Cape Verde, we sailed 54 days without sight of land. And the first land that we fell with was the coast of Brazil, which we saw the fifth of April, in the height of 33 degrees towards the pole Antarctic. And being discovered at sea by the inhabitants of the country, they made upon the coast great fires for a sacrifice (as we learned) to the devils; about which they use conjurations, making heaps of sand, and other ceremonies, that when any ship shall go about to stay upon their coast, not only sands may be gathered together in shoals in every place, but also that storms and tempests may arise, to the casting away of ships and men, whereof, as it is reported, there have been divers experiments.

The 7th day in a mighty great storm, both of lightning, rain, and thunder, we lost the canter, which we called the Christopher. But the eleventh day after, by our General's great care in dispersing his ships, we found her again, and the place where we met our General called the Cape of Joy, where every ship took in some water. Here we found a good temperature and sweet air, a very fair and pleasant country with an exceeding fruitful soil, where were great store of large and mighty deer, but we came not to the sight of any people; but travelling further into the country we perceived the footing of people in the clay ground, shewing that they were men of great stature. Being returned to our ships we weighed anchor, and ran somewhat further, and harboured ourselves between the rock and the main; where by means of the rock that brake the force of the sea, we rid very safe. And upon this rock we killed for our provision certain sea-wolves, commonly called with us seals. From hence we went our course to 36 degrees, and entered the great river of Plate, and ran into 54 and 53 1/2 fathoms of fresh water, where we filled our water by the ship's side; but our General finding here no good harborough, as he thought he should, bare out again to sea the 27th of April, and in bearing out we lost sight of our fly-boat wherein Master Doughty was. But we, sailing along, found a fair and reasonable good bay, wherein were many and the same profitable islands; one whereof had so many seals as would at the least have laden all our ships, and the rest of the islands are, as it were, laden with fowls, which is wonderful to see, and they of divers sorts. It is a place very plentiful of victuals, and hath in it no want of fresh water. Our General, after certain days of his abode in this place, being on shore in an island, the people of the country shewed themselves unto him, leaping and dancing, and entered into traffic with him, but they would not receive anything at any man's hands, but the same must be cast upon the ground. They are of clean, comely, and strong bodies, swift on foot, and seem to be very active.

The 18th of May, our General thought it needful to have a care of such ships as were absent; and therefore endeavouring to seek the fly-boat wherein Master Doughty was, we espied her again the next day. And whereas certain of our ships were sent to discover the coast and to search an harbour, the Marigold and the canter being employed in that business, came unto us and gave us understanding of a safe harbour that they had found. Wherewith all our ships bare, and entered it; where we watered and made new provision of victuals, as by seals, whereof we slew to the number of 200 or 300 in the space of an hour. Here our General in the Admiral rid close aboard the fly-boat, and took out of her all the provision of victuals and what else was in her, and hauling her to the land, set fire to her, and so burnt her to save the iron work. Which being a-doing, there came down of the country certain of the people naked, saving only about their waist the skin of some beast, with the fur or hair on, and something also wreathed on their heads. Their faces were painted with divers colours, and some of them had on their heads the similitude of horns, every man his bow, which was an ell in length, and a couple of arrows. They were very agile people and quick to deliver, and seemed not to be ignorant in the feats of wars, as by their order of ranging a few men might appear. These people would not of a long time receive anything at our hands; yet at length our General being ashore, and they dancing after their accustomed manner about him, and he once turning his back towards them, one leaped suddenly to him, and took his cap with his gold band off his head, and ran a little distance from him, and shared it with his fellow, the cap to one and the band to the other. Having despatched all our business in this place, we departed and set sail. And immediately upon our setting forth we lost our canter, which was absent three or four days; but when our General had her again, he took out the necessaries, and so gave her over, near to the Cape of Good Hope. The next day after, being the 20th of June, we harboured ourselves again in a very good harborough, called by Magellan, Port St. Julian, where we found a gibbet standing upon the main; which we supposed to be the place where Magellan did execution upon some of his disobedient and rebellious company.

The two and twentieth day our General went ashore to the main, and in his company John Thomas, and Robert Winterhie, Oliver the master-gunner, John Brewer, Thomas Hood, and Thomas Drake. And entering on land, they presently met with two or three of the country people. And Robert Winterhie having in his hands a bow and arrows, went about to make a shoot of pleasure, and, in his draught, his bowstring brake; which the rude savages taking as a token of war, began to bend the force of their bows against our company, and drove them to their shifts very narrowly.

In this port our General began to enquire diligently of the actions of Master Thomas Doughty, and found them not to be such as he looked for, but tending rather of contention or mutiny, or some other disorder, whereby, without redress, the success of the voyage might greatly have been hazarded. Whereupon the company was called together and made acquainted with the particulars of the cause, which were found, partly by Master Doughty's own confession, and partly by the evidence of the fact, to be true. Which when our General saw, although his private affection to Master Doughty, as he then in the presence of us all sacredly protested, was great, yet the care he had of the state of the voyage, of the expectation of her Majesty, and of the honour of his country did more touch him, as indeed it ought, than the private respect of one man. So that the cause being thoroughly heard, and all things done in good order as near as might be to the course of our laws in England, it was concluded that Master Doughty should receive punishment according to the quality of the offence. And he, seeing no remedy but patience for himself, desired before his death to receive the communion, which he did at the hands of Master Fletcher, our minister, and our General himself accompanied him in that holy action. Which being done, and the place of execution made ready, he having embraced our General, and taken his leave of all the company, with prayers for the Queen's Majesty and our realm, in quiet sort laid his head to the block, where he ended his life. This being done, our General made divers speeches to the whole company, persuading us to unity, obedience, love, and regard of our voyage; and for the better confirmation thereof, willed every many in the next Sunday following to prepare himself to the communion, as Christian brethren and friends ought to do. Which was done in very reverent sort; and so with good contentment every man went about his business.

The 17th of August we departed the port of St. Julian, and the 20th day we fell with the Strait of Magellan, going into the South Sea; at the cape or headland whereof we found the body of a dead man, whose flesh was clean consumed. The 21st day we entered the Strait, which we found to have many turnings, and as it were shuttings-up, as if there were no passage at all. By means whereof we had the wind often against us; so that some of the fleet recovering a cape or point of land, others should be forced to turn back again, and to come to an anchor where they could. In this Strait there be many fair harbours, with store of fresh water. But yet they lack their best commodity, for the water there is of such depth, that no man shall find ground to anchor in except it be in some narrow river or corner, or between some rocks; so that if any extreme blasts or contrary winds do come, whereunto the place is much subject, it carrieth with it no small danger. The land on both sides is very huge and mountainous; the lower mountains whereof, although they be monstrous and wonderful to look upon for their height, yet there are others which in height exceed them in a strange manner, reaching themselves above their fellows so high, that between them did appear three regions of clouds. These mountains are covered with snow. At both the southerly and easterly parts of the Strait there are islands, among which the sea hath his indraught into the Straits, even as it hath in the main entrance of the frete. This Strait is extreme cold, with frost and snow continually; the trees seem to stoop with the burden of the weather, and yet are green continually, and many good and sweet herbs do very plentifully grow and increase under them. The breadth of the Strait is in some places a league, in some other places two leagues and three leagues, and in some other four leagues; but the narrowest place hath a league over.

The 24th of August we arrived at an island in the Straits, where we found great store of fowl which could not fly, of the bigness of geese; whereof we killed in less than one day 3,000, and victualled ourselves thoroughly therewith. The 6th day of September we entered the South Sea at the cape or head shore. The 7th day we were driven by a great storm from the entering into the South Sea, 200 leagues and odd in longitude, and one degree to the southward of the Strait; in which height, and so many leagues to the westward, the 15th day of September, fell out the eclipse of the moon at the hour of six of the clock at night. But neither did the ecliptical conflict of the moon impair our state, nor her clearing again amend us a whit; but the accustomed eclipse of the sea continued in his force, we being darkened more than the moon sevenfold.[*]

[*] In this storm the Marigold went down with all hands.

From the bay which we called the Bay of Severing of Friends, we were driven back to the southward of the Straits in 57 degrees and a tierce; in which height we came to an anchor among the islands, having there fresh and very good water, with herbs of singular virtue. Not far from hence we entered another bay, where we found people, both men and women, in their canoes naked, and ranging from one island to another to seek their meat; who entered traffic with us for such things as they had. We returning hence northward again, found the third of October three islands, in one of which was such plenty of birds as is scant credible to report. The 8th day of October we lost sight of one of our consorts,[*] wherein Master Winter was; who, as then we supposed, was put by a storm into the Straits again. Which at our return home we found to be true, and he not perished, as some of our company feared. Thus being come into the height of the Straits again, we ran, supposing the coast of Chili to lie as the general maps have described it, namely north-west; which we found to lie and trend to the north-east and eastwards. Whereby it appeareth that this part of Chili hath not been truly hitherto discovered, or at the least not truly reported, for the space of twelve degrees at the least; being set down either of purpose to deceive, or of ignorant conjecture.

[*] The Elizabeth. Winter, having slight of the Admiral,
sailed home. The Golden Hind was thus left to pursue her
voyage alone.

We continuing our course, fell the 29th of November with an island called La Mocha, where we cast anchor; and our General, hoisting out our boat, went with ten of our company to shore. Where we found people whom the cruel and extreme dealings of the Spaniards have forced, for their own safety and liberty, to flee from the main, and to fortify themselves in this island. We being on land, the people came down to us to the water side with show of great courtesy, bringing to us potatoes, roots, and two very fat sheep; which our General received, and gave them other things for them, and had promised to have water there. But the next day repairing again to the shore, and sending two men a-land with barrels to fill water, the people taking them for Spaniards (to whom they use to show no favour if they take them) laid violent hands on them, and, as we think, slew them. Our General seeing this, stayed there no longer, but weighed anchor, and set sail towards the coast of Chili. And drawing towards it, we met near the shore an Indian in a canoe, who thinking us to have been Spaniards, came to us and told us, that at a place called Santiago, there was a great Spanish ship laden from the kingdom of Peru; for which good news our General gave him divers trifles. Whereof he was glad, and went along with us and brought us to the place, which is called the port of Valparaiso. When we came thither we found, indeed, the ship riding at anchor, having in her eight Spaniards and three negroes; who, thinking us to have been Spaniards, and their friends, welcomed us with a drum, and made ready a botija of wine of Chili to drink to us. But as soon as we were entered, one of our company called Thomas Moon began to lay about him, and struck one of the Spaniards, and said unto him, Abaxo perro! that is in English, 'Go down, dog!' One of these Spaniards, seeing persons of that quality in those seas, crossed and blessed himself. But, to be short, we stowed them under hatches, all save one Spaniard, who suddenly and desperately leapt overboard into the sea, and swam ashore to the town of Santiago, to give them warning of our arrival.

They of the town, being not above nine households, presently fled away and abandoned the town. Our General manned his boat and the Spanish ship's boat, and went to the town; and, being come to it, we rifled it, and came to a small chapel, which we entered, and found therein a silver chalice, two cruets, and one altar-cloth, the spoil whereof our General gave to Master Fletcher, his minister. We found also in this town a warehouse stored with wine of Chili and many boards of cedar-wood; all which wine we brought away with us, and certain of the boards to burn for firewood. And so, being come aboard, we departed the haven, having first set all the Spaniards on land, saving one John Griego, a Greek born, whom our General carried with him as pilot to bring him into the haven of Lima.

When we were at sea our General rifled the ship, and found in her good store of the wine of Chili, and 25,000 pesos of very pure and fine gold of Valdivia, amounting in value to 37,000 ducats of Spanish money, and above. So, going on our course, we arrived next at a place called Coquimbo, where our General sent fourteen of his men on land to fetch water. But they were espied by the Spaniards, who came with 300 horsemen and 200 footmen, and slew one of our men with a piece. The rest came aboard in safety, and the Spaniards departed. We went on shore again and buried our man, and the Spaniards came down again with a flag of truce; but we set sail, and would not trust them. From hence we went to a certain port called Tarapaca; where, being landed, we found by the sea side a Spaniard lying asleep, who had lying by him thirteen bars of silver, which weighed 4,000 ducats Spanish. We took the silver and left the man. Not far from hence, going on land for fresh water, we met with a Spaniard and an Indian boy driving eight llamas or sheep of Peru, which are as big as asses; every of which sheep had on his back two bags of leather, each bag containing 50 lb. weight of fine silver. So that, bringing both the sheep and their burthen to the ships, we found in all the bags eight hundred weight of silver.

Herehence we sailed to a place called Arica; and, being entered the port, we found there three small barks, which we rifled, and found in one of them fifty-seven wedges of silver, each of them weighing about 20 lb. weight, and every of these wedges were of the fashion and bigness of a brickbat. In all these three barks, we found not one person. For they, mistrusting no strangers, were all gone a-land to the town, which consisteth of about twenty houses; which we would have ransacked if our company had been better and more in number. But our General, contented with the spoil of the ships, left the town and put off again to sea, and set sail for Lima, and, by the way, met with a small bark, which he boarded, and found in her good store of linen cloth. Whereof taking some quantity, he let her go.

To Lima we came the 13th of February; and, being entered the haven, we found there about twelve sail of ships lying fast moored at an anchor, having all their sails carried on shore; for the masters and merchants were here most secure, having never been assaulted by enemies, and at this time feared the approach of none such as we were. Our General rifled these ships, and found in one of them a chest full of reals of plate, and good store of silks and linen cloth; and took the chest into his own ship, and good store of the silks and linen. In which ship he had news of another ship called the Cacafuego, which was gone towards Payta, and that the same ship was laden with treasure. Whereupon we stayed no longer here, but, cutting all the cables of the ships in the haven, we let them drive wither they would, either to sea or to the shore; and with all speed we followed the Cacafuego toward Payta, thinking there to have found her. But before we arrived there she was gone from thence towards Panama; whom our General still pursued, and by the way met with a bark laden with ropes and tackle for ships, which he boarded and searched, and found in her 80 lb. weight of gold, and a crucifix of gold with goodly great emeralds set in it, which he took, and some of the cordage also for his own ship. From hence we departed, still following the Cacafuego; and our General promised our company that whosoever should first descry her should have his chain of gold for his good news. It fortuned that John Drake, going up into the top, descried her about three of the clock. And about six of the clock we came to her and boarded her, and shot at her three pieces of ordnance, and strake down her mizen; and, being entered, we found in her great riches, as jewels and precious stones, thirteen chests full of reals of plate, fourscore pound weight of gold, and six-and-twenty ton of silver. The place where we took this prize was called Cape de San Francisco, about 150 leagues [south] from Panama. The pilot's name of this ship was Francisco; and amongst other plate that our General found in this ship he found two very fair gilt bowls of silver, which were the pilot's. To whom our General said, Senor Pilot, you have here two silver cups, but I must needs have one of them; which the pilot, because he could not otherwise choose, yielded unto, and gave the other to the steward of our General's ship. When this pilot departed from us, his boy said thus unto our General: Captain, our ship shall be called no more the Cacafuego, but the Cacaplata, and your ship shall be called the Cacafuego. Which pretty speech of the pilot's boy ministered matter of laughter to us, both then and long after. When our General had done what he would with this Cacafuego, he cast her off, and we went on our course still towards the west; and not long after met with a ship laden with linen cloth and fine China dishes of white earth, and great store of China silks, of all which things we took as we listed. The owner himself of this ship was in her, who was a Spanish gentleman, from whom our General took a falcon of gold, with a great emerald in the breast thereof; and the pilot of the ship he took also with him, and so cast the ship off.

This pilot brought us to the haven of Guatulco, the town whereof, as he told us, had but 17 Spaniards in it. As soon as we were entered this haven, we landed, and went presently to the town and to the town-house; where we found a judge sitting in judgment, being associated with three other officers, upon three negroes that had conspired the burning of the town. Both which judges and prisoners we took, and brought them a-shipboard, and caused the chief judge to write his letter to the town to command all the townsmen to avoid, that we might safely water there. Which being done, and they departed, we ransacked the town; and in one house we found a pot, of the quantity of a bushel, full of reals of plate, which we brought to our ship. And here one Thomas Moon, one of our company, took a Spanish gentleman as he was flying out of the town; and, searching him, he found a chain of gold about him, and other jewels, which he took, and so let him go. At this place our General, among other Spaniards, set ashore his Portugal pilot which he took at the islands of Cape Verde out of a ship of St. Mary port, of Portugal. And having set them ashore we departed hence, and sailed to the island of Canno; where our General landed, and brought to shore his own ship, and discharged her, mended and graved her, and furnished our ship with water and wood sufficiently.

And while we were here we espied a ship and set sail after her, and took her, and found in her two pilots and a Spanish governor, going for the islands of the Philippinas. We searched the ship, and took some of her merchandises, and so let her go. Our General at this place and time, thinking himself, both in respect of his private injuries received from the Spaniards, as also of their contempts and indignities offered to our country and prince in general, sufficiently satisfied and revenged; and supposing that her Majesty at his return would rest contented with this service, purposed to continue no longer upon the Spanish coast, but began to consider and to consult of the best way for his country.

He thought it not good to return by the Straits, for two special causes; the one, lest the Spaniards should there wait and attend for him in great number and strength, whose hands, he, being left but one ship, could not possibly escape. The other cause was the dangerous situation of the mouth of the Straits in the South Sea; where continual storms reigning and blustering, as he found by experience, besides the shoals and sands upon the coast, he thought it not a good course to adventure that way. He resolved, therefore, to avoid these hazards, to go forward to the Islands of the Malucos, and therehence to sail the course of the Portugals by the Cape of Buena Esperanza. Upon this resolution he began to think of his best way to the Malucos, and finding himself, where he now was, becalmed, he saw that of necessity he must be forced to take a Spanish course; namely, to sail somewhat northerly to get a good wind. We therefore set sail, and sailed 600 leagues at the least for a good wind; and thus much we sailed from the 16th of April till the third of June.

The fifth of June, being in 43 degrees towards the pole Arctic, we found the air so cold, that our men being grievously pinched with the same, complained of the extremity thereof; and the further we went, the more the cold increased upon us. Whereupon we thought it best for that time to seek the land, and did so; finding it not mountainous but low plain land, till we came within 38 degrees towards the line. In which height it pleased God to send us into a fair and good bay, with a good wind to enter the same. In this bay we anchored; and the people of the country, having their houses close by the water's side, shewed themselves unto us, and sent a present to our General. When they came unto us, they greatly wondered at the things that we brought. But our General, according to his natural and accustomed humanity, courteously intreated them, and liberally bestowed on them necessary things to cover their nakedness; whereupon they supposed us to be gods, and would not be persuaded to the contrary. The presents which they sent to our General, were feathers, and cauls of network. Their houses are digged round about with earth, and have from the uttermost brims of the circle, clifts of wood set upon them, joining close together at the top like a spire steeple, which by reason of that closeness are very warm. Their bed is the ground with rushes strowed on it; and lying about the house, [they] have the fire in the midst. The men go naked; the women take bulrushes, and kemb them after the manner of hemp, and thereof make their loose garments, which being knit about their middles, hang down about their hips, having also about their shoulders a skin of deer, with the hair upon it. These women are very obedient and serviceable to their husbands.

After they were departed from us, they came and visited us the second time, and brought with them feathers and bags of tabacco for presents. And when they came to the top of the hill, at the bottom whereof we had pitched our tents, they stayed themselves; where one appointed for speaker wearied himself with making a long oration; which done, they left their bows upon the hill, and came down with their presents. In the meantime the women, remaining upon the hill, tormented themselves lamentably, tearing their flesh from their cheeks, whereby we perceived that they were about a sacrifice. In the meantime our General with his company went to prayer, and to reading of the Scriptures, at which exercise they were attentive, and seemed greatly to be affected with it; but when they were come unto us, they restored again unto us those things which before we bestowed upon them. The news of our being there being spread through the country, the people that inhabited round about came down, and amongst them the king himself, a man of a goodly stature, and comely personage, and with many other tall and warlike men; before whose coming were sent two ambassadors to our General, to signify that their king was coming, in doing of which message, their speech was continued about half an hour. This ended, they by signs requested our General to send something by their hand to their king, as a token that his coming might be in peace. Wherein our General having satisfied them, they returned with glad tidings to their king, who marched to us with a princely majesty, the people crying continually after their manner; and as they drew near unto us, so did they strive to behave themselves in their actions with comeliness. In the fore-front was a man of goodly personage, who bare the sceptre or mace before the king; whereupon hanged two crowns, a less and a bigger, with three chains of a marvellous length. The crowns were made of knit work, wrought artificially with feathers of divers colours. The chains were made of a bony substance, and few be the persons among them that are admitted to wear them; and of that number also the persons are stinted, as some ten, some twelve, etc. Next unto him which bare the sceptre, was the king himself, with his guard about his person, clad with coney skins, and other skins. After them followed the naked common sort of people, every one having his face painted, some with white, some with black, and other colours, and having in their hands one thing or another for a present. Not so much as their children, but they also brought their presents.

In the meantime our General gathered his men together, and marched within his fenced place, making, against their approaching, a very warlike show. They being trooped together in their order, and a general salutation being made, there was presently a general silence. Then he that bare the sceptre before the king, being informed by another, whom they assigned to that office, with a manly and lofty voice proclaimed that which the other spake to him in secret, continuing half an hour. Which ended, and a general Amen, as it were, given, the king with the whole number of men and women, the children excepted, came down without any weapon; who, descending to the foot of the hill, set themselves in order. In coming towards our bulwarks and tents, the sceptre-bearer began a song, observing his measures in a dance, and that with a stately countenance; whom the king with his guard, and every degree of persons, following, did in like manner sing and dance, saving only the women, which danced and kept silence. The General permitted them to enter within our bulwark, where they continued their song and dance a reasonable time. When they had satisfied themselves, they made signs to our General to sit down; to whom the king and divers others made several orations, or rather supplications, that he would take their province and kingdom into his hand, and become their king, making signs that they would resign unto him their right and title of the whole land, and become his subjects. In which, to persuade us the better, the king and the rest, with one consent, and with great reverence, joyfully singing a song, did set the crown upon his head, enriched his neck with all their chains, and offered him many other things, honouring him by the name of Hioh, adding thereunto, as it seemed, a sign of triumph; which thing our General thought not meet to reject, because he knew not what honour and profit it might be to our country. Wherefore in the name, and to the use of her Majesty, he took the sceptre, crown, and dignity of the said country into his hands, wishing that the riches and treasure thereof might so conveniently be transported to the enriching of her kingdom at home, as it aboundeth in the same.

The common sort of people, leaving the king and his guard with our General, scattered themselves together with their sacrifices among our people, taking a diligent view of every person: and such as pleased their fancy (which were the youngest), they enclosing them about offered their sacrifices unto them with lamentable weeping, scratching and tearing their flesh from their faces with their nails, whereof issued abundance of blood. But we used signs to them of disliking this, and stayed their hands from force, and directed them upwards to the living God, whom only they ought to worship. They shewed unto us their wounds, and craved help of them at our hands; whereupon we gave them lotions, plaisters, and ointments agreeing to the state of their griefs, beseeching God to cure their diseases. Every third day they brought their sacrifices unto us, until they understood our meaning, that we had no pleasure in them; yet they could not be long absent from us, but daily frequented our company to the hour of our departure, which departure seemed so grievous unto them, that their joy was turned into sorrow. They entreated us, that being absent we would remember them, and by stealth provided a sacrifice, which we misliked.

Our necessary business being ended, our General with his company travelled up into the country to their villages, where we found herds of deer by a thousand in a company, being most large, and fat of body. We found the whole country to be a warren of a strange kind of coneys; their bodies in bigness as be the Barbary coneys, their heads as the heads of ours, the feet of a want [mole], and the tail of a rat, being of great length. Under her chin is on either side a bag, into the which she gathereth her meat, when she hath filled her belly abroad. The people eat their bodies, and make great account of their skins, for their king's coat was made of them. Our General called this country Nova Albion, and that for two causes; the one in respect of the white banks and cliffs, which lie towards the sea, and the other, because it might have some affinity with our country in name, which sometime was so called. There is no part of earth here to be taken up, wherein there is not some probable show of gold or silver.

At our departure hence our General set up a monument of our being there, as also of her Majesty's right and title to the same; namely a plate, nailed upon a fair great post, whereupon was engraved her Majesty's name, the day and year of our arrival there, with the free giving up of the province and people into her Majesty's hands, together with her Highness' picture and arms, in a piece of six pence of current English money, under the plate, whereunder was also written the name of our General.

It seemeth that the Spaniards hitherto had never been in this part of the country, neither did ever discover the land by many degrees to the southwards of this place.

After we had set sail from hence, we continued without sight of land till the 13th day of October following, which day in the morning we fell with certain islands eight degrees to the northward of the line, from which islands came in a great number of canoas, having in some of them four, in some six, and in some also fourteen men, bringing with them cocos and other fruits. Their canoas were hollow within and cut with great art and cunning, being very smooth within and without, and bearing a gloss as if it were a horn daintily burnished, having a prow and a stern of one sort, yielding inward circle-wise, being of a great height, and full of certain white shells for a bravery; and on each side of them lie out two pieces of timber about a yard and a half long, more or less, according to the smallness or bigness of the boat. These people have the nether part of their ears cut into a round circle, hanging down very low upon their cheeks, whereon they hang things of a reasonable weight. The nails of their hands are an inch long, their teeth are as black as pitch, and they renew them often, by eating of an herb with a kind of powder, which they always carry about them in a cane for the same purpose.

Leaving this island the night after we fell with it, the 18th of October we lighted upon divers others, some whereof made a great show of inhabitants. We continued our course by the islands of Tagulanda, Zelon, and Zewarra, being friends to the Portugals, the first whereof hath growing in it great store of cinnamon. The 14th of November we fell in with the islands of Maluco. Which day at night (having directed our course to run with Tidore) in coasting along the island of Mutyr, belonging to the king of Ternate, his deputy or vice-king seeing us at sea, come with his canoa to us without all fear, and came aboard; and after some conference with our General, willed him in any wise to run in with Ternate, and not with Tidore, assuring him that the king would be glad of his coming, and would be ready to do what he would require, for which purpose he himself would that night be with the king, and tell him the news. With whom if he once dealt, we should find that if he went to Tidore before he came to Ternate, the king would have nothing to do with us, because he held the Portugal as his enemy. Whereupon our General resolved to run with Ternate. Where the next morning early we came to anchor; at which time our General sent a messenger to the king, with a velvet cloak for a present and token of his coming to lie in peace, and that he required nothing but traffic and exchange of merchandise, whereof he had good store, in such things as he wanted.

In the meantime the vice-king had been with the king according to his promise, signifying unto him what good things he might receive from us by traffic. Whereby the king was moved with great liking towards us, and sent to our General, with special message, that he should have what things he needed and would require, with peace and friendship; and moreover that he would yield himself and the right of his island to be at the pleasure and commandment of so famous a prince as we served. In token whereof he sent to our General a signet; and within short time after came in his own person, with boats and canoas, to our ship, to bring her into a better and safer road than she was in at that present. In the meantime, our General's messenger, being come to the Court, was met by certain noble personages with great solemnity, and brought to the king, at whose hands he was most friendly and graciously entertained.

The king, purposing to come to our ship, sent before four great and large canoas, in every one whereof were certain of his greatest states (men of property or estate) that were about him, attired in white lawn of cloth of Calicut, having over their heads, from the one end of the canoa to the other, a covering of thin perfumed mats, borne up with a frame made of reeds for the same use; under which every one did sit in his order according to his dignity, to keep him from the heat of the sun; divers of whom being of good age and gravity, did make an ancient and fatherly show. There were also divers young and comely men attired in white, as were the others; the rest were soldiers, which stood in comely order round about on both sides. Without whom sat the rowers in certain galleries; which being three on a side all along the canoas, did lie off from the side thereof three or four yards, one being orderly builded lower than another, in every of which galleries were the number of fourscore rowers. These canoas were furnished with warlike munition, every man for the most part having his sword and target, with his dagger, beside other weapons, as lances, calivers, darts, bows and arrows; also every canoa had a small cast base mounted at the least one full yard upon a stock set upright. Thus coming near our ship, in order, they rowed about us one after another, and passing by, did their homage with great solemnity; the great personages beginning with great gravity and fatherly countenances, signifying that the king had sent them to conduct our ship into a better road. Soon after the king himself repaired, accompanied with six grave and ancient persons, who did their obeisance with marvellous humility. The king was a man of tall stature, and seemed to be much delighted with the sound of our music; to whom, as also to his nobility, our General gave presents, wherewith they were passing well contented.

At length the king craved leave of our General to depart, promising the next day to come aboard, and in the meantime to send us such victuals as were necessary for our provision. So that the same night we received of them meal, which they call sagu, made of the tops of certain trees, tasting in the mouth like sour curds, but melteth like sugar, whereof they make certain cakes, which may be kept the space of ten years, and yet then good to be eaten. We had of them store of rice, hens, unperfect and liquid sugar, sugar-canes, and a fruit which they call figo (plantains), with store of cloves.

The king having promised to come aboard, brake his promise, but sent his brother to make his excuse, and to entreat our General to come on shore, offering himself pawn aboard for his safe return. Whereunto our General consented not, upon mislike conceived of the breach of his promise; the whole company also utterly refusing it. But to satisfy him, our General sent certain of his gentlemen to the Court, to accompany the king's brother, reserving the vice-king for their safe return. They were received of another brother of the king's, and other states, and were conducted with great honour to the castle. The place that they were brought unto was a large and fair house, where were at the least a thousand persons assembled.

The king being yet absent, there sat in their places 60 grave personages, all which were said to be of the king's council. There were besides four grave persons, apparelled all in red, down to the ground, and attired on their heads like the Turks; and these were said to be Romans [probably Greeks] and ligiers [resident agents] there to keep continual traffic with the people of Ternate. There were also two Turks ligiers in this place, and one Italian. The king at last came in guarded with twelve lances, covered over with a rich canopy with embossed gold. Our men, accompanied with one of their captains called Moro, rising to meet him, he graciously did welcome and entertain them. He was attired after the manner of the country, but more sumptuously than the rest. From his waist down to the ground was all cloth of gold, and the same very rich; his legs were bare, but on his feet were a pair of shoes, made of Cordovan skin. In the attire of his head were finely wreathed hooped rings of gold, and about his neck he had a chain of perfect gold, the links whereof were great, and one fold double. On his fingers he had six very fair jewels; and sitting in his chair of state, at his right hand stood a page with a fan in his hand, breathing and gathering the air to the king. The same was in length two foot, and in breadth one foot, set with eight sapphires richly embroidered, and knit to a staff three foot in length, by the which the page did hold and move it. Our gentlemen having delivered their message and received order accordingly, were licensed to depart, being safely conducted back again by one of the king's council. This island is the chief of all the islands of Maluco, and the king hereof is king of 70 islands besides. The king with his people are Moors in religion, observing certain new moons, with fastings; during which fasts they neither eat nor drink in the day, but in the night.

After that our gentlemen were returned, and that we had here by the favour of the king received all necessary things that the place could yield us; our General considering the great distance, and how far he was yet off from his country, thought it not best here to linger the time any longer, but weighing his anchors, set out of the island, and sailed to a certain little island to the southwards of Celebes, where we graved our ship, and continued there, in that and other businesses, 26 days. This island is thoroughly grown with wood of a large and high growth, very straight, and without boughs, save only in the head or top, whose leaves are not much differing from our broom in England. Amongst these trees night by night, through the whole land, did shew themselves an infinite swarm of fiery worms flying in the air, whose bodies being no bigger than our common English flies, make such a show and light as if every twig or tree had been a burning candle. In this place breedeth also wonderful store of bats, as big as large hens. Of crayfishes also here wanted no plenty, and they of exceeding bigness, one whereof was sufficient for four hungry stomachs at a dinner, being also very good and restoring meat, whereof we had experience: and they dig themselves holes in the earth like coneys.

When we had ended our business here we weighed, and set sail to run for the Malucos. But having at that time a bad wind, and being amongst the islands, with much difficulty we recovered to the northward of the island of Celebes; where by reason of contrary winds, not able to continue our course to run westwards, we were enforced to alter the same to the southward again, finding that course also to be very hard and dangerous for us, by reason of infinite shoals which lie off and among the islands; whereof we had too much trial, to the hazard and danger of our ship and lives. For, of all other days, upon the 9th of January, in the year 1579 [1580], we ran suddenly upon a rock, where we stuck fast from eight of the clock at night till four of the clock in the afternoon the next day, being indeed out of all hope to escape the danger. But our General, as he had always hitherto shewed himself courageous, and of a good confidence in the mercy and protection of God, so now he continued in the same. And lest he should seem to perish wilfully, both he and we did our best endeavour to save ourselves; which it pleased God so to bless, that in the end we cleared ourselves most happily of the danger.

We lighted our ship upon the rocks of three tons of cloves, eight pieces of ordnance, and certain meal and beans; and then the wind, as it were in a moment by the special grace of God, changing from the starboard to the larboard of the ship, we hoisted our sails, and the happy gale drove our ship off the rock into the sea again, to the no little comfort of all our hearts, for which we gave God such praise and thanks, as so great a benefit required.

The 8th of February following, we fell with the fruitful island of Barateve, having in the mean time suffered many dangers by winds and shoals. The people of this island are comely in body and stature, and of a civil behaviour, just in dealing, and courteous to strangers; whereof we had the experience sundry ways, they being most glad of our presence, and very ready to relieve our wants in those things which their country did yield. The men go naked, saving their heads and loins, every man having something or other hanging at their ears. Their women are covered from the middle down to the foot, wearing a great number of bracelets upon their arms; for some had eight upon each arm, being made some of bone, some of horn, and some of brass, the lightest whereof, by our estimation, weighed two ounces apiece. With this people linen-cloth is good merchandise, and of good request; whereof they make rolls for their heads, and girdles to wear about them. Their island is both rich and fruitful; rich in gold, silver, copper, and sulphur, wherein they seem skilful and expert, not only to try the same, but in working it also artificially into any form and fashion that pleaseth them. Their fruits be divers and plentiful; as nutmegs, ginger, long pepper, lemons, cucumbers, cocos, figu, sagu, with divers other sorts. And among all the rest we had one fruit, in bigness, form and husk, like a bay berry, hard of substance and pleasant of taste, which being sudden becometh soft, and is a most good and wholesome victual; whereof we took reasonable store, as we did also of the other fruits and spices. So that to confess a truth, since the time that we first set out of our country of England, we happened upon no place, Ternate only excepted, wherein we found more comforts and better means of refreshing.

At our departure from Barateve, we set our course for Java Major; where arriving, we found great courtesy, and honourable entertainment. This island is governed by five kings, whom they call Rajah; as Rajah Donaw, and Rajah Mang Bange, and Rajah Cabuccapollo, which live as having one spirit and one mind. Of these five we had four a-shipboard at once, and two or three often. They are wonderfully delighted in coloured clothes, as red and green; the upper part of their bodies are naked, save their heads, whereupon they wear a Turkish roll as do the Maluccians. From the middle downward they wear a pintado of silk, trailing upon the ground, in colour as they best like. The Maluccians hate that their women should be seen of strangers; but these offer them of high courtesy, yea, the kings themselves. The people are of goodly stature and warlike, well provided of swords and targets, with daggers, all being of their own work, and most artificially done, both in tempering their metal, as also in the form; whereof we bought reasonable store. They have an house in every village for their common assembly; every day they meet twice, men, women, and children, bringing with them such victuals as they think good, some fruits, some rice boiled, some hens roasted, some sagu, having a table made three foot from the ground, whereon they set their meat, that every person sitting at the table may eat, one rejoicing in the company of another. They boil their rice in an earthen pot, made in form of a sugar loaf, being full of holes, as our pots which we water our gardens withal, and it is open at the great end, wherein they get their rice dry, without any moisture. In the mean time they have ready another great earthen pot, as set fast in a furnace, boiling full of water, whereinto they put their pot with rice, by such measure, that they swelling become soft at the first, and by their swelling stopping the holes of the pot, admit no more water to enter, but the more they are boiled, the harder and more firm substance they become. So that in the end they are a firm and good bread, of the which with oil, butter, sugar, and other spices, they make divers sorts of meats very pleasant of taste, and nourishing to nature.

Not long before our departure, they told us that not far off there were such great ships as ours, wishing us to beware; upon this our captain would stay no longer. From Java Major we sailed for the Cape of Good Hope, which was the first land we fell withal; neither did we touch with it, or any other land, until we came to Sierra Leona, upon the coast of Guinea; notwithstanding we ran hard aboard the cape, finding the report of the Portugals to be most false who affirm that it is the most dangerous cape of the world, never without intolerable storms and present danger to travellers which come near the same. This cape is a most stately thing, and the fairest cape we saw in the whole circumference of the earth, and we passed by it the 18th of June. From thence we continued our course to Sierra Leona, on the coast of Guinea, where we arrived the 22nd of July, and found necessary provisions, great store of elephants, oysters upon trees of one kind [mangrove], spawning and increasing infinitely, the oyster suffering no bud to grow. We departed thence the four and twentieth day.

We arrived in England the third of November, 1580, being the third year of our departure."

Bibliography

Bawlf, Samuel (2003) *The Secret Voyage of Sir Francis Drake, 1577–1580* Walker & Company

Hughes-Hallett, Lucy (2004) *Heroes: A History of Hero Worship* Alfred A. Knopf, New York.

Kelsey, Harry (1998) *Sir Francis Drake, the Queen's Pirate.*

Konstam, Angus and Peter Dennis (2011) *The Great Expedition – Sir Francis Drake on the Spanish Main 1585-86.*

Nichols, Philip (2010) *Sir Francis Drake.*

Pretty, Francis (2012) *Sir Francis Drake's Famous Voyage Round the World.*

Rodger, N. A. M. (1997) *The Safeguard of the Sea; A Naval History of Britain 660-1649.*

Stafford, Sir Julian (2012) Sir Francis Drake.

Sugden, John. (2012) *Sir Francis Drake.*

Wilson, Derek (1977) *The World Encompassed: Drake's Great Voyage, 1577–80.*

Made in the USA
Columbia, SC
05 July 2021